STORIES OF TEACHING

A Foundation for Educational Renewal

STEPHEN L. PRESKILL
University of New Mexico

ROBIN SMITH JACOBVITZ
University of New Mexico

Merrill
Prentice Hall

Upper Saddle River, New Jersey
Columbus, Ohio

Library of Congress Cataloging-in-Publication Data

Preskill, Stephen
    Stories of teaching : a foundation for educational renewal / Stephen L. Preskill, Robin Smith Jacobvitz.
      p. cm.
    Includes bibliographical references and index.
    ISBN 0-13-921248-5
    1. Teachers. 2. Teaching. 3. First person narrative. 4. Educational change. I. Jacobvitz, Robin Smith. II. Title.

LB1775 .P68 2001
371.102—dc21   99-086547

Vice President and Publisher: Jeffery W. Johnston
Editor: Debra A. Stollenwerk
Editorial Assistant: Penny S. Burleson
Production Editor: Mary Harlan
Design Coordinator: Diane C. Lorenzo
Cover design: Linda Fares
Cover art: Stephen Schildbach
Text design: Carlisle Publishers Services
Production Coordination: Kathy Davis, Carlisle Publishers Services
Production Manager: Pamela D. Bennett
Director of Marketing: Kevin Flanagan
Marketing Manager: Amy June
Marketing Services Manager: Krista Groshong

This book was set in Century Book by Carlisle Communications, Ltd. It was printed and bound by R. R. Donnelley & Sons Company. The cover was printed by Phoenix Color Corp.

Some ideas or descriptions were previously examined in "Narratives of teaching and the quest for the second self," by Stephen L. Preskill, 1998, *Journal of Teacher Education, 49,* 5.

10 9 8 7 6 5 4 3 2
ISBN: 0-13-921248-5

PREFACE

INTRODUCTION TO INSTRUCTORS

We have written this book for people who love great stories of teaching and who believe these stories are a powerful way to learn about the world of education. The stories we have chosen are designed to spark discussion about important educational issues and to provoke teachers to reexamine their assumptions about learning. We seek, above all, to engage and excite our readers and to immerse them, through the vehicle of stories, in the concrete particulars of everyday teaching. The stories explored in this book are written by superb teacher/writers who paint realistic and vivid portraits of classroom life. Their narratives sharply depict the stirring interactions that make contemporary teaching such challenging and exhilarating work. Furthermore, these stories underscore how much inspiring teachers can accomplish when they retain faith in the ability of learners to master even the most difficult academic material.

We have divided the teachers' stories in this book into six types of genres: narrative of social criticism, narrative of induction and apprenticeship, narrative of reflective practice, narrative of journey, narrative of hope, and narrative of freedom. We devote one chapter to each of the story types and incorporate discussions of at least three distinct narratives in each chapter. In these chapters, we explore the special problems of teaching presented by each genre. In the narrative of social criticism, for instance, we examine stories that highlight major social problems or that advance powerful critiques of schools. In the narrative of apprenticeship, we consider the unique challenges faced by beginning teachers, while in the narrative of reflective practice we focus on the teaching of Vivian Paley and her ability to hone her craft through careful and systematic reflection. The narrative of journey dwells on the autobiographies of teachers who have spent half their lives in education, whereas the narrative of hope reminds us that strategies for sustaining and perpetuating hope are a critical aspect of the craft of teaching. Finally, the narrative of freedom, like the narrative of reflective practice, centers on the lessons of a single, remarkable educator—bell hooks—and her uncompromising commitment to teaching as the practice of freedom.

In all of these chapters, we retell these stories in powerful and compelling ways but are especially intent upon drawing out lessons for novice and experienced teachers alike. A partial listing of the lessons we derive include that the best teachers:

- skillfully observe human interactions in classrooms
- carefully ground their teaching in a vision of a democratic community
- dedicate themselves tirelessly to their students' growth and welfare
- maintain challenging but flexible standards and are responsive to their students' individual needs
- learn constantly from colleagues and students and from their surroundings
- are stubbornly resilient and relentlessly affirming
- take risks and learn from mistakes and errors
- think continuously about their practices
- use dialogue and storytelling to help their students grow
- create secure places for learners
- are first and foremost learners themselves
- reflect on their own experiences as learners and use what they know about themselves to help others
- retain faith in the ability of all students to learn
- cannot conceive of teaching without a foundation in hope
- believe that human liberation is one of the enduring goals of all teaching

ORGANIZATION

Chapter 1 argues that reading outstanding teacher narratives by skilled teacher-writers is an invaluable way to prepare new teachers and to assist veterans in growing professionally. We also make a case for narrative as a way of knowing, and we offer more extensive descriptions of the six narrative forms or genres described above.

Chapter 2 considers teacher narratives from a historical perspective. We discuss eight narratives—four from the 19th century and four from the 20th century—each of which reflects its times. Together they indicate how perceptions of the leading educational challenges changed over time. These narratives become increasingly more focused on the specific problems of educating children well and on the connections between reflective teaching and the shaping of one's professional and personal identity.

Chapter 3 introduces the narrative of social criticism. We focus on four books that should stimulate readers to become more incisive and effective critics of schools. These are Jonathan Kozol's *Death at an Early Age* and his *Savage Inequalities*, Marva Collins' *Marva Collins' Way*, and Ira Shor's *When Students Have Power*.

Chapter 4 introduces the narrative of apprenticeship and induction. We examine three works that challenge readers to think about the value of educational mentors and the strategies teachers must adopt when such mentors are unavailable. These books are Robert Inchausti's *Spitwad Sutras*, James Herndon's *The Way It Spozed to Be*, and Patricia Schmidt's *Beginning in Retrospect*.

Chapter 5 analyses the relationship between reflection and action through the lens of five narratives of reflective practice by the acclaimed kindergarten teacher Vivian Paley. These books are *White Teacher, Kwanzaa and Me, The Boy Who Would Be a Helicopter, You Can't Say You Can't Play,* and *The Girl with the Brown Crayon.*

Chapter 6 focuses on the narrative of journey, a genre that is the closest to autobiography and often incorporates many elements of the other narrative forms already introduced. The books we discuss and interpret in this chapter include Mike Rose's *Lives on the Boundary,* Howard Gardner's *To Open Minds,* and Jane Tompkins' *A Life in School.*

Chapter 7 acquaints readers with the narrative of hope. This narrative form stresses the notion that education must retain a strong element of hope and faith if it is to have a long-term effect on students. The books examined in this chapter are Herb Kohl's *"I Won't Learn from You"* and his *Discipline of Hope,* Paulo Freire's *Pedagogy of Hope,* and Garret Keizer's *No Place but Here.*

Chapter 8 introduces the narrative of freedom. This form of narrative focuses on combating racism and promoting freedom as among the chief purposes of education. All of the narratives in this chapter are written by bell hooks, an experienced teacher, a college professor, a prolific author, and one of the leading philosophers of freedom writing today. The works we examine are *Teaching to Transgress, Bone Black,* and *Wounds of Passion.*

Chapter 9 is a significant departure from earlier chapters. We return to the issue of narrative knowing but focus our efforts on helping beginning and experienced teachers to think seriously about their own educational autobiographies. We include a variety of strategies and techniques to trigger reflection on past learning and teaching and to encourage readers to emulate the authors discussed in this book. We want teachers to begin to write their own narratives as learners and as educators and to experience the power of writing their own lives.

Chapter 10 synthesizes the findings from earlier chapters and reemphasizes the value of these stories for learning how to teach more effectively and live more fully. Also, we return to the themes of "wide-awakeness" and democracy and to some of the ways in which narratives of teaching can help educators to become the alert, critical, participatory, and caring pedagogues they must be in helping to foster a more just and equitable society.

At the conclusion of each chapter, summaries are included to help students remember key points, and a few brief questions follow to stimulate further dialogue and emphasize recurring themes.

USING THIS TEXT

This book can be used as a core or supplementary text in courses focusing on social and psychological foundations of education, curriculum and instruction, introduction to teaching, principles and practices of teaching, directed teaching, or the school in modern society. It would, of course, be ideal as well for more specialized courses focusing on autobiography, narrative, or the literature of educational reform and renewal.

Because this book focuses on the real-life stories of skilled teacher/writers, we think it offers a unique and valuable perspective on teacher education and professional development. We hope you agree.

ACKNOWLEDGMENTS

Steve Preskill is especially grateful to his coauthor Robin Smith Jacobvitz for her thoughtfulness, generosity, and hard work. This book would be greatly diminished without her fine contributions. Steve thanks his colleagues at the University of New Mexico for their support, especially Michael Morris, Breda Bova, Leroy Ortiz, Richard van Dongen, Tom Keyes, and Jan Gamradt. Special thanks also go to David Gruenewald, a graduate student at UNM who has been a strong booster of this project. Steve extends his gratitude as well to Audrey Thompson and Frank Margonis at the University of Utah and to George Otero and Lois Vermilya for being outstanding role models and great colleagues. He is particularly indebted to Stephen Brookfield for being a stimulating collaborator and a wonderful friend. Without the help of Debbie Stollenwerk, this project never would have gotten off the ground. We are most grateful to her. We also want to thank Kathy Davis for coordinating our manuscript into its final product. Finally, Steve dedicates this book to his wife Hallie. Her love and confidence remain his greatest sources of inspiration.

Robin Smith Jacobvitz thanks Steve Preskill for inviting her to work on this book. It has been a privilege to teach and to write with him. She is grateful to her parents, Patricia and Jack Smith, for encouraging her love of books and for bringing home Jonathan Kozol's first book more than 30 years ago. Robin thanks her students at the University of New Mexico for allowing her to be their teacher for almost 15 years. She also thanks her sister Claudia Smith; her brothers Jack and Chris Smith; Marguerite McCormack, Rebecca Reynolds Bannister, Sarah Woods, Jane Walker, Lori Connors-Tadros, and Judy Weinstein for their friendship; and Vickie Emery, Peter Chase, Miriam Levine, and Wayne Shrubsall for their assistance and good advice. Robin dedicates this book to her husband, Bob Jacobvitz. Without his constant love, patience, and support, it would have been impossible for her to do this work.

Special thanks goes to the following people who reviewed the manuscript: Myra J. Baughman, Pacific Lutheran University; Linda S. Beath, Central Washington University; Mary Lou Brotherson, Nova Southeastern University; Mary Ann Clark, Elms College; Jeanne Ellsworth, Plattsburgh State University of New York; Stephanie Evans, California State University, Los Angeles; Louise E. Fleming, Ashland University; Jane Hinson, State University of West Georgia; James Kauffman, University of South Carolina, Aiken; Johanna Nel, University of Wyoming; Karen Sanchez, Nova Southeastern University; Barbara Stern, Randolph-Macon Woman's College; Laura Wendling, California State University, San Marcos; Ann Whitaker, Northeastern Illinois University.

TO THE STUDENT

HOW THIS PROJECT GOT STARTED

It was almost 10 years ago when I first discovered the value of skillfully rendered stories of teaching and learning. Like Herb Kohl, who recalled in one of his own narratives a few special times in his life when a book just seemed to be waiting for him to pluck it from the shelf, my intellectual life was transformed one day while perusing Mike Rose's *Lives on the Boundary*. In clean, spare, eloquent prose, Rose tells the story of his life, focusing particularly on his experiences as a student and teacher. As Rose pieces together these details, a portrait emerges of an often troubled and neglected youth who is rescued by a few highly alert and caring teachers. These teachers, along with other mentors, help Rose become a scholarship student and develop into a consummate and dedicated teacher in his own right. In the process of constructing this story in all of its revealing specificity and concreteness, Rose also comments on the failures of American education generally and explores some of the instructional strategies and democratic dispositions needed to set it right. It is an awe-inspiring tour de force.

The pleasure and challenge of Rose's story led directly to my rereading or to reading for the first time Philip Lopate's *Being with Children*, James Herndon's *The Way It Spozed to Be*, Eliot Wigginton's *Sometimes a Shining Moment*, Jonathan Kozol's *Death at an Early Age*, Vivian Paley's *White Teacher*, and Garret Keizer's *No Place but Here*. Still others were devoured as they were published, including Howard Gardner's *To Open Minds*, Robert Inchausti's *Spitwad Sutras*, Kohl's *"I Won't Learn from You,"* and Stephen O'Connor's *Will My Name Be Shouted Out?* These are dramatic tales of growth, failure, dampened hopes, rebirth, and renewal. They show in great detail what it takes to teach well and to teach with heart. They underscore the notion that teaching is a terribly challenging profession and that it is impossible ever to get it right. They suggest as well that teaching is a calling of infinite possibility in which each new day is another chance to reach a disengaged student or to help a seemingly slow learner finally live up to his or her potential. They are fundamentally human stories. When told well by the most skillful of writers, they have the power to move us like any great imaginative literature. These stories of teaching are so compelling that you can't wait to share them with others, to single out the most dramatic and powerful parts, and to persuade others to become just as enthusiastic about them as you are.

My affection for these stories led me to assign a few of them in an introductory course for aspiring teachers that I was team teaching with Robin. Robin was already an avid reader of many of these narratives and introduced me to Jane Tompkins' *A Life in School*, Patricia Schmidt's *Beginning in Retrospect*, and a number of other powerful stories of teaching. Our mutual interest in these stories eventually inspired us to cowrite a textbook that would introduce new and veteran teachers to these wonderful narratives and help them to see their value as tools for professional development.

RETELLING TEACHER NARRATIVES TO MAXIMIZE THEIR EDUCATIONAL VALUE

In this book we seek to retell wonderful teachers' stories in ways that will educate and inspire people who care about teaching. We know of many books that claim to value narrative, but few get close enough to the details of the narratives themselves to shed light on why they move us, anger us, or enlighten us. In this book we want readers to feel they are in the presence of these teacher/protagonists, reliving their struggles and their triumphs and taking from the experience a renewed sense of the power and challenge of great teaching. We recommend that you read the narratives themselves, but it is also useful, at least initially, to have someone guiding you through them, underscoring the best parts and interpreting them for their maximum educational benefit. You will be introduced to more than 20 narratives that, in our view, have much to teach about what it takes to grow into teaching. They also alert you to the pitfalls and problems of learning to teach in institutions that are often inhospitable to imaginative, creative, inquisitive minds.

What does it take to teach in public schools? An enormous amount of persistence, courage, talent, and luck. And even then there is no guarantee of success or satisfaction. Teaching is hard work. Trying to balance the needs of dozens of students every day against the demands of subject matter and other pressures and working with students who suffer from every imaginable societal ill is exhausting, often discouraging work. But it can also be wonderful work, charged with the amazing and awe-inspiring drive that even the most downtrodden student frequently exhibits. Like no other educational literature, these stories capture the dilemmas and delights of great teaching—teaching that often goes against the grain of conservative public institutions.

EXCERPTS FROM TEACHER NARRATIVES

Although we assert that highlighting and interpreting some of the most enlightening and inspiring sections of these narratives has a special value for teachers, we know that reading the narratives directly has a power all its own. We have included excerpts from some first-rate teacher narratives. We hope as you read this book and learn from the stories we retell that you will also turn to these excerpts frequently to encounter the well-chosen words of these skilled teacher-writers. All of these authors have a distinctive style and approach and an enormous accumulation of experience and wisdom to share. The only way to get the fullest possible benefit from these narratives is to read them in their entirety. We hope that this book and the availability of these excerpts will motivate you to do just that.

READING TEACHER NARRATIVES AND THE PURSUIT OF EDUCATIONAL RENEWAL

We contend that these stories can help us become better teachers, and we claim that they can assist us in becoming more thoughtful and sensitive human beings. They spotlight not only the processes by which students learn but also the transformations that teachers undergo as they open themselves up to what their students and colleagues can teach them. These stories ultimately trace the self-renewal of these teacher/protagonists and the new identities that emerge from the lives they lead of wide-awake teaching and learning. These stories are about the call to teach, about an irresistible drive to commit one's life to other people's growth. The devotion these teachers give to their craft and to their students may seem a little crazy but quite endearing as well. These stories give us insight into the reasons why a few dedicated people are willing to devote themselves to an enterprise that can be so uncertain, messy, even chaotic. Hcrb Kohl calls life in teaching "joyful foolishness." This notion is an underlying theme of these stories.

As for the idea of educational renewal, it is a process of actively and continuously engaging in self-discovery that spurs new possibilities for deepening engagement between teachers and students. Each new encounter with a student or colleague or idea can leave the alert and eager teacher forever changed. The best teachers are wide open to new ideas and are always learning, and the acts of teaching and writing about teaching stimulate them to continue to grow. Educational renewal symbolizes the ongoing effort to construct an identity, to find a home in the world, to reach your potential as a person, and to see your image of yourself reflected in some form in the larger society. Educational renewal occurs when we free ourselves to widen our horizons and our choices and to set a more creative direction for our lives.

SIX GENRES OF TEACHER NARRATIVES

This book is a guide to reading these engaging teacher stories, and it provides an impetus to both novice and experienced teachers to write their own narratives. In studying these narratives, we have found they can be sorted into different narrative forms or genres that correspond to the skills, understandings, and attitudes teachers need to be effective. The types or genres we have identified include:

- the narrative of social criticism
- the narrative of induction and apprenticeship
- the narrative of reflective practice
- the narrative of journey
- the narrative of hope
- the narrative of freedom

We base the text on these different genres and use summaries, paraphrases, and excerpts from these narratives as means to discuss and explore what good teachers know and do.

As we have noted, we personally love many of these teacher narratives. We write this book to introduce these stories to prospective and experienced teachers, to get them to savor and appreciate the language and passions of these authors, and to encourage educators to use them as a springboard to better, more inspired, and more committed teaching. At their best, narratives of teaching provide accessible, compelling, and morally persuasive depictions of thoughtful teaching in all its ambiguity and complexity. They also have an immediacy that connects powerfully with the details of everyday experience, and they offer occasions to reimagine education's possibilities. Finally, the exploration of the narratives is an opportunity to relish those moments when deepened understanding and genuine human connection are put at the forefront of our pedagogical encounters and when simple joy in teaching and learning matters most.

Steve Preskill

BRIEF CONTENTS

CONTENTS

Stories as a Way of Knowing and Growing

READING OUTSTANDING TEACHER NARRATIVES

The more we work with both novice and veteran teachers, the more we grow convinced that reading narratives written by skilled teacher-authors can greatly enhance understanding of teaching and learning. Expertly crafted stories of teaching portray classrooms in all their vivid and concrete particulars and offer both prospective and experienced teachers a vicarious means to face the challenges of educating children well. These narratives encourage teachers to educate more creatively and resourcefully, and they engender new hope about the impact of teachers' work. The protagonists in these narratives grapple with all the difficulties that make teaching in contemporary schools so daunting, but their stories also highlight the imagination and commitment of teachers who see possibility in the most trying of circumstances. They reaffirm the role that teachers play in humanizing and democratizing students and in unleashing their ability to make a difference in the world. Furthermore, these narratives are guides to living well. They show that to foster student growth, teachers must experience their own ongoing self-development—their own continuing educational renewal. Thus, great teaching grows out of a clear and often reinvented sense of self, and the most moving teacher narratives chronicle the emergence of a better self and a better teacher.

From our point of view, the value of expertly written teacher narratives cannot be overestimated. Many scholars have argued that teachers should write their own stories and that other teachers should read them. But few have underscored the importance of narratives written by skilled, experienced teacher-writers who have special abilities to depict teaching in powerful and inspiring ways. These writers are superb storytellers who use their gifts to immerse readers in the dilemmas of teaching. Their carefully crafted stories arouse and instruct, heightening consciousness about habits of good living, learning, and teaching. They are vivid and concrete reminders that teachers must make hundreds of decisions every day that affect their students' futures. The pictures these writers paint with words sustain hope and restore faith in the process of education. They show that a teacher who works creatively and passionately with children, who strives to be caring and to pay attention, can make a decisive difference in the life of any child.

In this book, we examine more than 20 stories of teaching and learning, prime examples of artful and illuminating narratives that also deliver important lessons about the craft of teaching. Like all good writing, these stories are simple, direct, and highly engaging. But their surface simplicity disguises layers of complexity about education and making a life that we strive to explore and reveal. As Jane Isenberg (1994) points out in her unjustly neglected book about the impact of popular classroom chronicles on her own teaching and development, the best stories of teaching are

> plainly told by angry authors who describe the suffering of a disempowered constituency in the hope of ending that suffering. They are structured around crises of literacy, identity, and control and operate within constraints and conventions that are politically determined. (p. 105)

Isenberg likens these stories to slave narratives in that they are almost invariably occasions for the expression of rage. They focus on the formation of more authentic selves for both the teacher and students within the constraints of a hierarchical and racist society. Isenberg additionally contends that these stories have the advantages of being highly accessible to students, of being a means by which aspiring teachers can fantasize about actual teaching, and of being a vehicle for helping students "find their voices as poets, chroniclers, researchers, storytellers, critics, and biographers" (p. 127). This last point is especially important. Our affection for teacher narratives penned by skilled teacher-writers is based in part on our belief that these stories are a source of inspiration and excellence for teachers who are intent on composing their own lives as persons and professionals. We think these stories spur teachers to reflect on their work and make the continuous writing of their own stories a basis for honing their craft as teachers.

Until very recently, few educators have viewed teaching narratives as a source of instruction and enlightenment for aspiring and veteran teachers. Often, these stories have been dismissed as "merely entertainment, comic relief in the high drama of academic discourse" (Trimmer, 1997, p. x). As Joseph Trimmer states in the introduction to his collection of English teachers' short narratives, we might treasure stories for their wit and perspicuity, but we haven't trusted them as a means in themselves to teach and to learn.

Even among teacher educators who are most committed to using accounts of actual teaching experiences to enrich and complement educational theory, little attention has been paid to teachers' personal narratives (Carter & Doyle, 1996). It was striking to us that in the course of researching and reading teacher narratives for this book, we found so few references to Jane Isenberg's story of how teacher narratives shaped her professional identity. Scan these powerful words and consider how profoundly authors like Sylvia Ashton-Warner, Bel Kaufman, John Holt, and Herb Kohl have influenced her teaching:

> When, during the course of my recent musings, these teacher-authors reappeared in my consciousness, I recalled how they validated my affection for many of my students, as well as my horror at the biases and misanthropy of some of my colleagues; how they had shared their mistakes and triumphs in the classroom with me, thus helping me to recognize and acknowledge my own; how they had made me cry over the implacability of "the system" while at the same time showing me how to manipulate its constraints; and how they had taken me with them on their forays across cultural boundaries. (Isenberg, 1994, p. xiv)

As Carter and Doyle (1996) have recently shown in the *Handbook of Research on Teacher Education*, researchers and teacher educators are giving new prominence to biography in the preparation of teachers. They are discovering that the emerging identities and life histories of prospective teachers greatly influence the professional development of teachers—from the decision to teach, to the process of becoming a teacher, to the act of teaching itself. Carter and Doyle contend that several converging lines of thinking have contributed to this new perspective. Among others, they include: (1) critiques of the politics of teaching, (2) the prominence of feminist thinking in teacher education, and (3) a growing appreciation of narrative as both a form of inquiry and a form of theory about teaching.

With regard to the politics of teaching, Goodson (1994) has argued that studying teachers' lives and understanding how they experience their work is a way to place the teacher's voice at the center of reform efforts. He argues that teachers' stories can raise public consciousness about adverse conditions in schools and the complexity of teachers' work and give teachers a greater degree of control over the circumstances that either promote or impede learning. Furthermore, by writing and telling their own stories of life inside schools, teachers can generate new perceptions of schools and help to supplant the simplistic and misinformed rhetoric that often dominates public policy discussions.

Another critical perspective is one that views personal narratives as powerful instruments for maintaining and transforming teaching practices (e.g., Britzman, 1986, 1992). Britzman (1986) argues that when student teachers enter the classroom, their personal histories in such settings are evoked and deeply influence their practice. If the social and political contexts that shaped these histories are left unexamined, then, despite the student teacher's best intentions, "the cultural reproduction of authoritarian teaching practices" (p. 443) is likely to occur. We should add that the effect of understanding one's personal history is rarely simple or fast acting. As feminist writer Adrienne Rich (1979) put it, "The awakening of consciousness is not like the crossing of a frontier—one step and you are in another country" (p. 48). We revisit and revise our histories many times before the fullness of their force and meaning can be grasped.

The feminist perspective in educational theory is largely responsible for the popularity of the "voice" metaphor in current discussions of teacher education. In *Women's Ways of Knowing*, constructivist women—that is, those who incorporate personal knowledge with knowledge gained from others—are described as having developed a "narrative sense of self." They search for a voice in which to communicate to others their understanding of life's complexities. The feminist perspective in education particularly values life history as a source of knowledge and theory. Carter and Doyle cite Madeline Grumet's work, especially her book *Bitter Milk: Women and Teaching* (1988), as an example of educational scholarship that investigates the ways our own childhoods and our parenting practices are implicated in our practices as teachers.

What many of these researchers and theorists miss is that, if stories are to have their desired impact, they must be crafted carefully by skilled writers. As Martha Nussbaum (1995) demonstrates in her book *Poetic Justice*, good storytellers enjoy a special ability to frame events that unleash strong emotions, stirring and disconcerting us in ways that challenge convention and exacting an often "painful confrontation with one's own thoughts and intentions" (p. 5). She writes that such stories require us "to see and to respond to many things that may be difficult to confront [but] they make this process palatable by giving us pleasure in the very act of confrontation" (p. 6). Teacher narratives written by professional teacher-writers fit this description well. They encourage us to face our flaws and errors as teachers and human beings but, just as important, they also shed light on the ways in which institutions and systems often miseducate and diminish our children. At the same time, they raise awareness and increase understanding through a mode of presentation that is intrinsically interesting and widely accessible.

But Nussbaum makes an even stronger claim about stories that has direct relevance for teacher narratives. Stories written by good writers provide a foundation for building a moral and political theory that should become one of the bases for defining and measuring educational excellence. Stories make operational the values by which we should strive to live, and they concretely describe the interactions between teacher and students that we should expect in classroom settings premised on social justice and democracy. Furthermore, exposure to stories increases the reader's ability to feel deeply, to empathize with the experiences of others, and to become more fully human. When these stories focus on protagonists who are struggling with their emerging humanity, readers cannot help but reflect and perhaps act on the connections between their own personal identities and their aspirations to teach well.

Reading superb teacher narratives, like reading other wonderful books, is a way to live "more deeply, more fully, and with a more certain alliance with this human world" (Bauer, 1997, p. 11). As Michael Dorris (1997, p. xiv) so eloquently notes in his introduction to an edited volume about the impact of authors' early reading experiences, stories of all kinds affect us in at least four ways. First, they transport us from our own time and place to undiscovered and unimagined other worlds, leaving us forever changed and somewhat more capable of imagining and enacting a humane present. Second, good stories can give us a feeling of power, of enhanced knowing and appreciating that changes how we see those around us and ourselves. Third, Dorris refers to the "sense of independence" that readers experience when immersing themselves in wonderful books and the strengthened sense of self that often results from reading powerful, transforming literature. Finally, he mentions the "shock of connection" or recognition that occurs when encountering characters who may, on the surface, lack similarities to us but who, at a deeper level, share our anxieties, our hopes, and our passions. Dorris adds to this his conviction, which we endorse, that moving, disturbing, and thrilling reading "is a path into the great swirl of humanity, past, present, and future" (p. xiv). That books can help us to live more completely and that books are one invaluable doorway to the riches and wonders of the wider world are ideas we not only believe but exhort all teachers to adopt and practice as well.

Once we develop the habit of reading terrific teacher narratives, we will find ourselves drawn to these tales again and again. In Wayne Booth's (1988) words, these stories will become "the company we keep," an integral aspect of our pursuit of lifelong learning. We may even come to regard the protagonists and other characters in these stories as friends who give us pleasure, help us grow, and make our lives fuller and richer. Indeed, there is no reason why these narratives cannot give us pleasure the way that our leisure reading does, even as we recognize that it is a pleasure that often goes very deep and may reshape how we see ourselves. Like the friends who broaden our outlook and stretch our horizons, these stories, when read closely and repeatedly, can bring forth the best and truest selves that reside within all of us.

THE PURSUIT OF EDUCATIONAL RENEWAL

One of our central themes is that reading these narratives can change the kinds of people we are. They can foster the development of our second selves and stimulate a sense of educational renewal. The second self is a notion taken directly from Robert Inchausti's *The Ignorant Perfection of Ordinary People* (1991), an analysis of the lives of highly accomplished servant leaders like Mahatma Gandhi, Martin Luther King, Mother Teresa, and Lech Walesa. In extending themselves to make a difference in their communities, these leaders uncover new dimensions of themselves not previously discernible. For Inchausti, discovering and creating the second self is an "ethical accomplishment" (p. 12) as it is the self within our power to fashion from the choices we make and the everyday experiences we accumulate. Exploring and understanding the self has no real end in this conception and is reciprocally linked to our responsibility to continue to serve others and to live as fully and richly as possible. For Inchausti, it is not an arcane psychological self or an abstract academic one. Rather, it is a self that is "all around us, perpetually at hand in our families, our past, our public and private lives, our rites and our works, and in our possibilities and responsibilities. For it is in these concrete matters that the world addresses us, asks us who we are, and calls upon us to recollect our origins with gratitude and resolute love of life" (p. 12).

Inchausti argues that the work of making the self is the labor of a lifetime and that it occurs in concert with other selves, not in isolation from them. Ironically, our second self is most likely to emerge when we lose our sense of ourselves in service to others. We can answer the call to service in many important ways. Teaching stands out as one of the most ordinary yet extraordinary of vocations, one of the most selfless yet self-enhancing responses to this call.

The process of reconstructing the self is related to the search for meaning. Charles Taylor (1989) indicates that, in recent times, people have derived meaning from articulating and expressing their sense of what matters and from revising and expanding this sense throughout the course of their lives. Meaning and purpose, from this point of view, are not abstracted from experience but invented and discovered as a "manner of living ordinary life" (p. 23).

One way to understand this notion of the second self is to think of it as the self that builds upon but is different from the self one is born with. Our efforts to construct an identity, to reach and exceed our potential as human beings, and to make the choices that shape who we are and how we see the world are all part of the quest for the second self. It is a process of self-discovery, of enthusiastically pursuing personal and professional renewal. Furthermore, if these stories can spark individual renewal, the energy and excitement generated may contribute to systemic educational renewal as well.

In his book *This Rough Magic: The Life of Teaching* (1993), Daniel Lindley offers an intriguing stage theory of teaching that has direct bearing on the importance of the teacher's pursuit of educational renewal. Lindley contends that most teachers who are in the first stage as student teachers or as raw beginners simply struggle to get accustomed to spending many hours each day with children or adolescents. Their learning curves are steep as they figure out how to relate to young people, to discipline them, to use subject matter to engage them, and to accustom themselves to the constant noise, confusion, and clutter.

At the second stage, teachers have at least become competent. They have learned what to expect, more or less, from their students. They are more disciplined themselves and more savvy about the strategies needed to teach effectively and to motivate the different personalities that are arrayed before them. In this stage, which can begin during the first year and extend throughout a whole career, the heightened anxiety of the first-stage teacher is gone. A confidence and calm have set in that make teaching somewhat less frenetic, though no less challenging. As Lindley points out, many teachers never progress beyond this stage. These second-stage teachers have not discovered how to invest their teaching with their own unique perspectives, their own personal styles. At the third stage, which rarely emerges until the third or fourth year of teaching, Lindley maintains that teachers employ the established curriculum in such creative and special ways that wholly different relationships between teacher and subject matter and between teacher and students develop. As Lindley explains:

> Gradually the teacher herself is entering the work: She now feels herself to be an original, unique person, with a particular relationship both to the subject matter and to her students. Teaching becomes an idiosyncratically creative act, an extension and expression of her whole being. With this come moments of pure joy, or clarity, or fun that were previously only imagined. (p. 14)

We contend that when the teacher enters the work, when her or his original, unique perspective influences what is taught and how it is taught, the teacher's second self is emerging and that self is likely to continue to change, grow, and reemerge. This idea of the second self, or of the third-stage teacher, is very similar to what J. Glenn Gray (1984) calls the "moral artist." This is that wide-awake person who can never be fully plumbed or comprehended, who contributes a distinctive and often unpredictable constellation of talents and dispositions to every situation she or he encounters. As Gray says, this person's "hallmark is the open mind, the search for wider perspectives, the unfettered imagination. Such a person is never completely known or knowable for the simple reason that he is in the process of becoming, under way, not at the end of development. The fascination of a rich personality is one of the few inexhaustible phenomena in all experience. Again, like a work of art, every time we return to it, new facets are revealed" (p. 111).

PROFESSIONAL AND PERSONAL GROWTH THROUGH WELL-CRAFTED TEACHER NARRATIVES

Teachers reinventing themselves as moral artists can read and study skillfully crafted narratives that parallel their journeys. In this book we summarize, explore, and interpret teacher narratives that challenge and provoke readers to dedicate themselves to educational excellence and unrelenting self-renewal.

As Jalongo and Isenberg point out in their book *Teachers' Stories* (1995), narrative is both idiosyncratic and universal, particularistic yet familiar, illuminating the life experience of one person yet reminding us of our interconnectedness. As we read narratives of teachers' experiences, we can appreciate these stories for being concrete and unique retellings of another person's experience, even as we also see ourselves reflected in these accounts. This is an important dimension of their power and value and is related to another claim that Jalongo and Isenberg (1995) make for teachers' stories. They are a highly accessible, very engaging means to promote reflection on the complexity and highly contextualized nature of schooling and instruction. Stories embrace the messy, improvisational, unexpected qualities of teaching and learning. They also invite thought and discussion about the multiple meanings of good teaching. Stories of teaching encourage educators to generate their own views of what it means to teach well, building on and contributing to their hard-won self-knowledge. Who we are and who we become depends, in part, on the stories we read and the stories we construct about ourselves.

Practitioners and practitioners-to-be crave the authentic feel of stories even as they recognize that no story can capture the day-in, day-out struggle of teaching. Stories are accessible, attractive, and even seductive. They can woo us into thinking that the plotted, sometimes romantic nature of narrative is a substitute for the act of teaching itself. Yet, as Polkinghorne (1995) notes in his often-cited analysis of narrative, "plots function to select from the myriad of happenings those which are direct contributors to the terminal situation of the story" (p. 8). In the case of teaching stories, many of the details that are an integral part of every classroom experience are omitted for the sake of economy and narrative power. These stories have a point, after all, and the episodes included help the author drive home that point. Reading stories of teaching is not the same as observing a teacher in an actual classroom, nor are these stories substitutes for more theoretical or scientific approaches that are not hampered by the constraints of plot or the conventions of stories.

Nevertheless, stories have an undeniable power and value of their own that may even be central to the enterprise of education itself. Witherell and Noddings (1991) assert this claim with impressive directness:

> To educate is to take seriously both the quest for life's meaning and the meaning of individual lives . . . Through telling, writing, reading, and listening to life stories—one's own and others'—those engaged in this work can penetrate cultural barriers, discover the power of the self and the integrity of the other, and deepen their understanding of their respective histories and possibilities (pp. 3–4).

Our outlook and experiences parallel those of Witherell and Noddings. As teachers and professors of education, we have developed a deep appreciation for teacher narratives. We have watched our students fall in love with the best of these stories, fueling their aspirations to become great teachers. We have also seen how these stories captured our own imaginations and revitalized our own commitment to educational studies. We write this book to share with others our passion for these stories and to show how they have helped us in constructing a stronger sense of self and in renewing our obligation to the vocation of teaching.

SIX NARRATIVE FORMS

It is interesting and useful to exploit a variety of different kinds of narratives to help new and experienced teachers. We have found that these narratives can be divided into at least six forms or genres that represent important parts of the knowledge and dispositions preservice and in-service teachers should acquire to become better teachers. Among the possibilities discerned in the vast literature of teachers' stories are narratives of (1) social criticism, (2) apprenticeship and induction, (3) reflective practice, (4) journey, (5) hope, and (6) freedom.

Narrative of Social Criticism. One essential function of any teacher education program is to aid students in becoming more critical about the place of education in society and to gain new understanding of the school's historic role in maintaining an often unjust and inhumane status quo. Many students planning to pursue a career in teaching have little knowledge of how racism, bureaucratic insensitivity, and miseducation have plagued schools. No teacher can be a fully accomplished practitioner or an effective school leader without possessing a historical and sociological perspective on education and the ability to employ this perspective to critique the practices of the school and the larger society. Teachers must know how society has influenced and constrained the efforts of the school, and they must understand the ways in which many social forces have often prevented schools from fulfilling their democratic promise. As we have noted, narratives have an immediacy, concreteness, and dramatic impact that traditional historical and sociological analyses often lack (Brunner, 1994). They lend themselves well to reader self-reflection and they encourage thought processes that promote the development of personal and professional identity (Graham, 1991).

Narrative of Apprenticeship and Induction. As students develop the critical perspective needed to understand the larger context of schools and as they gradually generate their own vision for more humane and effective schooling, they will also find that they must learn the ropes of good teaching practice. The narrative of apprenticeship and induction focuses on the experience of emerging from novicehood and of doing so without compromising one's commitment to that original vision. This narrative form frequently recounts the efforts of skilled veterans to advise novices and to help them develop the practices they will need to flourish as teachers. It focuses on the struggles and challenges beginners face during student teaching and during the first full year of teaching and typically culminates in the protagonist's successfully meeting these challenges and learning the "reflective stance that is so crucial to masterful teaching" (Jalongo and Isenberg, 1995, p. 40). But it may also end with novice teachers still searching for success and meaning, particularly when they have been unable to identify a mentor to whom they may serve as apprentices. Interestingly, this period in a teacher's life is roughly equivalent to Lindley's first stage of teaching.

Narrative of Reflective Practice. Once the first year or so is over and the apprenticeship has ended, teachers must continue to hone their skills. One of the most noteworthy ways for them to do this is to reflect regularly and insightfully on their everyday practices. The best teachers spend much time thinking about their teaching—what they are doing, why they are doing it, and how they can do it better. The narrative of reflective practice focuses on teachers who are self-critical in constructive ways and who apply what they learn to their work in schools. Vivian Paley's many books are among the best examples of the narrative of reflective practice. Paley models the process of subjecting every facet of her teaching to her unyielding critical eye. These narratives take the reader inside the mind of the teacher to show how the teacher's standards influence evaluation of her own practices and how she acts on these evaluations to create a classroom that is more just, equitable, and humane.

Narrative of Journey.   As teachers go from novices to veterans, they must find ways to sustain their enthusiasm and commitment. The narrative of journey gives teachers an opportunity to reflect on their whole careers, their whole lives. It is a chance to consider once again who they are, how a career in teaching has contributed to their identity, and whether the day-to-day work of a teacher continues to bring fulfillment. This genre brings together all of the elements that make these stories such powerful and useful guides for both novice and experienced teachers. Not simply a series of anecdotes about teaching, these stories are full-fledged autobiographies in which we witness the protagonists growing as students and thinkers and later as teachers and "moral artists." Reading such narratives may be an occasion to reexamine one's life and profession and to do what needs to be done to make teaching as exciting and life-enhancing a vocation as possible. The narrative of journey incorporates all of the other narrative forms by calling on teachers to reflect on their pasts and renew their futures.

Narrative of Hope.   This narrative form is an elixir against despair. It accentuates optimism, imagination, and a sense of wonder as foundations for strong education. It reminds us of the paradox that what we do can make a difference for individual children and adults, even though these efforts cannot be satisfactorily assessed or encompassed. The narrative of hope helps us to rediscover the purpose and meaning of education and to take pleasure in the smallest improvements and the most modest accomplishments of our students. It impresses upon us that teachers must maintain their optimism to be effective stewards of their students' present and future lives. The narrative of hope helps teachers and students to imagine possible worlds and to acquire the tools to act on those imaginings. It parallels Dewey's notion of "democratic faith"—that all children can learn and even flourish if only the right conditions are established and suitable pedagogies employed.

Narrative of Freedom.   Like the narrative of hope, this is a genre of attitude and tone as much as it is of practice and conduct. It is an especially inspiring form that calls teachers to see the chief object of their work as the unleashing of their students' abilities within the context of an increasingly more just and nonracist society. This form of narrative focuses on freedom, on giving people the skills and attitudes needed to shed the fetters of conventional practice, and on fostering individual and collaborative accomplishments that previously seemed out of reach. It focuses on critique and hope, on reflection and bold action. It portrays a way of being in the world that eschews limits and constraints and embraces possibility, compassion, and love. It is a form of narrative that openly expresses rage about the past while actively building on emerging conditions to shape a more caring, equitable, and emancipatory future. bell hooks' books, particularly her most autobiographical ones, are prime examples of the narrative of freedom. Her focus as a teacher is to create free spaces within an oppressive environment. She exhorts us to use our own teaching to create a more just and loving world.

Almost like stages in a teacher's life, these narrative forms incorporate many of the skills and dispositions teachers at all stages of their careers require to sustain themselves and to make their work worthwhile. Although most narratives may be strongly identified with a particular form or genre, many also incorporate elements of all the other forms as well. For example, the narrative of apprenticeship and induction often includes a strong social critique and portrays a great deal of reflective practice. As we have already noted, the narrative of journey is almost by definition a hybrid of many of the other narrative forms. As with any typology, it can be instructive and useful to define teacher narratives by these categories, but in the end such categorizing is at least somewhat contrived.

THE VALUE OF SUMMARIZING AND INTERPRETING TEACHER NARRATIVES

In chapters 3 through 8 we recount and examine the most powerful and useful stories from the books that we think best represent these genres and to which teachers are most likely to respond favorably. We provide a guide to reading these stories and an analysis of what they can contribute to one's professional knowledge and personal development. We encourage you to read the original narratives in full, and we have included some excerpts from these narratives to give you a flavor of how these authors write. In addition, we emphasize the great value in experiencing and thinking about highlights from narratives in juxtaposition to other narratives of the same genre. What it means to apprentice oneself to a mentor, to be a reflective practitioner, or to promote hope, to use three examples, is deepened when these issues are explored from a few different but related perspectives. Each of these narratives contains many wonderful stories. We have identified some of the most engaging and meaningful of these "stories within stories" to help you to see why teachers at all levels of experience need to include this "teacher lore" (Schubert, 1991) within their pedagogical repertoires.

Narratives written by skilled writers who are also accomplished teachers can be likened to the work of "educational connoisseurs." As Schubert (1991) explains it, these are individuals "who have considerable experience in educational situations and who have developed sophisticated levels of perception and discrimination, similar to connoisseurship in the arts" (p. 208). They have developed special abilities to "observe, describe, evocatively interpret and evaluate" (p. 209) the art and craft of teaching and, through their writing, they offer compelling visions of teaching and learning that shape the thought and action of readers and practitioners.

We highlight the work of widely acclaimed educational connoisseurs who not only have a deep understanding of teaching and learning but also have a highly refined sense of how to convey through their writing what they have discovered from experience. Drawing on some of the preliminary findings of William Schubert's Teacher Lore Project (1991, p. 220), we find that these teachers appear to share a number of characteristics. The most salient of these characteristics or qualities are that these teachers:

1. Maintain a sense of mission about the importance of teaching.
2. Exhibit a love of and compassion for students.
3. Find ways to build on student strengths.
4. Exhibit a clear sense of meaning and direction and are in the process of revising the same.
5. Guide their work with a quest for that which is worthwhile and just.
6. Are actively involved in self-education.

We will refer to these points throughout this book and return to them in more detail in the concluding chapter to examine the ways in which these teacher-authors have exemplified and strived to foster in others these characteristics.

CONCLUSION

Teachers' stories written by skilled teacher-writers are a powerful source of inspiration and knowledge. They stimulate teachers to reflect deeply on their lives and their profession. Like all excellent storytelling about teaching, the stories we single out in this book meet the criteria that Thomas Barone (1992) establishes for a narrative of "enhanced professionalism." First, they are accessible and engaging for most readers, regardless of their background. Second, they are compelling, showing teachers posing familiar problems and resolving them with a sense of "wearied elation" (p. 20) in the end. Third and probably most important for our purposes, they are morally persuasive, resulting in "the reconstruction of a portion of the reader's value system" (p. 20). Barone explains the moral power of great stories with a claim that fits our own experience when reading the best of these stories. Good stories, he writes, "enable readers to gaze in fresh astonishment upon a part of their world they thought they already seen. They also allow readers to be better acquainted with people they thought they had already known" (p. 20). Few experiences are as familiar as going to school, yet these stories, in the hands of "educational connoisseurs," help us to reenvision education's possibilities and its realities and to hasten our quest for educational renewal.

STUDY QUESTIONS

1. How can reading teachers' stories enhance your development as a teacher?
2. What are some of the advantages of stories as a means of educating teachers?
3. What is the "second self" and how does this concept relate to the development of teachers?
4. What are some of the educational issues you expect to find discussed in these teachers' stories?
5. What values do you expect to find expressed in these narratives?
6. How might reading these stories help you in your teaching career?

REFERENCES

Barone, T. (1992). A narrative of enhanced professionalism: Educational researchers and popular storybooks about school people. *Educational Researcher, 21*(8), 15–24.

Bauer, M. D. (1997). A more certain alliance. In M. Dorris & E. Buchwald (Eds.), *The most wonderful books: Writers on discovering the pleasures of reading* (pp. 9–11). Minneapolis, MN: Milkweed Editions.

Booth, W. (1988). *The company we keep: An ethics of fiction.* Berkeley, CA: University of California Press.

Britzman, D. (1986). Cultural myths in the making of a teacher: Biography and social structure in teacher education. *Harvard Educational Review, 56,* 442–456.

Britzman, D. (1992). The terrible problem of knowing thyself: Toward a poststructural account of teacher identity. *Journal of Curriculum Theorizing, 9*(3), 23–46.

Brunner, D. D. (1994). *Inquiry and reflection: Framing narrative practice in education.* Albany, NY: State University of New York Press.

Carter, K. & Doyle, W. (1996). Personal narrative and life history in learning to teach. In J. Sikula (Ed.), *Handbook of research on teacher education* (2nd ed., pp. 120–142). New York: Macmillan.

Dorris, M. (1997). Introduction. In M. Dorris & E. Buchwald (Eds.), *The most wonderful books: Writers on discovering the pleasures of reading* (pp. xiii–xv). Minneapolis, MN: Milkweed Editions.

Goodson, I. (1994). Studying the teacher's life and work. *Teaching and Teacher Education, 10*(1), 29–37.

Graham, R. (1991). *Reading and writing the self: Autobiography in education and the curriculum.* New York: Teachers College Press.

Gray, J. G. (1984). *Re-thinking American education: A philosophy of teaching and learning.* Middletown, CT: Wesleyan University Press.

Grumet, M. (1988). *Bitter milk: Women and teaching.* Amherst, MA: University of Massachusetts Press.

Inchausti, R. (1991). *The ignorant perfection of ordinary people.* Albany, NY: State University of New York Press.

Isenberg, J. (1994). *Going by the book: The role of popular classroom chronicles in the professional development of teachers.* Westport, CT: Bergin and Garvey.

Jalongo, M. R. & Isenberg, J. P. (1995). *Teachers' stories: From personal narrative to professional insight.* San Francisco, CA: Jossey Bass.

Lindley, D. A. (1993). *This rough magic: The life of teaching.* Westport, CT: Bergin and Garvey.

Nussbaum, M. (1995). *Poetic justice: The literary imagination and public life.* Boston: Beacon Press.

Polkinghorne, D. E. (1995). Narrative configuration in qualitative analysis. In J. A. Hatch & R. Wisniewski (Eds.), *Life history and narrative* (pp. 5–23). London: Falmer.

Rich, A. (1979). When we dead awaken: Writing as re-vision. In A. Rich, *On lies, secrets, and silence* (pp. 33–49). New York: Norton.

Schubert, W. (1991). Teacher lore: A basis for understanding praxis. In C. Witherell & N. Noddings (Eds.), *Stories lives tell: Narrative and dialogue in education* (pp. 207–233). New York: Teachers College Press.

Taylor, C. (1989). *Sources of the self: The making of the modern identity.* Cambridge, MA: Harvard University Press.

Trimmer, J. (Ed.). (1997). *Narration as knowledge: Tales of the teaching life.* Portsmouth, NH: Boynton/Cook.

Witherell, C. & Noddings, N. (1991). Prologue: An invitation to our readers. In C. Witherell & N. Noddings (Eds.), *Stories lives tell: Narrative and dialogue in education* (pp. 1–12). New York: Teachers College Press.

2

A Historical Perspective on Teacher Narratives

At least since the beginning of the 19th century, American educators have told stories about their experiences as teachers in schools. Employing fiction or autobiographical narrative, they have recounted tales of classroom power struggles, recalled yarns of overcoming adverse physical and social conditions, and set down memories of winning over whole communities reluctant to support public education. These stories strike a powerful chord with readers. Emerging in every decade, sometimes to wide acclaim, they continue to attract an audience because they capture something universal about people's experiences in schools. In addition to imparting a great deal about everyday life in classrooms and about how getting an education has changed over time, they are especially successful in delving into the sorrows and joys of careers in teaching. Sometimes they focus on novices struggling to survive, other times on the veteran looking back on a lifetime of service and endeavoring to make meaning out of it all. Invariably, the events chronicled and the anecdotes recounted are transformative moments when new understanding emerged or deepened appreciation occurred. They are, like so much autobiographical literature, stories of change, maturation, and self-revelation. They remain one of the starting points for students of the history of education who want to investigate the development and evolution of teaching as a craft and profession.

AUTOBIOGRAPHY OF DANIEL PAYNE

Although teacher narratives go back a long way, these stories did not become a distinct and recognizable genre until common schools were institutionalized in American life, roughly the period from 1830 to 1890. During this era, dozens of stories were written by teachers from all parts of the country about the trials, tribulations, and delights of shaping young minds. Ironically, one of the most affirming of such accounts was written by an African American named Daniel Payne (Cohen & Scheer, 1997), a lifelong educator who became President of Wilberforce College. Long before his tenure at Wilberforce, however, he directed a successful school for free, black children in antebellum Charleston, South Carolina.

Payne's early and unquenchable passion for learning and study is one of the themes of his autobiography. He recounts a boyhood apprenticeship in which he ate his meals hurriedly to leave extra time for reading, and remembers that he would often read late into the night and then arise at 4 in the morning to study some more.

Payne's formal education is brief. For three years, he attends a school for free, black children where he learns reading, arithmetic, writing, spelling, and history. He is left ignorant of geography and English grammar, however, as these subjects are not taught in schools for "colored" children. Despite the limitations of his formal education, Payne opens his own school in 1829 at the age of 19. Although he initially attracts only three students to this school, each of whom pays him 50 cents a month, he soon establishes the leading school for free, black children in Charleston, with enrollment growing to more than 30 students by the mid-1830s. His success is largely attributable to the heroic commitment he makes to his own learning. Lacking knowledge of geography, he purchases a text about cartography and is soon constructing his own maps and teaching what he has learned to his students. Ignorant of the most basic principles of English grammar, he memorizes an entire textbook on the subject but still does not fully understand it until he reviews the text two more times. Only then is he able to articulate and practice its rudiments and thus introduce grammar into his school curriculum. On another occasion, Payne acquires a Greek grammar and learns the Greek alphabet within a day. Three days later he translates a chapter of the gospel of Matthew from Greek into English. He studies and masters large parts of Euclid, investigates the foundations of botany, and surveys much of what is known at that time about the other natural sciences.

Payne's inexhaustible thirst for knowledge carries over into his teaching. An early proponent of experiential education, he cleans and stuffs a wide variety of local game and hangs them up on the walls of his classroom for examination and study. In his autobiography, Payne recalls a vivid example of "hands-on" learning: "I bought a live alligator, made one of my pupils provoke him to bite, and whenever he opened his mouth I discharged a load of shot from a small pistol down his throat. As soon as he was stunned, I threw him on his back, cut his throat, ripped open his chest, hung him and studied his viscera till they ceased to move" (p. 60). Payne becomes so renowned, especially as a teacher of science, that other schoolmasters in the Charleston area seek him out and Payne happily teaches them what he has learned. Daniel Payne is arguably a pioneer in the field of professional development for educators.

LOCKE AMSDEN BY DANIEL P. THOMPSON

Another experienced teacher from the same era used fiction rather than autobiography to tell his story (Cohen & Scheer, 1997). Daniel Pierce Thompson's novel *Locke Amsden* features the eponymous hero, who is hired to teach in a rural New England community in the mid-1840s. Amsden boards in the home of an illiterate but thoughtful local resident with whom he engages in a searching conversation about the advantages of advanced education. Amsden modestly assures his host that learned people are no better able to answer the big questions in life than are the uneducated.

The next day Amsden meets his students for the first time. They are surprisingly orderly, even timid in his presence. It turns out that Amsden's brother has circulated the rumor that Locke has a fiery temper and is easily riled. As Amsden observes his students' nervous tentativeness, he is quietly amused by the effect of his brother's words. Instead of having to take time to establish discipline, usually the first responsibility of schoolmasters in such rural communities, he can concentrate on the lessons of both the mind and the heart. His first object is to develop in his students a love of learning, and he does so by getting to know their strengths and weaknesses and by using humor, praise, provocation, and puzzlement. Soon the students are interested less in rough sports and bullying their weaker peers and more in the riddles of nature and the problems of arithmetic Amsden poses daily. Parents notice the change in their children and are pleased, and Amsden's unlettered host observes that within a month the new schoolmaster "had done more towards making good thinkers of his scholars than any of their former instructors had done in a whole winter" (p. 96).

All is well until the day one of Amsden's older students openly defies his authority. Amsden is about to chastise the student publicly in accordance with the procedures of the time when he reconsiders and wonders if a private intervention wouldn't produce a more desirable effect. That evening Amsden visits the home of the offending student and invites his father to participate in devising an appropriate consequence. The father at first declines, responding that this is one of the things for which the schoolmaster is being paid. But when Amsden explains that he thinks the father's presence will be beneficial, the schoolmaster, the father, and the son all travel to the schoolhouse to administer the punishment. Amsden does most of the talking in explaining the seriousness of the student's transgression, but the father also offers helpful observations and suggestions. After an hour-long exchange, the student accepts the error of his ways and pledges to be on good behavior for the rest of the term.

This disciplinary interlude is extraordinary for at least three reasons. First, it is private. The teacher eschews the public humiliation that is advocated at the time. Second, it does not involve corporal punishment, which, after all, is the standard form of chastisement at that time. Third, and perhaps most exceptional, Amsden involves the parent in the disciplinary action. Thompson intends his novel to be both an accurate rendering of common schools and a reform tract attacking the most entrenched and inhumane practices in schools. This story is like many teacher narratives of the past and the present, meant to enlighten at least as much as to amuse.

EDWARD EGGLESTON'S *THE HOOSIER SCHOOLMASTER*

Still another writer from this period renowned for his stories of teaching is Edward Eggleston, who published his best seller *The Hoosier Schoolmaster* in 1871. Setting his story in the Midwest, Eggleston described events from his own Indiana boyhood and based many of the schooling episodes on his brother's experiences as a teacher. Although fictional like Thompson's stories, his novel is an accurate depiction of rural community life of the 1840s and 1850s. When this book was published in the early 1870s, it was enormously popular and remains one of the best-known narratives of teaching from the 19th century.

When Eggleston wrote his story, children were expected to attend the free, publicly supported common schools. However, the students themselves often resisted these expectations, especially the older, male children who continued to struggle with reading and other basics. Consequently, the most popular stories about schooling from this era, including Eggleston's, involve an intrepid teacher who endeavors to win the respect of his students and to keep them in attendance at the public school.

The Hoosier Schoolmaster is the story of a teacher named Ralph Hartsook and his efforts to gain the confidence of the small Indiana community of Flat Creek. At first, Ralph is labeled a bookish, stuck-up alien with little understanding of the hardships of country living. In those days teachers usually boarded in different people's homes during the school year. The Means family is the first one that Ralph gets to know. The father is a school trustee, and the son is a muscular and rebellious student named Bud. Ralph quickly gains Bud's admiration when he goes night hunting with him and, in a tussle, overcomes a recalcitrant raccoon. The next day breaks rainy and cold and is given over to more sedentary pursuits. Ralph sits with the family and spins story after story. With animation and enthusiasm he recounts the tales of Sinbad, Gulliver, Robinson Crusoe, and many others. The Means family, starved for such entertainment, hangs on every word. They develop new respect for this strange young man from afar.

Despite his rapport with the Means family, Ralph's first efforts as schoolmaster are not successful. Echoing the notion that teachers must know themselves well to teach their students effectively, Eggleston wrote of Ralph: "He was not master of himself, and consequently not master of anybody else" (p. 20). After a few difficult days, Ralph resolves to be a bulldog—unruffled but tenacious—taking "hold in such a way that nothing should make him let go" (p. 20). When Ralph's students attempt to upset him by trapping a puppy inside his desk, he remains calm, spots the offending student, and firmly directs him to deposit the dog outside the schoolroom. A few days later, a different student who remains intent on humiliating the schoolmaster loosens a floorboard near Mr. Hartsook's desk in hopes that he will fall through the flooring and tumble into the pond waiting just below. But Ralph learns of the mischief planned for him and spends most of the day avoiding the misplaced plank and hatching his own scheme. Finally, the opportunity presents itself and Ralph induces the boy who loosened the board to fall into his own trap. As he pulls the boy from his watery fate, Mr. Hartsook playfully scolds his charges for being so cruel toward one another and warns them that such behavior will no longer be tolerated. The pupils can only marvel at the schoolmaster's cleverness and placidity and prepare to do whatever he requests.

Ralph must face one more test—the community spelling bee. A source of both enlightenment and recreation, the "spelling school" is one of the few events that brings the entire community together. It is also a reminder to the citizens of rural Flat Creek that "the chief end of man is to learn to spell" (p. 24). The schoolmaster must demonstrate his mastery in this most significant of all academic pursuits. As if to underscore the point, the host of the event begins the festivities by announcing that Webster's speller is the greatest of texts, perhaps surpassing even the Bible.

The competition begins. Ralph holds his own against most of the spellers, but there is one rival who seems unbeatable. Jim Phillips enjoys no distinction other than a marked ability to spell. As each increasingly difficult word is announced, Jim spells it coolly and confidently. With far more at stake but with far less assurance, the schoolmaster holds on until something unexpected occurs. When Jim Phillips is asked to spell "theodolite," he does so with the same air of confidence but mistakenly inserts a y where the i should be. He sits down as the schoolmaster triumphantly spells the word without error. In defeating Jim Phillips, Ralph seems to overcome the last barrier between him and the respect he so fervently seeks. But then a new rival appears named Hannah Thomson. A little known but attractive young woman, she outspells the schoolmaster on the word "daguerreotype" and leaves not only with the new respect of the community but also with the admiration of Ralph Hartsook, who escorts her home. Though his honesty will be disputed many times and his efforts to woo Hannah repeatedly stymied, Ralph's ability as a teacher is never again questioned. As realistic as *The Hoosier Schoolmaster* may be in its depictions of schooling and teaching, it is, in the end, a typical period melodrama. Its chief attractions are the budding romance between Ralph and Hannah and the unlikely events that result in a triumphant finale for Ralph Hartsook.

THE JOURNALS OF CHARLOTTE FORTEN

A final narrative from the 19th century especially worth inclusion here is the teaching journal Charlotte Forten kept between 1854 and 1864. It is a concrete and detailed portrait of a young African American woman intent on proving that she is the intellectual equal of any other person, black or white, female or male. It is significant also for the firsthand account it provides of the South Carolina Port Royal Experiment, in which teachers like Forten educated freed slaves to realize new possibilities for themselves.

The journal opens when Charlotte is 16 and has just graduated from grammar school. She enrolls in a normal school at Salem, Massachusetts, and revels in the intellectual adventures the school and community provide. Her journal is full of references to the new books she discovers and the wonderful ideas she encounters. It is also crammed with a litany of famous speakers whose lectures she eagerly seeks out. Hardly a leading New England abolitionist is omitted. She hears the fiery Wendell Phillips, the uncompromising William Lloyd Garrison, the erudite O. B. Frothingham, and the beloved Ralph Waldo Emerson. All offer her the cognitive stimulation and sustenance she so mightily craves. Immediately after her graduation in 1856 from the normal school at Salem, she accepts a position as a teacher, but the experience pales in comparison to the yeasty intellectual environment to which she has become accustomed.

The chief negative note is sounded on September 12, 1855. It concerns the racial hatred she faces in the integrated but still bigoted environment of Massachusetts. She writes:

> I wonder that every colored person is not a misanthrope. Surely we have everything to make us hate mankind. I have met girls in the schoolroom. They have been thoroughly kind and cordial to me. Perhaps the next day met them in the street—they feared to recognize me. Others give the most distant recognition possible. I, of course, acknowledge no such recognitions, and they soon cease entirely. These are but trifles, certainly, to the great public wrongs which we as a people are obliged to endure. But to those who experience them, these apparent trifles are most wearing and discouraging. Even to a child's mind, they reveal volumes of deceit and heartlessness, and early teach a lesson of suspicion and distrust. Oh! It is hard to go through life meeting contempt with contempt, hatred with hatred, fearing, with too good reason, to love and trust hardly anyone whose skin is white. (p. 74)

Her first year of teaching leaves her frustrated and ill. Indeed, the journal entries from this period either omit all reference to actual teaching or cast it disparagingly. Occasionally, she observes how boisterous or undisciplined the children are. Frequently, she notes that teaching has a depressing, dispiriting effect on her. At one point, she exclaims: "I find a teacher's life not nearly as pleasant as a scholar's" (p. 82). After less than 2 years of teaching, she resigns her position in Salem and returns to her native Philadelphia to recuperate, to work for the antislavery cause, and to do some limited substitute instructing. The outbreak of the Civil War revitalizes her interest in teaching and excites her desire to use the pulpit of education to serve ex-slaves.

Within less than a year of the war's onset, the ideal opportunity for Charlotte emerges when the island of Port Royal, off the coast of South Carolina, is captured by Union forces and made the site of a great educational experiment. The ex-slaves, who outnumber the whites 10 to 1, are unusually isolated from other settlements and have been forced to live under quite adverse conditions. The organizers of the Port Royal community have two main goals: to demonstrate that the ex-slaves have a great capacity to learn and to show that, with proper training, the freedmen can fight in combat against the Confederacy. Charlotte Forten plays a prominent role in carrying out the first goal but is no less interested in the second.

Arriving at Port Royal in late 1862, Charlotte's enthusiastic commitment to serving the black children of the community is evidenced in many of her journal entries. In one long entry from November 30, she characterizes her students very positively, in marked contrast to the torment of her teaching assignment in Massachusetts. She refers to one student as "bright, eager to learn," and another as a "good-natured, easy soul." Still another she calls "a very cunning little creature" (p. 160). A few days later she notes that she is responsible for an immense number of students—58 to be exact—but adds that she likes a large school, finding it very "inspiriting" (p. 165). Although it is important to note that Charlotte is joyously responding to a true call, she also has never encountered such a highly motivated group of learners before. Observers of the scene unanimously agree that the recently liberated African Americans eagerly consume every morsel of learning their teachers serve up.

Although her tenure in the South lasts only a year and a half, Charlotte Forten's days there are fruitfully spent. She is instrumental in making the Port Royal experiment work. Thousands of African American children enroll in the schools and successfully learn to read, write, and compute. Thousands of the children's parents go to church schools, in which Charlotte volunteers, to learn English. Young black men train for army service and serve bravely. Charlotte knows many of these soldiers; she recalls the 54th regiment the most clearly. Not long after she sees them off, the soldiers bravely storm the Confederate battery at Fort Wagner only to be tragically cut down by rebel forces. A further sign of progress is that, within 2 years of the inception of the Port Royal experiment, many black families buy land and set up businesses in the Beaufort area. Despite centuries of enslavement, the freedmen adapt rapidly and soon make it on their own. Charlotte Forten counts this development, too, as part of her mission and part of her victory. Never again will teaching matter so much to her or be so dear to her students.

These narratives are some of the best-known stories of teaching from the 19th century. They take place in rural, agrarian settings, and they reflect the romantic and upbeat temperament of the times. Like many of the histories that would be written about this period, these stories, with the possible exception of Forten's, are optimistic, even triumphalist renderings of how publicly supported education prevails, bringing enlightenment and knowledge to every benighted corner of a burgeoning nation. Of course, the truth is far more complex and subtle, but these stories nevertheless offer a concrete picture of teaching practice that many readers still find compelling.

LEONARD COVELLO'S *THE HEART IS THE TEACHER*

The most celebrated teacher narratives of the first half of the 20th century shift the focus from the country to the city and present more nuanced and mixed pictures of teachers' struggles to educate an increasingly diverse and multifaceted populace. One of the best known of these narratives is Leonard Covello's *The Heart is the Teacher* (1958). It highlights Covello's rise from a poor, Italian immigrant family to a position as one of the leading public educators in New York. This story is one of the first modern teacher narratives. It focuses almost entirely on teaching and related educational issues and simultaneously chronicles Covello's growth as an educator and as a person. It also symbolizes an important shift in the demographics of the United States. The early 20th century ushers in a new era of industrialization and urbanization, and the rapid social change associated with this period poses one of the greatest challenges that Covello faces as an educator.

Arriving in New York in 1896 at the age of 9, Leonard and his family settle in a tenement flat in the East Harlem section of the city, which becomes the site of his home and the locus of his work for the next 60 years. His own experiences in school as a recent immigrant from Italy do not go well. He knows no English when he enters the "soup schools" of New York, and he endures months of instruction in almost total bafflement. Soup schools, entirely segregated from the public school system, are so named because they serve a thin gruel at lunchtime intended to sustain their poor immigrant clients for the remainder of the school day. The soup, however, is often not enough to sustain the students during the incessant rote memorization and choral recitation rigidly imposed by most teachers. While many students learn and are promoted to the regular public school system, others find the drill and the memorizing so burdensome that they are lost to the public schools forever.

Although Leonard eventually enjoys some success and goes on to the public school, he hates this boring routine. Far more satisfying to him is the relationship he develops with Miss Anna C. Ruddy, a local Christian missionary who runs a kind of settlement house called the Home Garden in Leonard's East Harlem neighborhood. It is at the Home Garden that Leonard blossoms. Here he studies the Bible with Miss Ruddy and forms a club under her guidance to read books, produce plays, and organize songfests. Although outside the Home Garden he is part of a gang that often gets into scrapes with rival gangs, Miss Ruddy and her Home Garden provide the balance and the modeling that Leonard so desperately needs.

Despite Miss Ruddy's valiant efforts, Leonard drops out of school in his early teens. Although his justification is that his mother is suffering from a long illness and his family needs the additional income, he also dislikes school. He can't see where it is leading, and he receives neither guidance from school officials nor any encouragement to give it another try. As he tells his friends upon leaving school for what appears to be the last time: "Nobody knows we're alive inside there, except maybe one or two teachers. They don't even know when you come and when you go. They should worry if I ever come back" (p. 53). From this experience he learns that educators must nurture their students and persevere whenever setbacks occur or misfortune takes hold.

Within a year Leonard returns to school with renewed vigor and confidence. He finally masters the English language and writes for the school newspaper, joins the literary club, and plays an active role in the debating society. To earn extra money, he gives English lessons to Italian immigrants. The absence of Italian studies from the high school curriculum is a continuing disappointment, but getting an education emerges as the most important thing in his life. His concern about the expense of college is alleviated when he earns a special scholarship. In 1907, 20-year-old Leonard Covello enrolls at Columbia University.

Leonard majors in French. Even at the college level, prejudice against the study of Italian remains. Covello will work to overcome this bias many years later. While at Columbia, he applies himself to a wide range of required courses, but he is disappointed by what he encounters. The courses lack a unifying principle, he tells a friend, and demand little hard thinking. There are lectures and quizzes "but not enough real teaching and little rapport between student and instructor. . . There is no contact of minds. You feel that the professor is niggardly about the knowledge he hands out—as if he were afraid he might give too much at one time. You go to a lecture and listen and simply accept" (p. 69).

As was often the case with Covello, he finds other, more informal ways to enrich his mind. At the East Harlem YMCA, which essentially takes the place of Miss Ruddy's Home Garden after her death, he meets John Shedd and Leone Piatelli, two men who share a deep respect for the language and culture of Italy. Together, they have a formative influence on Covello's intellectual life. They awaken Leonard to the beauty and timelessness of Dante, and they help him to see that Italy's quest for unification and liberty parallels America's journey. But more than anything, they teach him that there is no conflict between a love of ideas and a desire to serve others, that they are mutually energizing and entirely complementary pursuits. This lesson shapes the rest of his life.

After graduating from Columbia in 1911 with a Phi Beta Kappa key in hand, Covello considers advanced work in French and a future teaching at the college level. But when an opportunity arises to teach high school French, he seizes it and devotes most of the rest of his life to working with high school students. Although he enjoys the work immediately, it takes him a while to adjust to his new position. He begins with a traditional view of the teacher—that it is his responsibility to convey knowledge to the students and their job to receive it passively. He makes no allowances for the different experience and ability levels of the students he teaches; he plans lessons that cover too much ground at too rapid a pace, and he assigns homework that is, for most students, too difficult and too exacting. Although he grows increasingly effective, he remains dissatisfied. He confides to his friends Shedd and Piatelli that, although he enjoys the work, the human element is missing. He teaches French without getting to know his students as people, he laments. Moreover, he finds that learning French is the least important thing in many of his students' lives. He yearns to play a role, not just as a teacher, but also as a confidante, advisor, and advocate for his students' aspirations.

One of the strategies Covello explores to enliven the education he provides for his students, many of whom are first and second generation Italians, is to champion Italian as a legitimate course of study at the high school level. Like many current advocates of multiculturalism who want students to see their backgrounds, histories, and traditions reflected in the school curriculum, Covello seeks to introduce Italian primarily to help Italian students develop a new appreciation for their language and culture. This mission becomes an important part of his life's work and eventually transforms Leonard Covello into an academic pathfinder and an educational leader of the first rank.

Because of the intervention of World War I, the death of his first wife, and a post-War flirtation with a career in advertising, Covello does not begin to implement his dream until 1920. In that year he teaches the first class in Italian at De Witt Clinton High School, and, as he points out in his autobiography, it may have been the only class in Italian offered in the entire country at that time. He also creates the first Italian Department in the city, making it not only a challenging academic environment, but also a place where students from all over the East Side can go for help, support, or advice. Although Leonard contemplates many alternate careers during his first few years of teaching, with the creation of the Italian Department his commitment to public education never wavers again. In the teaching of Italian to the Italian youth of the East Side of New York, he finds his professional niche.

With time, Covello makes another great discovery, one that educators of today seem to be relearning daily. Teaching for Covello is not just a transaction between a teacher and a student; it is an exchange that involves the student's whole family, and even the entire community of which the student is a part. The implications of this insight are far-reaching. It means teachers and administrators must get to know the background and culture of their students' families. It means they must understand the neighborhoods in which these students live and relate what they teach to the experiences their students have outside school. And it means teachers must be as responsive to what their students have to teach them, as the students themselves remain open to their teachers' knowledge and wisdom.

In attempting to carry out these goals, Covello makes a close study of the Italian family in America and even offers a course on the subject at New York University. Covello teaches the course many times and gains a reputation as an expert on the subject. He also becomes increasingly sensitive to the issues of racial and ethnic minorities in schools. At a time when few mainstream educators are concerned about diversity and multiculturalism, Covello contributes to a 1938 text titled *Racial and National Minorities in the United States*, which became the basis for many courses on intercultural understanding. As Tyack and Hansot (1982) point out in their brief portrait of

Covello, his interest in the Italian community eventually extends to include all ethnic groups. His vision, actively pursued for the rest of his life, culminates in the notion "that the school itself should mobilize neighborhood people to bring about social justice" (p. 210).

After many years as a teacher, Leonard Covello plays an important role in establishing the Benjamin Franklin High School in the East Harlem section of New York. He is named its first principal and serves for 22 years. His work as a principal is an extension of what he has done as a teacher. He brings the community into the school and the school into the community. He encourages his students and teachers to work in the community and to use it as a basis for what they are learning. Courses focusing on current social problems and on the promise and practice of American democracy are commonplace. Invariably, such courses also require students to complete a community service project. While Covello contends that linking the curriculum closely to life in the neighborhoods is paramount, he labors as well to maintain academic rigor and to prevent Benjamin Franklin High from degenerating into a vocational or technical institution. Recalling his own experience in school, he insists that every student be given every opportunity to prepare for college. While not opposed to thoughtfully structured vocational education programs, he advocates required courses that give students a broad background and keep their post-high school options open.

Leonard Covello was ahead of his time, and contemporary educators continue to study his work for new ideas and fresh inspiration. His narrative stands out because it chronicles his professional growth as it examines the ways in which the most progressive educators were responding to the challenges of an increasingly diverse and complex society.

ANGELO PATRI'S *A SCHOOLMASTER OF THE GREAT CITY*

Another 20th century story of teaching in New York by another Italian immigrant is Angelo Patri's *A Schoolmaster of the Great City* (1921). Devoting almost no space to his early life, Patri plunges the reader into his first year of teaching when he is responsible for instructing 66 children ranging in age from 8 to 15. Largely ignorant of both subject matter and pedagogy, Patri imposes a strict discipline on his students. The administration of the school is so impressed with the new teacher's methods that he is "promoted" to an even more difficult class comprised of 50 "misfits." In this case, harsh discipline not only does not work, it seems to make the students even more hostile. One strategy is effective, however—stories. Stories of his early life in Italy, stories of Patri's father prevailing over a wolf that threatens the family sheep, stories of anything and everything engage and enthrall his students.

But stories are all Patri has to draw on. After two years of teaching he is still floundering, unable to uncover a method or a process that allows him to enjoy relatively consistent success. Only after going back to the university to discover the works of John Dewey does Patri develop an underlying philosophy that makes sense to him: "I realized then that the child must move and not sit still: that he must make mistakes and not merely repeat perfect forms: that he must be himself and not a miniature reproduction of the teacher. The sacredness of the child's individuality must be the moving passion of the teacher" (p. 15).

Patri finds that, with this philosophy in mind, he can make education more meaningful for his students. But successful as he is, he feels constrained by the traditional bureaucratic expectations of most of the principals for whom he works. He yearns to direct his own school. His aspiration is eventually realized and he assumes the principalship of a large school in Manhattan.

He sets to work shaping a new vision for the school. Overwhelmed by the monotony in the classrooms he visits, he encourages creative expression in composition, drawing, movement, and athletics. He invites teachers to introduce students to real things in nature and the community, rather than to rely exclusively on book learning and the exploration of abstractions. One teacher who misconstrues Patri's approach offers a lesson on robins. She encourages her students to discuss the subject openly and to draw what they feel, but they do all of this without ever leaving the classroom. Patri explains that the first step must be to go outdoors and to observe robins in their natural surroundings and then to follow up as creatively as possible.

Following Dewey again, Patri focuses on developing the whole child. He doesn't want them just to read and write and compute, he also wants them to sing and cook and act out stories and find joy in what they discover and learn. To a parent who laments the lack of homework that his child is assigned, Patri warns that such work in excess can dampen the spirit and distract the student from learning the things most meaningful for her. Patri also insists that school be not just preparation for some later challenge but a wonderful way to make the most of the present. He discourages parents who seek to promote children prematurely to higher grades to accelerate their progress, and he urges them to see their children's present placement as an opportunity to deepen and enrich what they already know and understand.

Like Covello, Patri recognizes that schools often fail to take advantage of what parents and the outside community can contribute. Rather than hold routine parent meetings, community members are invited to attend concerts, informative lectures, and dramatic performances, many of which are hosted by teachers. Gradually they lead to other meetings and more opportunities for parents to get involved in planning and problem solving. In time parents reciprocate and invite teachers into their homes to socialize and to make further plans for collaboration. Through all of this, Patri encourages teachers and parents to see themselves as natural allies and as true partners in the education of the children.

Perhaps Patri's most valuable contribution to an understanding of the conditions that make education work is the emphasis he places on the intellectual and emotional development of teachers. In his first days as a teacher, he felt stifled intellectually in that there were no opportunities for him to learn or to share his greatest passions. He writes: "There is no bondage so deadly as that which prohibits intellectual liberty" (p. 155). In his own school he seeks to unleash the teachers' strengths, to make their interests and their growth an important mission of his school. He does this not just to satisfy teachers but also to let teachers use their "best talents in behalf of the children" (p. 155).

Patri discovers and exploits the hobbies of his teachers. The lover of flowers conducts the nature study, the music lover organizes the chorus, the avid reader facilitates the discussion of literature, and so on. This simple change generates an unprecedented level of intellectual energy in the school. When the idea of reading poetry to the children is proposed, for example, one teacher seems to explode out of her seat with excitement. She is particularly fond of Robert Louis Stevenson and enthusiastically recites the poetry to her colleagues that she regards as appropriate. She also identifies verses that go well with music, that can be presented dramatically, and that can be paired effectively with illustrations. Stevenson's songs and later the poetry of many other writers form the basis for regular Friday morning assemblies. By the end of the year, all of the children have learned a few poems, and many have memorized almost all of the verse presented during the assemblies.

In the end, Patri claims five things must be changed to make schools the vital, joyful institutions they are meant to be. These five suggestions remain timely. First, schools must be places where a child's individual genius can be developed and cultivated. Second, teachers must be encouraged to find inspiration in their work, to collaborate with others, to view their teaching as a creative, even artistic, enterprise, and to keep their own intellectual aspirations high. Third, each school must break free of the inhibiting bonds of the bureaucracy and create its own spirit and ethos. Fourth, the walls separating the school and the home must be broken down and a new relationship formed in which the school becomes part of the entire community's efforts to educate and uplift its populace. Finally, educators must develop a new attitude toward the child in which every student is viewed as having a capacity to learn and where the problem of education is not located in the child but in identifying methods and strategies that work for everyone.

CAROLYN PRATT'S *I LEARN FROM CHILDREN*

A contemporary of Patri's, Carolyn Pratt shows how to make many of these changes a reality. She accomplishes this under very different conditions—a small, private school in New York—but her story, aptly titled *I Learn from Children*, is instructive on how to create a stimulating and liberating environment for children and adults alike.

A native of Fayetteville, New York, Pratt begins teaching at the age of 17 in a one-room school and continues to teach in the Fayetteville area for a number of years before receiving a scholarship in 1892 to study kindergarten methods at Columbia's Teacher's College. Hoping to discover why children seem to lose their natural desire to learn as they get older, she quickly becomes disillusioned with the prevailing view that the school's chief function is to discipline and regulate students. She enrolls in the manual training department, reveling in the opportunity to use tools and to make useful things. But here too she is disappointed in that she learns the steps involved in constructing something but never gets the satisfaction of actually completing a project. Upon graduation, she accepts a position at the Normal School for Girls in Philadelphia where she teaches her students much as she had been taught but with the "depressing conviction that I was helping to perpetuate a system which had no real educational value" (p. 13).

She resigns from the Philadelphia school and moves back to New York City in search of a more meaningful way to nurture children. For years, she teaches part-time in a private school and in two different settlement houses. No longer constrained by the manual training exercises and locksteps imposed by the Normal School, Pratt encourages her students to pursue projects of their choice and to persevere as long as the projects remain interesting and fruitful. Her only rule, "work or leave the shop," results in children who industriously and joyfully engage in the entire work of production and who are introduced to a "fascinating world into which they walk with confidence in their own powers" (p. 17).

Then, as the historian Lawrence Cremin (1961) characterizes it, Carolyn Pratt undergoes her "conversion experience" (p. 203). It happens as she observes an imaginative 6-year-old maneuvering his toy trains. She is struck by how inventively he uses whatever materials are at hand to provide a setting for the train set and by how absorbed he is in furnishing the sounds and sights necessary to make the scene as authentic as possible. Pratt exclaims: "It seemed to me that this child had discovered an activity more satisfying to him than anything I had ever seen offered to children" (p. 19). Cremin adds that, in this simple moment, "Miss Pratt saw the vision of a new school: a child-sized community in which the inhabitants, through play, might grasp the essential truths of the universe" (p. 204).

In 1914 she opens her school in a three-room apartment in Greenwich Village and welcomes her first six students, all of whom are preschoolers. At first called the Play School and later the City and Country School, Pratt commits from the beginning to a school "with no fixed limits," that takes "shape under the children's own hands . . . is as wide and high as their own world," and grows "as their horizons" stretch (p. 40). The entire city is their classroom. Whether to the docks or the train station or the local butcher, each day is devoted to a journey that becomes fuel for the children's imaginations. At first, simple blocks suffice as substitutes in school for ships or steam engines, but hand-made replicas are soon in demand. With Pratt's assistance, the children learn to use tools and to fashion increasingly sophisticated models with their own hands. Through all of this, Pratt advocates a minimal amount of adult interference. The children are far more capable, she cautions, than most adults realize, since adults rarely give children the margin for error and the room to experiment that they need to figure things out for themselves. Similarly, adults' inclination to answer every question children ask must be curbed, since "the answer which the child has found for himself is the one which has meaning for him" (p. 45). Moreover, the most productive response to many questions is another question that neither the child nor the adult can immediately answer. Only then can both child and adult enjoy a collaborative encounter that is truly meaningful.

As the years go by, Pratt's school grows rapidly. Featured prominently in John and Evelyn Dewey's *Schools of Tomorrow* (1915), the Play School is soon swarming with curious educators and prospective parents. In the fall of 1921, the school moves to a roomier location to accommodate a much larger student body ranging in ages from 5 to 8. Pratt gradually takes on a small staff to teach the different grade levels and to be the school's recognized specialists in music, art, literature, and biology. Pressed by scholars to articulate the school's mission and purpose, Pratt fears that her innovative and even improvisational style will be reduced to formulas and pat answers. In collaboration with the staff, however, she confirms that the school is based in part on recognition of the integral relationship between freedom and interest. Freedom by itself is valueless and only takes on meaning when used to do something positive as "determined by the child's interest in what he" wants to do. The freest child, Pratt affirms, is the one "most interested in what he is doing, and at whose hand are the materials for his work or play." Freedom, discipline, and even cooperation are irrelevant unless tied to activity that has meaning for the child. "Freedom to work, and the discipline to work, both individual and group work," Pratt avers, "these were the values on which the children thrived and grew" (p. 68).

There is perhaps no better example of how deeply young children crave the discipline of work than the story of the 8-year-olds in Carolyn Pratt's school who take on jobs. Always open to what they are learning by observing the children, Pratt and her staff conclude that, with the older children, blocks, toys, and other representations of the adult world will no longer do. They need real jobs in which they can be of service to others. The children are offered the chance to establish and run a store that sells school supplies. They eagerly take up the challenge. First, there is construction work, carving the store out of one corner of the classroom and facing it out into the hallway so that passersby are attracted to the goods for sale. Second, they take out a loan and purchase the necessary supplies to be sold. Third, the children must run and maintain the store. This last is constantly refined as visits to nearby stationery stores provide them with new marketing ideas and as the demand to master reading and computing skills is quickly satisfied. Open for 30 minutes every morning, the store is operated by a rotating committee. Another rotating committee balances the accounts.

This work has an enlivening effect on the whole school. The demand for spending money grows rapidly, as does interest in the products being sold. Before long, the 8-year-olds visit paper mills to see how one of their best-selling products is made and even tour a docked steamer just in from the Amazon that is loaded down with the rubber used to make the erasers they sell. These trips lead to unanticipated forays into history, geography, and economics. This episode confirms Pratt's claim that the discipline of work is a doorway into the world.

JULIA WEBER GORDON'S *MY COUNTRY SCHOOL DIARY*

Julia Weber Gordon's *My Country School Diary* seems to represent a surprising return to the bucolic idylls of the 19th century but is more a reminder that highly progressive one-room schoolhouses continued to flourish well into the 20th century. Gordon's diary of her four years of teaching in the country school is important because it documents the everyday workings of a rural school in the 1930s and because it is maintained by an educator of the first rank. In an introduction to Gordon's book, John Holt notes that Miss Weber (her name before she married after the 1946 publication of this book's first edition) lacked money and resources, but her enthusiasm and ingenuity created a "learning environment of great variety and richness" (p. xv). Her diary remains one of the most detailed accounts ever compiled of one teacher's practices.

Weber's first entries are composed during the summer of 1936, just before she assumes responsibility for the one-room country school in rural New Jersey. She reproduces a class list containing the names of the 28 children assigned to her. The ages of the children range from 5 years, 4 months to 15 years, 8 months. Undaunted by the staggering spread of their developmental levels, Weber identifies two chief purposes for the first year: "to learn as much as possible about the needs and abilities of the children" and "to begin to meet these needs and to develop these abilities through such opportunities as arise in our daily living together and through the resources near at hand in the community" (p. 3).

Within a month Weber familiarizes herself with the family backgrounds and the learning capacities of her students. She notes that the 28 children come from 12 different families, and she observes that virtually all the children are economically poor and academically limited. But, as she catalogues their strengths and weaknesses, she notes that most of the children have excellent attitudes and are highly capable scholastically.

Paralleling actions of other progressive educators like Covello, Patri, and Pratt, Julia Weber makes the world immediately outside the school an important aspect of the curriculum. She often takes the children into the community to study its history and to investigate the ways local people make a living. She also invites community members, especially the elderly, to tell stories of how life in the area has changed over time. Such a generous and inclusive impulse contributes to making the school an important, even indispensable part of the community's life and gives the children a sense that their education is not remote from the world but a rich and enriching aspect of it.

Another outstanding feature of Weber's teaching is the remarkable number of skills she models and encourages the children to try for themselves. As John Holt has comprehensively shown, the list is diverse and extensive, though probably not out of reach for an ambitious pedagogue. Some of the things she can do include an ability to: play the harmonica and the piano, perform Indian and folk dances, sing songs in many languages, design and build a playhouse, make and manipulate puppets, fashion paper windmills, produce scale drawings, identify a variety of plants, grow flowers, sew, cook, make salt crystals, construct furniture for the playhouse, identify and compare fabrics, spin thread, and weave with simple looms (see p. xviii in Holt's introduction.) All of these and quite a few other skills are put to good use in her stimulating school.

But perhaps most interesting of all is the way in which Weber thoughtfully records criticisms of her own teaching and carefully documents her own personal and professional growth. Discipline is an ongoing concern, especially among the older boys in the school. In the first years, two boys in particular chronically stir up trouble. At one point while chiding them once again for their inappropriate behavior, she notes that, by the time she is done, the boys are hanging their heads in shame. In her diary, she takes herself to task and exclaims: "Sometimes I think I talk too much" (p. 56). At another point, Weber expresses her admiration for two thoughtful and experienced visitors from the community who immediately command the respect of the children by speaking calmly and clearly about the objectives of their visit. She adds, perhaps too self-disparagingly, "I'd like to be able to do that" (p. 66).

Early in her second year the unruliness arises again. She considers adopting a more autocratic style and admits she has made many mistakes. She is unsure about the value of maintaining her commitment to democratic practices. But in the end, she decides that the children must learn to govern themselves and be active participants in making the school more useful for them. A few months later, most of the discipline problems have been resolved, but Weber comments that the children seem to have reached some sort of plateau. The sense of progression, of growth, that is so important to her just doesn't seem to be present. She observes: "I know that I am not using in my teaching all that I know about good education. It's terribly hard. To know the words is one thing, but to be able to translate the words into action is a much more difficult thing" (p. 120).

It is this inclination to critique herself, to reflect thoughtfully on her own practices, that leads to a breakthrough midway into the second year. With the help of an assistant, Weber settles on a unit focusing on the surrounding community, with a special emphasis on the dairying industry so important to this part of New Jersey. The students do some preliminary research and then generate key questions, which become the basis for the unit. Weber restrains her tendency to answer the questions for the children and tries to let the questions stand to pique the children's curiosity and to lead out to still more provocative queries. Over time, these questions lead to not only intensive study of dairying but also to investigation of economics, transportation, applied science, and nutrition. Weber notes that because the children study a subject that can be witnessed firsthand within their community, it has more meaning for them. Books become tools and resources used along with discussion to prepare the children for careful observation. After completing the observations, the children talk and write about what they have seen and thus enhance their overall understanding. As Weber puts it, "Not only have they been helped to find meaning in their immediate environment, but their environment has been extended, their horizon broadened" (p. 142).

At the end of the second year, Weber comments that her efforts to educate the children have been a struggle. She notes, however, that she has learned more and has helped the children to improve. She reaffirms her commitment to democratic process and to the strong sense of group membership that she is striving to develop in the children.

Her entries launching the third year are positive and optimistic. She notes that teachers have a picture of the kind of life they want their students to lead that broadens as the teacher's life broadens as well. She implies that, as instruction proceeds, one of the dynamics is the teacher's own growth and that teaching improves and deepens in proportion to the teacher's ability to develop as a person and learner. Even for Weber in the 1930s, the quest for the second self is seen as an important part of professional development.

Although the third year gets off to a particularly good start, Weber's habit of self-criticism does not abate. In one October entry, she reflects on what has been accomplished and decides that an unsatisfactory unit on the fruit industry must be brought to a rapid conclusion. In its place she plans a unit on the textile industry, which becomes one of her greatest triumphs. At first it does not seem to go well. According to her own analysis, she "doled out subject matter in nicely organized form" without giving the children an opportunity to experiment, to question, and to expand on their own senses of what is valuable or aesthetically pleasing (p. 166). She begins again by having the children examine their own clothing to ascertain the materials used to produce them. They proceed to a series of cloth scraps and attempt to identify which ones are cotton, which wool, and which synthetic. They are puzzled by the different types of cotton, for instance, and wonder how they can be certain what they are handling. Weber explains that it is practically impossible to sort them out with the naked eye, a pronouncement that leads naturally enough to procuring a microscope.

Once the scraps have been thoroughly examined and studied, the children ask to do their own weaving. Unassembled looms are ordered and put together with virtually no intervention from Weber. The weaving begins. Through it all, Weber observes the children closely. At one point, she notes that a stimulating experience is a good way to engage the children, but that it should be an experience that will "open up possibilities for growth and for further experiences. It should arouse curiosity and set up strong purposes which will impel the children to learn" (p. 173). John Dewey could hardly have said it better.

The weaving leads naturally to rich, provocative questions that touch on many disciplines. One student answers a question about the sources of wool by making a map of the world with descriptions of the different animals that yield wool. A question arises about how the price of wool is affected by the kinds of animals available to furnish the wool. This leads to questions about the conditions that influence price, including labor-saving machinery. This in turn leads to historical investigations about how the price of wool plummeted in the 18th century when weaving machines were first introduced. Weber enthusiastically welcomes this process of posing questions and, despite the temptation to bring it to a close, keeps it going for several weeks. The excitement of the students remains at a surprisingly high pitch. The textile unit, begun in January, is still going strong in April.

At the beginning of her fourth and last year, Weber is more upbeat than ever. She has learned a great deal and she is acutely aware of this. Her pleasure in her own learning and in observing the increasing breadth of the students' understanding is intoxicating. In a highly revealing moment, she writes at some length:

> All those good things that I want for the boys and girls I teach are coming for me, too. I too am becoming increasingly aware of my capacities and of my place in the world. I study hard and listen to those who have had other and more experiences than I and I think I know the meaning of every word they say. I try, often painfully and discouragingly, to test these words and to turn them into action, again and again, and suddenly all the words take on new meaning. I realize that I did not really know before, but now I do. I am also aware that many of the things I now think I know, will take on new and fuller meaning as I continue to experience consciously. I have found that I can learn to do things I never did before. I too can meet life creatively and help to make it a better place for me and my fellow man. It is the most wonderful, most encouraging and hopeful feeling one can have! (p. 197)

CONCLUSION

Weber's words provide a fitting conclusion to this chapter. Despite teaching in an environment that many would regard as isolated and parochial, she not only found her path as a teacher, she found herself as well. But to the extent that she did find herself, it was a hard-won discovery and one that she must make again and again. Becoming a teacher, like the making of the self, is a life-long project; it is never fully done. Although Weber understood this more clearly than the teachers from the other 20th century narratives, they all grasped it to some degree. It is this understanding, above all else, which sets the modern teacher narrative apart. As we discuss teachers' stories of the last 30 years, we encounter this theme repeatedly.

Teaching is an unfathomably difficult craft. The best teachers recognize this; their stories highlight it. But these teachers keep pushing on, doing all they can to master its complexities. They do so because they love teaching and because it is part of who they are and who they are becoming. For these teachers, learning to teach is an irresistible part of the continuing quest for one's second self and the enduring pursuit of educational renewal.

STUDY QUESTIONS

1. The formal and informal education of teachers in the United States has changed dramatically since the 1800s. Describe some of the differences in the preparation of the teachers in these historical narratives and that of teachers today.
2. These historical narratives include those of teachers in both rural and urban settings. How are the issues teachers confront in rural settings similar to or different from those in urban settings?
3. What educational values do these teachers espouse? How similar or different are their values compared with those of contemporary teachers?
4. How similar or different are the educational issues faced by these teachers compared with those faced by teachers today?
5. How do these teachers engage in their own professional development? What kinds of opportunities for professional development are available to teachers today?
6. Why is Julia Weber's diary regarded as perhaps the first modern teacher narrative?

REFERENCES

Cohen, R. M., & Scheer, S. (Eds.). (1997). *The work of teachers in America: A social history through stories.* Mahwah, NJ: Lawrence Erlbaum Associates.

Covello, L. (1958). *The heart is the teacher.* New York: McGraw-Hill.

Cremin, L. (1961). *The transformation of the school.* New York: Vintage.

Dewey, J., & Dewey, E. (1915). *Schools of tomorrow.* New York: E. P. Dutton.

Eggleston, E. (1871). *The hoosier schoolmaster.* Bloomington, IN: Indiana University Press.

Forten, C. L. (1953). *A free Negro in the slave era: The journal of Charlotte L. Forten.* R. A. Billington, Ed. New York: Collier Books.

Gordon, J. W. (1970). *My country school diary.* New York: Dell Publishing.

Patri, A. (1921). *A schoolmaster of the great city.* New York: Macmillan.

Pratt, C. (1948). *I learn from children.* New York: Simon and Schuster.

Tyack, D., & Hansot, E. (1982). *Managers of virtue.* New York: Basic Books.

3

The Narrative of Social Criticism

Teachers must become effective social critics of schools. Too often educators don't realize how savagely racism, miseducation, and bureaucratic insensitivity have plagued American public schools. As emerging social critics, teachers need greater understanding of the school's historic complicity in maintaining and perpetuating ignorance and injustice. They must become informed advocates of the role schools can play in creating a more democratic society. Teachers should develop new appreciation for the exceptional schools that have successfully paired educational excellence and equity, and they should understand what a few remarkable educators have done to oppose and resist conditions and practices that impede learning.

Although historical and sociological analyses play important parts in enlightening novices and veterans alike, narratives of social criticism have an immediacy, a concreteness, and a dramatic impact that enrich more traditional approaches. Narratives incorporate complex sequences of events that show how schools inhibit learning, and they document the ways in which the best efforts of outstanding educators are sometimes negated by a suffocating and insensitive system.

Since much of the social criticism of schools is based on a conflict model in which the interests of two or more contending groups are at odds, narrative is especially well suited to portray the origins of these conflicts and the measures attempted to deny, squelch, or resolve the differences. Additionally, narratives spur readers to reflect on their own experiences with conflict and to fashion a professional identity that includes risk taking and a willingness to confront the most counterproductive aspects of the system.

No teacher can be a fully accomplished practitioner or an effective educational leader without the ability to analyze educational policies and to explain how the inequalities of the larger society are reflected in the school's practices. Narratives of social criticism are stories that underscore the failure of many schools to fulfill their democratic promise; at the same time, these narratives offer insight into the experiences of individual educators who dare to be different. These narratives focus on courageous and uncompromising educators who, despite the resistance of those in power, create more democratic environments for children and adults and who realize their dreams of a more inclusive and humane learning community. In the process of challenging the system, the protagonists of these narratives learn a great deal not only about the limits of educational reform and the power of progressive educational change, but also about themselves.

JONATHAN KOZOL: SAVAGE INEQUALITIES THEN AND NOW

Jonathan Kozol's book *Death at an Early Age* (1967) still has an enormous impact on readers. Kozol tells a vivid story of his year teaching fourth grade in the Boston Public Schools and delivers a stinging indictment of an educational system designed to control and to stigmatize children rather than stimulate and educate them.

The first chapter, about a troubled African American youngster named Stephen, sets the tone for the entire book. A ward of the State of Massachusetts, Stephen is the foster child of a family who abuses him. He is distracted and emotionally disturbed, and he does poorly in almost all of his subjects. He excels only in art and spends much of his time drawing and sketching, though his work is almost never in accord with the expectations of the Art Teacher. Still, his artwork shows verve and imagination, and he especially enjoys sharing it with Kozol, who thinks Stephen's artwork is the best in the class. But because Stephen's style is unconventional and unresponsive to the Art Teacher's instructions, he constantly incurs her wrath. "Garbage! Junk!" she shrieks upon receiving his unorthodox project. "He gives me garbage and junk! And garbage is one thing I will not have." Reminding us of the source of the title for his book, Kozol intones, ". . . she did not know or care anything at all about the way in which you can destroy a human being. Stephen, in many ways already dying, died a second and third and fourth and final death before her anger" (p. 4).

This is only the beginning of a book that repeatedly employs this kind of detail to describe the racism pervading one school and, by extension, the entire system. The reader meets many teachers and administrators, a few of whom are blatantly bigoted, but most of whom exhibit a more subtle and insidious prejudice. The most interesting of these is the Reading Teacher, who plays the role of foil to Kozol's own inexperienced but "creatively insubordinate" (Ayers, 1993, pp. 129–130) persona.

The Reading Teacher claims she has a complete lack of prejudice. With Kozol's probing a portrait emerges of a person with some deeply rooted racist assumptions. How these assumptions influence her thinking with respect to school policies, and how Kozol resists these policies, makes up a significant part of the dramatic tension in this book.

Kozol finds that, to help some of the least privileged black students, he must spend time with them outside of school. The Reading Teacher advises him not to pursue outside connections with black children. Yet she sees nothing wrong with maintaining such contact with white children herself. Kozol proposes that he take his class to an exhibit on Egypt at the Boston Museum of Fine Arts in preparation for a unit he would be teaching on the subject. The Reading Teacher first brightly recalls the days, presumably before the school became predominantly African American, when such outings were commonplace and were part of a rich, imaginative curriculum at the school. Then, returning to the present day, she scolds Kozol for even suggesting such an idea with the students they currently have. On another occasion Kozol recommends that a talented young black artist in the school be given a scholarship to an outstanding summer program in Cambridge. The Reading Teacher again demurs, unable to see why a lesser program cannot suffice.

Their differences frequently touch on curricular issues. For example, Kozol wants to teach a lesson on the historical connections between the cotton gin and slavery, but the Reading Teacher views this as inadvisable on the ground that it is wrong to remind the children of their slave origins. She even goes so far as to state: "I don't want these children to have to think back on these years later on and to have to remember that we were the ones who told them they were Negro" (p. 68).

Since virtually no biographies of black people are available in the school library, Kozol brings in a few copies of a life history of Martin Luther King, Jr. The Reading Teacher objects, arguing that since the school is not all-black, it would be unfair to the few white children in attendance to impose these materials upon them. Somehow the extent of the curricular injustices to black children does not disturb her.

The differences between the Reading Teacher and Kozol are heightened not long after he agrees to take over a fourth-grade class, which had been taught for five months by an irresponsible and incompetent instructor. At first, Kozol falters in struggling to reach these children who have been so badly neglected: in desperation, he resorts to shouting and intimidation. But he quickly restores their spirit and curiosity, primarily because, as he writes, "I came into the room knowing myself to be absolutely on their side." Refusing to assign blame to the students for the troubles that have burdened them during the school year, he shows his support for them in every way he can and "openly expresse[s] dissatisfaction with the stupidity of a school system that had cheated them" (p. 162).

The first writing assignment that Kozol gives his new students precipitates another conflict with the Reading Teacher. When he asks them to provide descriptive reports of the physical environment of the local school or neighborhood, he is pleased when they write surprisingly detailed and perceptive essays about the tragic deterioration that surrounds them. The Reading Teacher is outraged, however, because she is sure that Kozol has planted images of decline and degradation in the students' minds and that such descriptions were far from the students' thoughts until prompted by Kozol's assignment. As with her prohibitions against teaching about slavery, the Reading Teacher seems to be saying that educators should not be the ones to alert the students to the fact that their school is falling down around them. Most serious of all is the inability of the Reading Teacher to confront the glaring contradictions of such educational neglect in a democratic society; she must instead find fault in Kozol or even in the children.

The physical and moral decay that permeates the school is one of Kozol's most emphatically developed themes. Everything about the school is old, broken down, and seemingly beyond repair. When it's hot, many of the windows cannot be opened; when the weather is cold and windy, the brittle, rotting window frames occasionally give way, not only endangering the children but also making the rooms unbearably cold. Few of the desks have escaped some kind of disrepair: most desktops lack hinges, many tops are missing altogether, desk legs are wobbly, desk chairs squeak or lack back support. Much of the blackboard space is unusable, and the few available boards are worn down to almost nothing. The lighting is poor: many of the fluorescent lights emit an eerie glow or flicker interminably. To top it off, the textbooks are ancient. Most are hopelessly out of date and few have all their pages intact.

It is within this depressing and disorienting environment that Kozol must find ways to engage his students. He brightens the classroom walls with the playful modern paintings of Paul Klee and Joan Miro. The Art Teacher warns that the children will be put off by these paintings. But many of these paintings fascinate the children, motivating them to learn more and to emulate their style.

Kozol introduces some of his favorite poetry to his fourth graders. They eagerly read poems by Yeats and Frost, which are thought to be too difficult for these children. But again, just when he thinks he is making progress, he is informed by a person in authority that the poems he chose are not part of the fourth-grade curriculum and should not be studied. This sequence of events becomes routine: try something inventive and different, get an enthusiastic response from the students, and then wait for the magic wand of the bureaucracy to wave it all away. The absurdity doesn't make it any easier for the teacher who is admonished for this misstep. But just a few moments of reflection reveal what is really going on. To be innovative in this way is to threaten "the standardized condescension on which the entire administration of the school is based." Such threats are best handled by keeping the curriculum basic and predictable and by maintaining low expectations for the children. By focusing on limits and emphasizing curricular and disciplinary boundaries, "many children are tragically and unjustifiably held back from a great many of the good things that they might come to like or admire and are pinned down instead to books the teacher knows and to easy tastes that she can handle" (p. 193).

Of all the poems Kozol introduces to the children from outside the fourth-grade curriculum, the one that has the greatest impact is "Ballad of the Landlord" by the African American poet Langston Hughes. In just 33 lines, the poem captures the dilemmas that many of the black children face in their own neighborhoods. It tells of a landlord who will not repair his black tenant's deteriorating apartment, of the tenant who out of desperation threatens the landlord, and of how the press reports the incident as an unprovoked threat from a dangerous Negro. The children like the poem so much that most of them take it home on mimeographed sheets that Kozol provides and commit it to memory. Most clamor to recite the poem before the entire class. It speaks to them in ways that the standard curriculum does not.

When word gets out that Kozol has used the Hughes poem, retribution is swift. First the principal of the school castigates him for teaching an unauthorized poem and then later in the day informs him he is fired. When Kozol attempts to discover from the principal if it is the Hughes poem or another action that led to the firing, he is told that his dismissal came from central administration. The next day, the administrator responsible for Kozol's dismissal informs him that no poem that is not in the official Course of Study can be read to students without prior permission. Kozol further learns that any piece of literature about Negroes cannot be used if it involves suffering. When Kozol points out that this would rule out almost the entire body of black literature, he is told that only literature that "accentuates the positive or describes nature or tells of something hopeful" (p. 202) may be taught. The utter absurdity of such a restriction stuns Kozol, but he has also come to expect it. It is part of the stark reality of teaching in a bureaucracy where learning is one of the lowest priorities.

The differences between Kozol and the Reading Teacher culminate with Kozol's dismissal. The dismissal generates a great deal of publicity and splits the community and the school wide open. Although the school board and the administration take a strong stand against Kozol's actions, most of the parents show their support for Kozol. The Reading Teacher sides entirely with Kozol's opponents and tells him that her main concern is with the welfare of the white community, not the black children who never see their experiences reflected in the school's program.

If the Reading Teacher is viewed as a symbol of the bureaucracy that daily towers over life in the Boston Public Schools, then Kozol's battle with her takes on a new dimension and affords his narrative a special analytic sharpness. He is engaged in nothing less than a war for the hearts and minds of the children. Yet each successive encounter with the Reading Teacher shakes his confidence and dims his hopes for the future. Despite the apparent futility of resistance, Kozol goes on resisting. He is a self-styled "intellectual guerrilla" (1981, p. 3), quietly subverting the mindless rules and regulations that the school has established to maintain control. Even though his resistance finally results in his dismissal from the Boston Schools, Kozol keeps pushing. He is driven by an uncompromising vision of equity, decency, excellence, and truth that no contrived respect for authority can diminish.

Teachers should not forget Kozol's experience, despite the despair and futility he expresses. Too often, school districts allow the "managerial imperative" (Cuban, 1988) to obscure the real purposes of education and the real reasons for answering the call to teach. Getting clear about who we are and getting clear about meaningful purposes of education are part of the same process. The conditions that are the source of genuine education are also what help us to grow as teachers. Stimulating the love of learning, piquing interests that last a lifetime, and welcoming and nurturing the gifts that children bring with them into the classroom are the preeminent purposes of education, and unless teachers resist the bureaucratic impulse to subvert these purposes, everything else they do will come to nothing. Kozol's story reminds us of the need to maintain our critical perspective, to counteract policies and practices that diminish students, and to articulate alternative visions that address our common humanity and our need to make meaning together.

For those who might argue that Kozol's story is a thing of the past, it is instructive to read his more recent collective portrait of six of the most impoverished school districts in the United States, titled *Savage Inequalities* (1991). In the opening of this book, Kozol recalls his Boston experiences as a fourth-grade teacher, experiences that he eventually turns into his prize-winning narrative *Death at an Early Age.* He mentions that this work led him to other research and writing projects that were only marginally related to schooling. In 1988, realizing that he missed being in classrooms, he visits more than 30 communities and their schools to learn about the current state of American education. What he discovers stuns him. Segregation is worse than ever: most of the urban schools he observes are 95 to 99 percent nonwhite. Furthermore, he does not locate any school in the United States where there are "nonwhite children in large numbers truly intermingled with white children" (p. 3).

Most disillusioning of all, the urban, largely nonwhite schools that Kozol visits lack the most basic educational necessities. Rooms freeze in the winter without heat and swelter in the summer without air conditioning. Few spaces escape some sort of serious damage. Bathrooms are frequently unusable and cafeterias are often unsanitary. Books are at a premium in both classrooms and libraries, and those that are available remain hopelessly out of date. Kozol is struck by how "extraordinarily unhappy" these schools are. More like prisons than public institutions of learning, most of these schools, with their steel grates guarding the windows, are patrolled by police officers and are regarded by cabdrivers as war zones to be avoided. They barely resemble schools at all but seem instead to be designed as holding pens for hostile young people impatient to burst into adulthood.

Perhaps the most devastating portrait is the one that opens Kozol's book. It focuses on the predominantly African American community of East St. Louis, Illinois, just across the Mississippi River from St. Louis, Missouri. Chemical plants pump fumes into the air all day and all night long. East St. Louis is a city with an inordinately high childhood asthma rate, no systematized care for expectant mothers, and not even regular garbage pickup.

The schools in East St. Louis are another sign of the waste and neglect that seem to be everywhere. Sewage backup is a frequent cause of school closure, staff paychecks are regularly delayed for at least 2 weeks, class sizes are skyrocketing as a result of mandated layoffs, and those teachers who hang on don't have enough chalk or paper. East St. Louis High School has a machine shop that can't be used because there is no one to teach in it, and the physics laboratory is decades out of date and lacks running water. Although the chemistry laboratory does have adequate equipment, the Bunsen burners cannot be used because, with class sizes ballooning, there are too many students for one instructor to supervise.

Kozol visits one of the school's most celebrated educators, Irl Solomon, a history teacher. Despite the severity of the school's problems, Solomon says it is not the worst high school in the city. Still, he has only one outdated history text to give to each student. Solomon must provide any other materials out of his own pocket. He furnishes magazines, books, videotapes, and the VCR on which to play the tapes, without any supplement from the school's budget. After 30 years of teaching, Solomon makes $38,000, significantly less than he can earn in the city of St. Louis. He notes that, of the 33 students who start out in his 11th-grade American history class in the fall, perhaps two thirds remain come spring. The attrition rate is far worse for freshmen and sophomores. He indicates with sadness that only a tiny fraction of the students at East St. Louis High enjoy the advantages of a strong and challenging academic program.

Sam Morgan, the high school's principal, tells Kozol that the school needs to be renovated. Thousands of dollars are lost due to faulty windows and an uncontrolled heating system. The school needs new typewriters and computers, updated science labs, and a larger library. Most of the books were acquired second-hand from a Catholic school that closed down. But none of these modest desires are to be satisfied; there just isn't any money.

When Kozol meets with the superintendent of the East St. Louis schools, Lillian Parks, she doesn't excuse the neglect and deterioration, nor does she make it seem less than it is. Parks notes: "Gifted children are everywhere in East St. Louis, but their gifts are lost to poverty and turmoil and the damage done by knowing they are written off by their society. Many of these children have no sense of something they belong to. They have no feeling of belonging to America. Gangs provide the boys, perhaps, with something to belong to. . . ." With equal eloquence, Parks describes the plight of the girls. "There is a terrible beauty in some of these girls—terrible, I mean, because it is ephemeral, foredoomed. The language our children speak may not be Standard English but there still is wisdom here. Our children have become wise by necessity" (p. 34).

East St. Louis is a terrible reminder of how badly we neglect many of our children and of how excruciatingly difficult it is to sustain hope when the most basic requirements are absent. It is also a symbol for those who believe that great teaching or renewed effort can redeem even the worst situation. Decent facilities, adequate funding, and a safe environment are the necessary foundation from which good education springs. Without these basics, children cannot learn. It is a tribute to the courage and perseverance of the people of East St. Louis that they continue to struggle to provide a decent education for their children. That the United States allows school districts like those in East St. Louis to operate without the help they desperately need is a sad commentary on the outmoded formulas we continue to rely on to finance education.

MARVA COLLINS: CRITIQUE AND ACTION

Although Kozol's accounts of American education are incisive and powerful, they hold out little hope for the future. This quality is both a strength and a weakness. Kozol's narratives teach us that tinkering will not alleviate the grave problems that plague American schools. Only a renewed public commitment to educational equity and a radical redistribution of revenues that forces the richest communities to share their wealth with the poorest will make a difference, he insists. Short of this dramatic transformation, there seems to be little that educators and local communities can do to improve America's system of schooling. Thus, it is fitting to turn here to the experiences of Marva Collins, a master teacher who has imparted to thousands of students the educational foundation they need to become lifelong learners and productive members of society. Her sharp critique of American education, and her efforts to counteract its worst effects, is the subject of the book she cowrote with Civia Tamarkin titled *Marva Collins' Way* (1990).

Marva Collins is born in Monroeville, Alabama, on August 31, 1936. Her father, who owns a grocery store and a funeral parlor, is one of the leaders of the African American community. He becomes the parent to whom Marva feels especially close: he always has a supportive word or a ready ear. Marva works long hours in the grocery store alongside her father, waking at dawn to help him open the store and returning in the late afternoon to count the income for the day. In the evening, Marva sits snugly in her father's arms while they review the local newspaper's accounts of recent events or read aloud together from a favorite book.

Although she lives with the burdens of jim crow racism—racist epithets and separate facilities for every imaginable activity—Marva never faces the threat of racial violence until the day she accompanies her father to a cattle auction and he outbids white buyers from huge meatpacking conglomerates. He is literally backed into a corner and warned to never again return to the auction. Marva watches as her father refuses to back down and promises to return and retaliate against anyone threatening to do him harm. When Marva and her father are free of these racist buyers, he tells her: "I made an honest bid. If you believe in what you do, then you don't ever have to fear anyone" (p. 37). From this experience and others like it, Marva acquires a quiet confidence and determination that serve her well as a teacher and an unrelenting critic of public schools.

Marva learns from her own schooling primarily what not to do. When she is in first grade, she writes the numeral 2 backwards and is rebuked with a rap on the knuckles each time she commits this simple error. As a result she becomes adamant in her own teaching that the students' mistakes be regarded as a natural part of the learning process and that they be used as a basis for help. Putting self-confidence and self-esteem at the top of her list of educational objectives, Collins insists that every action enhance the child's sense of well-being. It becomes her strategy to treat errors as opportunities to promote her students' development, not to put them down or punish them.

Unfortunately, much of Marva's schooling is designed to bring her down and to limit her aspirations. Escambia County Training School is a typical segregated school: the emphasis is less on the liberal arts and more on "practical pursuits." Girls are expected to take home economics, which, in Marva's mind, is the school's way of communicating the message that black women should confine themselves to domestic or service employment. Having acquired a certain amount of feistiness from observing her father, she informs the principal that she considers the course both degrading and inappropriate for her. For whatever reason, he lets the issue pass, making Marva Collins one of the few girls in that period to graduate from Escambia without a course in home economics.

Eager to continue her education, Collins goes to Clark College in Atlanta. The experience has little impact on her, attributable to the rather poor preparation she receives in high school and to the fact that she is immature and unsure what to do with her life. She majors in secretarial science and, upon graduation, teaches business courses to high school students in Alabama. The principal at the school where she teaches in those first years is a superb educator. He teaches her how to read to her students, how to discern when they do not understand the material, and how to use this information to help them. After two years of teaching in Alabama, she realizes that she has a gift for teaching but is also interested in taking up some new challenges. During a visit to Chicago in 1959, she vows to settle down there.

Owing to a teacher shortage, Marva easily secures a position teaching elementary school in the Chicago Public Schools. Although she lacks experience teaching young children, she finds that she readily adapts to her second-grade students. It doesn't take her long to realize that the standard Board of Education curriculum underestimates the ability of her students. Like Kozol, she adds new activities and readings. Drawing on her childhood memories, she introduces a series of fables and fairy tales by Aesop, the Grimm Brothers, La Fontaine, Hans Christian Andersen, and Tolstoy. She finds that these supplemental readings not only raise the interest level of her students, but they also provide occasions for the children to think about and discuss important issues. Their discussions touch on such fundamental concerns as the meanings of happiness and wisdom and the expectations for leading a moral life. Like Vivian Paley, Collins has the children write and draw about these stories and make dramatic productions out of them. It is a year of experimentation, discovery, and gentle subversion of the standard curriculum. Apparently, Marva's changes go unnoticed or are not considered significant enough to warrant protest.

After a few years off to raise her children, Collins takes a full-time position at Delano Elementary School in Chicago and remains there from 1963 to the mid-1970s, primarily teaching second grade. At first her professional life at Delano is rich and enlightening, due largely to the principal's high standards and instructional leadership. His faculty workshops are legendary for demonstrating his grasp of a wide range of English poetry and for the dramatic flourishes he uses to keep his audience engaged and interested. Marva follows his example and begins using poetry and other classic literature in her own teaching. Above all, she notes, the principal shows her "that a good teacher is one who continues to learn along with the students" (p. 55).

But the good times at Delano don't last. A more traditional principal who seems to care only about maintaining discipline and keeping order takes over. His sole injunction to Collins is to keep the shades on her windows even. It appears that his job has nothing to do with the quality of education offered or how effectively teachers deliver instruction. Teaching, Collins finds, is the last thing on his mind. Indeed, like Garret Keizer, who detests all the obligations that keep teachers from teaching, Collins discovers that:

> Teaching was the last priority, something you were supposed to do after you collected the milk money, put up the bulletin boards . . . straightened the shades and desks, filled out forms in triplicate, punched all the computer cards with pre-test and post-test scores, and charted all the reading levels so they could be shipped downtown to the Board of Education. (p. 56)

Collins is shocked by the school district's obsession with test scores. Nothing seems to matter except scores on standardized examinations. They are studied, probed, graphed, and ranked, but in the end they aren't used to hold educators accountable, nor to help students advance, nor to rethink curriculum. The tests are a major part of the educational pretense that seems to overshadow the Chicago schools.

Collins also grows convinced that the so-called "look-say" method of reading is holding students back. The method relies on the memorization of a carefully specified sight-word vocabulary. Teachers pair these sight words with a reading text series like the Dick and Jane books and gradually build their students' ability to master an increasing number of similar words. The claim is that this method avoids the drudgery of traditional phonics and allows students to read meaningful texts almost from the beginning. Collins is a severe critic of look-say. She wonders how students can acquire the ability to read without an intensive and comprehensive program that shows them how to sound out most words. But phonics is only a start for Collins. What she wants more than anything else is for her students to develop a love of reading and to acquire a taste for great literature. She reads to them and with them constantly. She uses excerpts from the works of Emerson, Bacon, and Thoreau and gives the words and ideas of these writers a central place in her classroom and curriculum.

Collins teaches more than reading, writing, and arithmetic. She concerns herself with every aspect of her students' lives. She helps them maintain good hygiene, and she teaches them to use acceptable manners, to develop healthy posture, and to wear flattering clothes. Most of all, she relates all of these concerns to the development of their character and their self-esteem. She believes that she must educate the whole child and that this commitment obliges her to teach many things outside the standard curriculum.

Unfortunately, her philosophy of education conflicts with that of her colleagues. Many of them resent Collins for being too flamboyant, for working such long hours, and for demanding so much more of her students than any other teacher. She is frequently attacked for being a persistent critic of standard practices at Delano. She condemns the adopted textbook series for "dumbing down" the curriculum and for selling the students far too short. She also takes on the school's administration for putting bureaucratic procedure ahead of teaching and learning. And she openly admonishes principals for prizing superficial harmony over thoughtful critique and for avoiding risks.

But Collins doesn't criticize just the local schools. She knows that many problems stem from a nationwide textbook industry eager to exploit the latest fad and to make a large profit off the most recent innovation. As she says in her book:

> There is a lot of money to be made from miseducation, from the easy to read easy to learn textbooks, workbooks, teacher manuals, educational games and visual aids. The textbook business is more than a billion-dollar-a-year industry and some of its biggest profits come from "audio-visual aids"–flash cards, tape cassettes and filmstrips. No wonder the education industry encourages schools to focus on surface education. (p. 59)

Some of Collins' colleagues become deeply antagonistic and the principal grows increasingly less sympathetic, despite the fact that Collins proves she is a superb teacher. One day, she and her class set out on a field trip to a fast-food restaurant, a trip which is part of her teaching unit on food and for which she has observed all the proper procedures for getting permission. As they are leaving, the principal suddenly cancels the trip because faculty resentment against her has reached a new high. Collins takes her children on the trip anyway, proclaiming that the principal has made a promise to support her and that she will not disappoint the children. After that, her relationships with the principal and with her colleagues are beyond repair. Not long after this incident, two notes appear in her mailbox that essentially read: "You think you're so great. We think you're nothing" (p. 70).

Collins contemplates giving up teaching as a career. This changes, however, when a group of women active in Chicago's West Side and dissatisfied with the performance of the public schools urge Collins to become the director of a private elementary school they are organizing. With the generous assistance of the Alternative Schools Network and Daniel Hale Williams University, a local community college, the new school is launched.

When the term begins, only four children are enrolled. To be gravely discouraged, perhaps even ready to give up on the whole project, would not be surprising. Collins, however, has no such thoughts. On that first day alone, they recite not the Pledge of Allegiance but the Pledge to Ourselves, which says: "This day has been given to me fresh and clear. I can either use it or throw it away. I promise I shall use this day to the fullest, realizing it can never come back again" (p. 84). They read from Emerson's "Self-Reliance" and talk about the connections between getting an education and leading a good life. They read from Proverbs and talk more about education for knowledge, wisdom, and vision and for securing a good livelihood. They do some phonics drills, perform some math exercises, discuss place value, and read together again, this time from Aesop's Fables. In the process of reading Aesop, they review the etymology of key words, go over unfamiliar vocabulary, discuss Greek history, and define fable. They also have an extensive and wide-ranging discussion about the multiple meanings of the fables they read. At the end of the day, Collins distributes to each of the four children math and phonics homework especially designed to address the needs of each child.

In all of this work, Collins never talks down to children and always strives to challenge them while also engaging them. She believes in drill, memorization, and practice, but she does not let these things get in the way of exploratory learning, creative projects, and, most of all, thoughtful discussion in which each child has the chance to give her or his opinion and to learn from the views of others. She writes, "The one thing all children finally wanted was the chance to be accepted for themselves, to feel some self-worth. Once they felt it, children became addicted to learning, and they had the desire to learn forever" (p. 92).

The teaching and learning patterns established on that first busy day are repeated again and again as the year progresses. By February of the first year, 13 children daily arrive at the West Side school to learn Marva's lessons. Now, the ages of the children range from 7 to 12, and the challenges of maintaining an effective one-room schoolhouse grow increasingly acute.

Despite the difficulty in doing so, Collins insists on treating each child as a distinct and unique individual. She condemns the common practice in public schools of relying on psychological reports and cumulative files to label and stigmatize children. She hates the tendency of many educators to stereotype children according to social class, or neighborhood, or their parents' marital status. And she becomes especially incensed when people tell her that ghetto children don't need the classics, just some good vocational training. Such opinions recall her own childhood when black girls were expected to take home economics to prepare them for careers as domestic servants. Again, though, Collins is perceptive enough to recognize that this tendency to label and to stereotype is not primarily the fault of the schools themselves but of societal practices in which categorizing and classifying are viewed as the most effective way to manage people. Moreover, Collins' understanding of learning is sophisticated. The problem, she affirms, is often not in the child at all but in the learning environment, the teaching approach, or even in an antagonistic relationship between instructor and student. Collins tends to see teaching and learning as a highly complex, multifaceted set of arrangements and relationships. To assume that the child is at fault when learning doesn't occur strikes her as hopelessly simplistic and, at times, even cruel.

Collins' approach to education is an interesting blend of liberal and conservative, progressive and traditional. She rejects all aspects of cookie-cutter education in which every child is treated alike and expected to meet identical standards. She comes to know every child well and tailors the schooling each will receive to the specific needs, experiences, and skill levels of the child. She also values her students' perspectives and finds a great deal of time during each day to give students a chance to air their views and to learn from others. At the same time, she wants every child to master the curriculum, and she is willing to employ drill, intensive practice, and memorization to reach some of these objectives. She embraces what she calls a balanced approach in which there is no necessary conflict between stimulating creativity or critical thinking and learning by rote. Cognitive skills can be developed and sharpened, she insists, even as feelings and attitudes are also respected and nurtured. (See Cuban, 1998, on how the ongoing debate between progressives and traditionalists sometimes obscures the most important school reform issues.)

Eventually this balanced but highly rigorous and engaging approach wins Marva Collins allies from all over the country. At first, only the Chicago media publicize her successes, but soon nationally distributed periodicals and even television programs shower Collins with praise. Although some of this exposure leads to sharp criticism as well, Collins becomes an educational celebrity and her school continues to blossom as a result. By the early 1980s, the enrollment has swelled to 200 children with over 500 on a waiting list. To this day, Marva Collins continues to prosper as one of the country's best-known teachers.

More than anything, she becomes known as an educator who is unalterably committed to using classic literature to impart reading skill and taste, to teach ethics and morality, and to prove to her students that they are capable of mastering anything, no matter how challenging. As she has said:

> The great books were their greatest teacher. While there are critics who claim the classics are too difficult for younger students to read— that an eleven year old, for example, can't understand anything as complicated as *The Brothers Karamozov*—I have found that great literature not only teaches students to read but also makes them thirsty for more and more knowledge. These books are over the head of the student reader; that is the purpose of reading them. We read to stretch the mind, to seek, to strive, to wonder, and then to reread. We discuss the ideas contained in these books with others, and we temper our own thoughts. The great books are great teachers because they demand the attention of the reader. The mundane content of second-rate literature turns students off from reading forever. (p. 178)

Here in a nutshell is not only Marva Collins' philosophy of education, but her critique of public schools as well. The schools do not challenge or engage students enough, and they do not build a thirst for more learning. Far too often they are holding pens, way stations, baby-sitting institutions that forget how precious and wonderful real learning and profound understanding can be. It remains Marva Collins' unalterable mission to affirm the difficulty of genuine learning, while also insisting that, with the right help and under the right conditions, everyone can learn the most challenging material. Additionally, she avers few things are as satisfying as proving to oneself and to others that even the most formidable educational obstacles can be overcome.

IRA SHOR AND A NARRATIVE OF STUDENT EMPOWERMENT

Ira Shor presents a very different view of the problems of current educational practice and of the strategies needed to address those problems in his 1996 book *When Students Have Power*. At first glance, the book appears to be a straightforward tale of Shor's struggle to democratize his teaching and to share power with his students in authentic ways. It is this, but it is also a critique of the educational and social practices of contemporary American society that make strong democracy and genuine power sharing excruciatingly difficult. It systematically analyzes all the signs and symbols, rituals and rules, norms and expectations that undermine careful thought, open discussion, and bold action in American schools.

Ira Shor has taught English for 20 years at the City University of New York at Staten Island. During that time he has become one of the leaders of a school of educational theory and practice called critical pedagogy. As one of its most articulate progenitors, Shor has documented the ways in which schools and other large institutions silence students and prevent them from exploring and analyzing their own and the larger society's most pressing problems. Shor has also become a leading advocate of the use of dialogue and other pedagogical means to empower students. With *When Students Have Power* Shor has written his most engaging narrative and has recorded in unprecedented detail the unpredictable turns his students take as he bravely follows the implications of his own philosophy and practice. As Shor himself puts it:

> I advise myself to search for the untested and unpredictable openings at the margins and in the cracks of the group I was approaching, where I might find territory less captured by the status quo, where some critical thought, civic ideals, and democratic relations were possible even in conservative times. For teachers like me, this experimental search for transformative openings involves a risk-taking 'praxis' (action relating theory to practice, in a specific context that challenges limiting situations). The story in this book is about the surprises I encountered as a result of some action against the limits. (p. 3)

The course in which this experiment is carried out focuses on utopias. Ironically, the class is held in a dark, drab, artificially lit basement chamber, which for Shor symbolizes the low expectations that this Staten Island institution holds for its working class clientele. In recounting the first day of this class, Shor captures the shared characteristics of the working class students who file into his class—their modest ambitions, their cynicism about politics, their poorly paid work, their moonlighting, their resiliency, their street smarts without academic smarts, and their suspicion of professors and other authority figures. Yet Shor is also quick to note that, although these characteristics are typical of many of his students, they do not begin to "exhaust all of their individual differences" (p. 7). Shor admires these students, describing them as "complicated, smart, tough, humorous, enterprising and capable, expressing a range of voices and personalities" (p. 9).

As Shor indicates, the story begins as students enter the classroom and strategically choose their seats. The chairs that are available to students are cheap and uncomfortable; they contrast sharply with the plush, expensive chairs the faculty, and especially the administration, have purchased for themselves. Even the chairs convey the message that the students are weak, disempowered, and unimportant compared with the people who run the college. The arrangement of the chairs—in straight rows with the teacher's distinctive chair and desk in the front—reinforces the power differential between instructor and students. The students are aware (if only subconsciously) that this arrangement is meant to control them and to undermine their autonomy, and most of them resist it by placing themselves as far as possible from the teacher's location. Shor refers to these far-flung classroom reaches as "Siberia, East and West" and observes that, when students position themselves in this way, they defer to the instructor while also trying to subvert her or him. "They appear to be rejecting authority and submitting to it at the same time," he notes (p. 12). Shor explains that this Siberian Syndrome is a manifestation of how the school marginalizes and mistreats many students. For the most part, school has been not only a disempowering experience, but an unpleasant and disheartening one as well. For too many of these students, school has made them feel less intelligent, less able, and less confident. They keep coming back to take advantage of the vocational and economic benefits that school ostensibly confers, but they become suspicious when teachers claim that the chief purpose of education is to stimulate thought or to get students to appreciate the intrinsic value of learning.

Once the students position themselves in the classroom, Shor argues that what the teacher does next sets an important tone for the entire term. To introduce the content of the course or to review the syllabus without addressing the underlying conflicts that exist between students and teacher is to perpetuate the inequalities and disaffection under which students have labored for so long. At the same time, most students have virtually no experience with power sharing in classrooms; to expect students to make constructive use of newfound authority without preparation jeopardizes Shor's experiment in critical education. He must therefore use his "institutional authority to ease into a process of shared power" (p. 19).

One way Shor does this is by moving to Siberia, invading the students' space and sitting face to face with the most resistant learners, thereby bringing attention to an ingrained habit. Shor invokes Vygotsky's "Law of Awareness" in this regard and notes that, when routinized, unquestioned behavior is interrupted, the opportunity arises "to notice it, question it, and consider alternatives" (p. 22). Discussion ensues about the ways in which classroom seating reflects power relationships in the classroom, broaching a formerly taboo subject. Over time, Shor finds that, by varying his own placement in the classroom, he can bring attention not only to the Siberian Syndrome but also to the phenomenon of what Shor calls the "Scholasticons" (p. 12), those students who sit near the front and eagerly engage the teacher's questions and comments but who also are more directly subject to the instructor's power and authority.

Shor issues a warning worth pausing over. It is much easier for a tall, imposing, white professional male like Shor to invade Siberia without suffering negative consequences than it is for a woman or person of color to do so. Persons who are on the margins or who are regarded as weak by others can expect an especially inhospitable reception any time they bring attention to ingrained habits or to power relations that are often uncomfortable to reflect on. Strategies such as "invading Siberia" should be carried out with caution and with the distinct recognition that they may backfire and create even more interpersonal tension. There are benefits, then, that accrue to white males in a patriarchal society even when they are attempting to transform the very power relations that advantage them in the first place.

Of course, bringing attention to classroom seating is only the beginning of the slow process of introducing critical education into a course and moving toward authentic power sharing. How course content is chosen and studied, how the class is run, reflected upon, and assessed, and how conflicts are handled and resolved are open for negotiation. All of these things are affected by the ways in which classroom discourse is handled. Shor refers to the work of Nan Elsasser and Patricia Irvine that calls for four major changes in the creation of new speech communities in classrooms. These include:

1. Students reading, speaking, and writing their own language along with Standard English
2. Students and teachers jointly constructing curricula to address issues they agree are important
3. Students and teachers producing knowledge that is valuable for them and others
4. Students and teachers "initiate and/or support actions which challenge inequitable power relations in and out of the classroom" (p. 30)

Shor's strategy is to begin the class by giving students as active a role as possible and by restraining his own participation. He calls this "frontloading student expression" (p. 41; also see *Empowering Education*, 1992), which he contrasts with "backloaded teacher commentary." It means holding back commentary on a syllabus and the expectations of the teacher and making room for students' voices right from the start. But it also means posing questions about important matters for the students, and about the university and utopias, that get the students thinking through some of the issues from the course and talking with one another regarding some of their leading concerns. If Shor speaks at all during this first class, it is to engage the students both individually and in small groups with the questions he has posed or to synthesize near the end of the class (backloading) some of the recurring themes brought up by the students. He may also introduce some general information about utopias that will help the students in reflecting on their own questions and comments. As Shor puts it, he assumes an "interrogative rather than a declarative posture in the rhetorical setting" (p. 42).

The students are encouraged in small groups, without the interference of the teacher, to generate their own thoughts and their own themes about the course topic—utopias. When the small groups have completed their work, they are encouraged to report back to the large group about their findings. Shor makes a special effort to show his students that he is listening carefully to what each group says by taking copious notes. This, he says, shows that he respects their ideas. Later, he adds, he will refer to these contributions, often using the students' exact words to reaffirm that what they have to say really matters. This practice is, of course, a complete reversal of what the students are, for the most part, used to. They expect the teacher's words to be given special consideration; putting a premium on student speech and ideas is a significant shift for most students. Again, it sets the tone for the rest of the course in which the contributions of students will be held in high regard.

There is no conflict, however, between elevating the importance of student thought and reserving space for Shor himself to make some original commentary. What is inviolate in this experiment in critical, democratic education is the right of students to critique the teacher's comments or anything else about the class they find unsatisfactory. As Shor observes, it is not democratic or critical if students are ignored, silenced, or punished in making their criticisms public for general discussion. "By bringing conflict and alienation out into the open," Shor affirms, "I hope to interfere with the formation of Siberia" (p. 57).

In a chapter titled "Escaping Siberia," Shor recounts how he attempts to create in the class "a small social system for experimental change" (p. 64). The first issue they take up is the placement of the chairs in the classroom. While recognizing that forming the chairs into a circle does not, by itself, result in a more progressive class, Shor prefers a circle because it upsets the balance of power relations, shifting the focus from the instructor to the students. A circle greatly increases the possibility of multivocal, multilateral dialogue; keeping the chairs in rows does not. Shor's students do not always agree, however, and Shor is himself aware of how the circle can intrude on the privacy of individual participants. Nevertheless, on balance, it is the arrangement he prefers, and he is relieved when the students opt for the circle.

After additional deliberations about class participation procedures, the class takes up the issue of grading and evaluation. Long a user of learning contracts, Shor distributes his list of criteria that students will need to meet to earn an A, B, or C. His intent in using such contracts is to provide an opportunity for students to reflect on their work in the class and to give them some say in how they will contribute. He wants them not only to make some choices but also to do some questioning about the criteria themselves, and to take charge, at least to a degree, of their own education. Once he can demonstrate that he means what he says, the students, who are at first quite hesitant, avidly debate the criteria of the learning contracts. In various ways, they question the expectation to participate actively in discussion, they challenge the notion that attendance should be required, and they seek to redefine tardiness. In all of these areas and others, Shor listens patiently to what they have to say and ends up compromising on most of them. But he also reaffirms the importance of negotiating these issues and reemphasizes that critical, democratic education does not oblige the teacher to accept whatever the students want. Both the students and the teacher retain a strong voice and a right to criticize anything, but neither has the right to prevail on every issue.

One of the most interesting issues that Shor and the class members debate is the requirement that students attend class. One student named Angela argues persuasively against any attendance requirement. She bases her claim on past college experience in which her presence in class made little or no difference. As long as she mastered the lecture notes acquired from a friend and studied the assigned reading carefully, she could "ace" the examinations and get the highest possible grade. Attendance, she had learned, is irrelevant. Shor's counter-argument is that his class is different and that every student's voice is needed to negotiate the curriculum effectively, to share power productively, and to "build mutual discussion" (p. 111). Although Angela accepts Shor's explanation, she goes on to other issues. She gets Shor to agree to extend the time at the beginning of class before a student is counted as tardy and she works out a slightly earlier dismissal time. Shor does not anticipate how literally students like Angela will claim their "protest rights," but he nevertheless views the process as a healthy and necessary exercise in learning to share power.

While mildly frustrated and surprised by some of the students' demands, Shor is unrelenting in his desire to negotiate every issue with his students. To keep the conversation about how the class is conducted as fresh as possible, Shor organizes an "after-class group" composed of volunteers interested in gathering for about 20 to 40 minutes following the regular class to critique Shor's teaching and the course content. For Shor, it is a transformational experience. Twice a week the students cast aside their inhibitions and criticize Shor's teaching in profound and insightful ways. No aspect of his instruction is left unexplored; no part of his attempt to establish meaningful and lasting relationships with his students goes unanalyzed. Although painful in many ways, these critiques help him to become a more alert, sensitive, and responsive teacher. But the after-class group also yields two more benefits. First, he is enabled to hold his students to a higher standard. As Shor says, "by accepting student discipline, a power-sharing teacher then becomes democratically (not institutionally) authorized to make higher demands on the students because students have been authorized to make higher demands on the teacher" (p. 125). Second, by agreeing not just to critique but also to plan and coconstruct the course, the after-class group lightens Shor's burden; he is no longer solely responsible for how the class is going. In the process, as Shor notes, the after-class group becomes the "teacher's friend" (p. 126).

All of this power-sharing gradually leads to two marked differences in student behavior. One is that students in general, not just in the after-class group, become more willing to subject the class to tough, thoughtful criticisms. The three texts for the class (for instance, B. F. Skinner's *Walden II*, Ernest Callenbach's *Ecotopia*, and *50 Simple Things You Can Do to Save the Earth*) are comprehensively assessed, with Skinner's pedantic approach receiving the harshest evaluation. Some students find *50 Simple Things* to be too simplistic and not worth the time that is spent on it. The students reflect on the class more probingly and holistically and are increasingly able to offer defensible and persuasive arguments about their preferences. The second difference is that the students grow more effective in systematically criticizing the policies and practices of the university and the larger society. They begin to view these policies and practices through the lenses of democracy, community, and environmental sustainability, and, for the most part, find them wanting. But their criticisms become less personal and idiosyncratic and more closely connected to the good of the whole.

When Shor asks the after-school group to develop an alternative evaluation form for the class—an interesting exercise in itself, especially when it is compared with the standard university form (see pp. 201–203 of his book for complete copies of the two forms)—the group first settles on two central questions:

1. Has this class opened you up to new ideas and changed your way of thinking?
2. Do you feel motivated to take action in student or civic government or in other classes to change things? (p. 197).

Their answers focus, for the most part, on a new willingness to question the status quo, to interrogate widely accepted assumptions, to imagine alternative ideas and actions, and to be more skeptical of "official" pronouncements. To the extent that Shor is striving to get his students to think about themselves, their class, and their community more critically, the responses he receives on the evaluation form indicate that he is quite successful.

Predictably, there are also a fair number of criticisms of how the class is run. One of the recurring concerns that Shor hopes to address in the future is the reading list. Of the three books, all of which Shor assigns without input from the students, only *Ecotopia* wins wide acclaim. His plan in subsequent classes is to expand the reading list and to give the students the prerogative to choose the most appropriate texts in the most helpful order.

Adaptations such as these are designed not just to get the students to think more critically and to take charge of their own learning, but to recreate the entire educational process. The line between teacher and student blurs and a new model emerges in which, as Freire (1970) says, the teacher and students "become jointly responsible for a process in which all grow" (p. 67). In Shor's words, "In a concrete way, the students had become teachers, clarifying for themselves what they had learned and experienced while also teaching me how to become a better teacher" (pp. 214–15).

One wonders: did the writing of this narrative about the utopias class also teach Shor new things about his teaching and about himself? Did his work with the students and the process of recalling and reconstructing the events from this class help Shor in questing after his second self? There is every reason to think so. On the final page of *When Students Have Power*, Shor proudly includes the evaluation of Angela, the student who sharply negotiated with him about some of the requirements of the course. She emphasizes how much she learned and observes that Shor pushed her mind "to its outermost limits" (p. 221). Shor then refers to their exchanges about how difficult it is to sustain one's commitment to being a change-agent. Shor expresses concern that, with age and the mounting obligations of adulthood, enthusiasm for social change tends to disappear. Angela steadfastly refuses to allow this to happen and agrees to meet Shor 20 years hence to see if their common fire continues to burn bright. Shor brings the book to a close with this final, affirming sentence: "I hope her desires for social change stay warm, bright, and alive, and so do mine" (p. 221).

CONCLUSION

All of the narratives featured in this chapter—by Kozol, Collins, and Shor—are stories of unrelenting moral and social commitment. They all focus on how to eliminate the conditions that inhibit student growth and on strategies for promoting the values and actions that help human beings to learn and to flourish. They all include systematic analyses of the ways in which schools and other institutions limit the development of intellectual independence and individual agency, and they all offer concrete suggestions for creating authentic communities of learning. They are realistic about how much can be accomplished by one teacher or one class, but they remain committed to doing what they can on both a local and global level to institute lasting change. Finally, they know that their experiences are not unique, and that their struggles are a symbol for the thousands of teachers and students who resist daily an often-deadening status quo. They continue to engage in this struggle, however, and to document it carefully, primarily because they know it is the right thing to do, but also because they know that they must. It is part of who they are and who they are becoming. It is part of the story of their lives and their quest for a higher self, which is inextricably tied to their ongoing pursuit of a more decent society.

In summary, we conclude that *social critic teachers:*

Observe and analyze classrooms to identify teaching practices that inhibit learning and to advocate for changes that promote human growth.

Observe and analyze social institutions to uncover conditions that impede human flourishing and to push for changes that foster educational renewal.

Thoughtfully ground their educational ideas and teaching practices in a powerful vision of a more humane, democratic society and a more caring, equitable school.

Love what they teach and do not hesitate to communicate their passion for subject matter to students.

Dedicate themselves to their students' welfare, learning, and growth.

Maintain high but flexible standards that are sensitive to the needs of individual learners.

STUDY QUESTIONS

Kozol

1. Describe the differences between the Reading Teacher's and Jonathan Kozol's views on what should be taught to children. If you found yourself in Kozol's position, how would you respond to the Reading Teacher's remarks?
2. Why does Kozol describe the physical conditions of the school where he teaches and, later, of the schools that he visits? How would you cope with the physical condition of the school?
3. Why do most of the parents of Kozol's students support him while the school board and administrators in his school oppose him? Do you think that parental support of the kind that Kozol received would make more or less of a difference today, or would there be no difference in the outcome today?

Collins

1. Why does Marva Collins recount her experiences as a young girl in her story of her teaching career?
2. Why did the other teachers in the Chicago public school ostracize Collins? How would you cope with other teachers' attempts to "put you in your place"?
3. Collins started a private school after being discouraged with the way the public schools operated. What are the specific issues that a private school might be better able to address than a public school? What are some of the limitations of private schools?

4. Why does Collins advocate a "great books" curriculum for young children?

Shor
1. What methods does Ira Shor use to enable his students to explore issues of power in their education?
2. How does Shor evaluate his teaching? His students' learning?
3. How is the quest for educational renewal exemplified in Shor's story?

REFERENCES

Ayers, W. (1993). *To teach: The journey of a teacher.* New York: Teachers College Press.

Collins, M., & Tamarkin, C. (1990). *Marva Collins' way.* New York: Putnam.

Cuban, L. (1988). *The managerial imperative and the practice of leadership in schools.* Albany, NY: State University of New York Press.

Cuban, L. (1998, January 28). A tale of two schools. *Education Week, 17,* 20, 48, 33.

Freire, P. (1970) *Pedagogy of the oppressed.* New York: Seabury Press.

Kozol, J. (1967). *Death at an early age.* Boston: Houghton Mifflin.

Kozol, J. (1981). *On being a teacher.* New York: Continuum.

Kozol, J. (1991). *Savage inequalities.* New York: Crown.

Shor, I. (1992). *Empowering education.* Chicago: University of Chicago Press.

Shor, I. (1996). *When students have power.* Chicago: University of Chicago Press.

Death at an Early Age

You check around the classroom. Of forty desks, five have tops with no hinges. You lift a desk-top to fetch a paper and you find that the top has fallen off. There are three windows. One cannot be opened. A sign on it written in the messy scribble of a hurried teacher or some custodial person warns you: DO NOT UNLOCK THIS WINDOW IT IS BROKEN. The general look of the room is as of a bleak-light photograph of a mental hospital. Above the one poor blackboard, gray rather than really black, and hard to write on, hangs from one tack, lopsided, a motto attributed to Benjamin Franklin: *"Well begun is half done."* Everything, or almost everything like that, seems a mockery of itself.

Into this grim scenario, drawing on your own pleasures and memories, you do what you can to bring some kind of life. You bring in some cheerful and colorful paintings by Joan Miro and Paul Klee. While the paintings by Miro do not arouse much interest, the ones by Klee become an instantaneous success. One picture in particular, a watercolor titled "Bird Garden," catches the fascination of the entire class. You slip it out of the book and tack it up on the wall beside the doorway and it creates a traffic jam every time the children have to file in or file out. You discuss with your students some of the reasons why Klee may have painted the way he did and you talk about the things that can be accomplished in a painting which could not be accomplished in a photograph. None of this seems to be above the children's heads. Despite this, you are advised flatly by the Art Teacher that your naïveté has gotten the best of you and that the children cannot possibly appreciate this. Klee is too difficult. Children will not enjoy it. You are unable to escape the idea that the Art Teacher means herself instead.

For poetry, in place of the recommended memory gems, going back again into your own college days, you make up your mind to introduce a poem of William Butler Yeats. It is about a lake isle called Innisfree, about birds that have the funny name of "linnets" and about a "bee-loud glade." The children do not all go crazy about it but a number of them seem to like it as much as you do and you tell them how once, three years before, you were living in England and you helped a man in the country to make his home from wattles and clay. The children become intrigued. They pay good attention and many of them grow more curious about the poem than they appeared at first. Here again, however, you are advised by older teachers that you are making a mistake: Yeats is too difficult for children. They can't enjoy it, won't appreciate it, wouldn't like it. You are aiming way above their heads. Another idea comes to mind and you decide to try out an easy and rather well-known and not very complicated poem of Robert Frost. The poem is called "Stopping By Woods on a Snowy Evening." This time, your supervisor happens to drop in from the School Department. He looks over the mimeograph, agrees with you that it's a nice poem, then points out to you—tolerantly, but strictly—that you have made another mistake. "Stopping By Woods" is scheduled for Sixth Grade. It is not "a Fourth Grade poem," and it is not to be read or looked at during the Fourth Grade. Bewildered as you are by what appears to be a kind of idiocy, you still feel reproved and criticized and muted and set back and you feel that you have been caught in the commission of a serious mistake.

On a series of other occasions, the situation is repeated. The children are offered something new and something lively. They respond to it energetically and they are attentive and their attention does not waver. For the first time in a long while perhaps there is actually some real excitement and some growing and some thinking going on within that one small room. In each case, however, you are advised sooner or later that you are making a mistake. Your mistake, in fact, is to have impinged upon the standardized condescension on which the entire administration of the school is based. To hand Paul Klee's pictures to the children of this classroom, and particularly in a twenty-dollar volume, constitutes a threat to this school system. It is not different from sending a little girl from the Negro ghetto into an art class near Harvard Yard. Transcending the field of familiarity of the administration, you are endangering its authority and casting a blow at its self-confidence. The way the threat is handled is by a continual and standardized underrating of the children: They can't do it, couldn't do it, wouldn't like it, don't deserve it. In such a manner, many children are tragically and unjustifiably held back from a great many of the good things that they might come to like or admire and are pinned down instead to books the teacher knows and to easy tastes that she can handle. This includes, above all, of course, the kind of material that is contained in the Course of Study.

Try to imagine, for a child, how great the gap between the outside world and the world conveyed within this kind of school must seem: A little girl, maybe Negro, comes in from a street that is lined with car-carcasses. Old purple Hudsons and one-wheel-missing Cadillacs represent her horizon and mark the edges of her dreams. In the kitchen of her house roaches creep and large rats crawl. On the way to school a wino totters. Some teenage white boys slow down their car to insult her, and speed on. At school she stands frozen for fifteen minutes in a yard of cracked cement that overlooks a hillside on which trash has been unloaded and at the bottom of which the New York, New Haven and Hartford Railroad rumbles past. In the basement, she sits upon broken or splintery seats in filthy toilets and she is yelled at in the halls. Upstairs, when something has been stolen, she is told that she is the one who stole it and is called a liar and forced abjectly to apologize before a teacher who has not the slightest idea in the world of who the culprit truly was. The same teacher, behind the child's back, ponders audibly with imagined compassion: "What can you do with this kind of material? How can you begin to teach this kind of child?"

Gradually going crazy, the child is sent after two years of misery to a pupil adjustment counselor who arranges for her to have some tests and considers the entire situation and discusses it with the teacher and finally files a long report. She is, some months later, put onto a waiting-list some place for once-a-week therapy but another year passes before she has gotten anywhere near to the front of a long line. By now she is fourteen, has lost whatever innocence she still had in the back seat of the old Cadillac and, within two additional years, she will be ready and eager for dropping out of school.

Once at school, when she was eight or nine, she drew a picture of a rich-looking lady in an evening gown with a handsome man bowing before her but she was told by an insensate and wild-eyed teacher that what she had done was junk and garbage and the picture was torn up and thrown away before her eyes. The rock and roll music that she hears on the Negro station is considered "primitive" by her teachers but she prefers its insistent rhythms to the dreary monotony of school. Once, in Fourth Grade, she got excited at school about some writing she had never heard about before. A handsome green book, brand new, was held up before her and then put into her hands. Out of this book a teacher read a poem. The poem was about a Negro—a woman who was a maid in the house of a white person—and she liked it. It remained in her memory. Somehow without meaning to, she found that she had done the impossible for her: she had memorized that poem. Perhaps horribly, in the heart of her already she was aware that it was telling about her future: fifty dollars a week to scrub floors and bathe little white babies in the suburb after an hour's streetcar ride. The poem made her want to cry. The white lady, the lady for whom the maid was working, told the maid she loved her. But the maid in the poem wasn't going to tell any lies in return. She knew she didn't feel any love for the white lady and she told the lady so. The poem was shocking to her, but it seemed bitter, strong, and true. Another poem in the same green book was about a little boy on a merry-go-round. She laughed with the class at the question he asked about a Jim Crow section on a merry-go-round, but she was also old enough to know that it was not a funny poem really and it made her, valuably, sad. She wanted to know how she could get hold of that poem, and maybe that whole book. The poems were moving to her.

This was a child in my class. Details are changed somewhat but it is essentially one child. The girl was one of the three unplaced special students in that Fourth Grade room. She was not an easy girl to teach and it was hard even to keep her at her seat on many mornings, but I do not remember that there was any difficulty at all in gaining and holding onto her attention on the day that I brought in that green book of Langston Hughes.

Of all the poems of Langston Hughes that I read to my Fourth Graders, the one that the children liked most was a poem that has the title "Ballad of the Landlord." The poem is printed along with some other material in the back part of this book. This poem may not satisfy the taste of every critic, and I am not making any claims to immortality for a poem just because I happen to like it a great deal. But the reason this poem did have so much value and meaning for me and, I believe, for many of my students, is that it not only seems moving in an obvious and immediate human way but that it *finds* its emotion in something ordinary. It is a poem which really does allow both heroism and pathos to poor people, sees strength in awkwardness and attributes to a poor person standing on the stoop of his slum house every bit as much significance as William Wordsworth saw in daffodils, waterfalls and clouds. At the request of the children later on I mimeographed that poem and, although nobody in the classroom was asked to do this, several of the children took it home and memorized it on their own. I did not assign it for memory, because I do not think that memorizing a poem has any special value. Some of the children just came in and asked if they could recite it. Before long, almost every child in the room had asked to have a turn.

All of the poems that you read to Negro children obviously are not going to be by or about Negro people. Now would anyone expect that all poems which are read to a class of poor children ought to be grim or gloomy or heartbreaking or sad. But when, among the works of many different authors, you do have the will to read children a poem by a man so highly renowned as Langston Hughes, then I think it is important not to try to pick a poem that is innocuous, being like any other poet's kind of poem, but I think you ought to choose a poem that is genuinely representative and then try to make it real to the children in front of you in the way I tried. I also think it ought to be taken seriously by a teacher when a group of young children come in to him one morning and announce that they have liked something so much that they have memorized it voluntarily. It surprised me and impressed me when that happened. It was all I needed to know to confirm for me the value of reading that poem and the value of reading many other poems to children which will build upon, and not attempt to break down, the most important observations and very deepest foundations of their lives.

4

The Narrative of Induction and Apprenticeship

Regardless of how well they are prepared or how much promise they appear to have, novice teachers must sooner or later face the trial by fire of real teaching. Hardship and struggle may predominate during this induction phase, but teachers who persevere and continue to learn will discover that the time spent with students is as profound and illuminating as anything they have ever done. This is especially true if they already love the subjects they teach and if, over time, they acquire affection for their students as well. Few combinations are as powerful as teaching the things you revere to people for whom you care deeply. When, as Parker Palmer (1998) says, you also develop the experience and maturity to teach in a manner that is true to your own growing self, then teaching can become an irresistible calling.

The narratives to be examined in this chapter depict failure and triumph, setback and growth. They underscore the notion that teaching is challenging and difficult work, never fully learned or mastered. These narratives also show that, in time and with help, teachers can become better at turning their classrooms into sites hospitable to questioning, collaborative inquiry, and meaningful learning.

Indeed, the most thoughtful beginning teachers must fortify themselves for the ceaseless struggle against educational meaninglessness. That is, they must maintain a high level of what Maxine Greene (1978) calls "wide-awakeness" to resist the tendency to teach unreflectively—to follow tradition, regardless of its value or purpose. They must combat the deadening routines, the conventional opinions, and the irrelevant content that obstruct growth. They must strive to construct places for learning that engage students' hearts and minds and that encourage them both to question the world and to find their place within it. Teachers like Robert Inchausti, James Herndon, and Patricia Schmidt frame their stories in just these terms: as interruptions of the conventional and usual and as quests for both collective meaning and self-renewal.

ROBERT INCHAUSTI: LEARNING TO TEACH FROM A MASTER

Arriving at an all-male Catholic high school fresh out of graduate school to teach English to ninth-grade boys, Robert Inchausti is a self-confessed intellectual snob. He aspires to be a noted interpreter of literary texts, not a lowly instructor of 14-year-old boys. For him, this kind of teaching is beneath contempt; the intellectual demands are nonexistent and the psychic costs are far too punishing. Furthermore, he knows almost nothing about pedagogy and even less about adolescents. In the course of his story, however, he not only learns a great deal about this work, he also comes to value it deeply, largely through the wise intervention of his intellectual and pedagogical mentor, Brother Blake. He also learns a great deal about himself, discovering that the assertion of his own distinctive identity is part of learning to teach well and of making his teaching a sublime and powerful experience for students. Turning teaching into a truly transformative process, Inchausti finds, is a rare and mysterious calling. It becomes a way of rediscovering himself and of transcending that self, of experiencing and analyzing the conflicts of everyday life and rising above them.

Early in his teaching apprenticeship, Inchausti barely copes with his out-of-control ninth-grade class. Each day before school he feels panic washing over him: dizziness, empty feelings in the pit of his stomach, and a mounting terror invade his body. His feeble efforts to enforce classroom rules seem to only worsen the situation. One day, the Dean of Discipline, aptly named Mr. Strapp, takes over Inchausti's class to demonstrate the sort of authoritarian toughness Strapp believes is called for. But, despite some skill in using long pauses punctuated by bellowed threats and intimidating gestures, the Dean plays on the students' fears, pure and simple. Despite his own inexperience, Inchausti knows immediately that this performance has nothing to do with educating children or with helping them to become more sensitive human beings.

Mike Morton, an iconoclastic colleague for whom Inchausti shows a grudging respect, offers a unique explanation for why Inchausti and others are plagued by discipline problems. Arguing that the faculty don't really know how to teach and the students don't really know how to learn, Morton contends that the students resist the faculty to learn how to beat the system and to create alternative visions for themselves. But the system relentlessly reasserts itself. "The only thing we offer them," Morton insists, "is the intolerable option of becoming like us" (p. 19). Intrigued but confused, Inchausti asks why Morton keeps teaching. "To survive them," Morton asserts. "Only then do we become their teachers: heroic counterexamples to their unexamined lives" (p. 19).

Although Inchausti learns a thing here and there from educators like Mr. Strapp or Mike Morton, it is Brother Blake who helps him to see teaching in a completely new light. From their very first encounter, Brother Blake helps Inchausti understand that everything in a classroom—student behavior, discipline, writing, text interpretations, character development, and more—is related and that it is up to the teacher to help the students to see the connections. Interestingly, Mr. Strapp and Brother Blake are ideological opponents who see education in diametrically different ways. Whereas Strapp wonders how students can be better prepared for college, Brother Blake teaches students to be "more passionate than prepared, less defended and more willing to take risks. . . ." He seeks to make them open to new experience, to develop their ability to analyze and their capacity to feel awe. In the end, he says, "we want them to surprise us by their futures, not live out some ambitious high school administrator's dream of a successful life" (p. 36). Now here, Inchausti exclaims, is a view of education that excites and inspires. Brother Blake understands what really goes on in classrooms. He is the only colleague "not hiding behind clichés, the only one still intellectually alive" (p. 35).

While still enduring his students' behavior problems, Inchausti invites Brother Blake to observe a lesson on the book *Lord of the Flies*. As usual the same students create disturbances, while other students, eager to discuss the novel, openly express their frustration with their peers. Brother Blake takes note of this frustration and, with Inchausti's permission, interrupts the lesson. He asks Jim, one of the most serious students, why he doesn't do anything to stop the other students' inappropriate behavior instead of depending on the teacher to intervene. Jim takes offense at being held responsible for others' misbehavior, but Brother Blake quickly explains that it is not a matter of responsibility so much as it is learning to deal with those who interfere with the rights of others. Brother Blake then uses the novel to support his contention. "Think of Ralph on the island in *Lord of the Flies*," he begins.

> Without the adults there to protect him, he wasn't able to take leadership away from Jack. He was the only one there who could communicate with Simon and Piggy and make their gifts useful to the group, but he wasn't able to put Jack in his place, so he wasn't able to lead. (p. 39)

Jim asks whether Brother Blake means that he is like Ralph. Brother Blake, wanting Jim to feel the full power of their situation and the connections between literature and classroom life, replies assertively, "You are Ralph. And you'll never get off the island if you just sit around waiting for some adult to rescue you. I know it's hard. Barbarians like Jack are everywhere. But that is what it means to be on your quest" (pp. 40–41).

With these brief exchanges, Brother Blake teaches Inchausti and his students some important lessons. First, school life is important; it is not an interruption in real life or just preparation for real life, but a significant part of being in the present and an invaluable part of becoming a more fully realized human being. Second, he shows them that the students, through their actions, can make a difference in how all of them experience classroom life. Third, he affirms that what they read and study has a bearing on who they are and on how they choose to live their lives. In addition to these lessons, Inchausti learns that spontaneous, impassioned teaching that capitalizes on unplanned occurrences in the classroom can have a decisive impact on students' attitudes, sometimes greater than even the most scrupulously planned instruction. Indeed, time and respect for this kind of spontaneity must be carefully guarded. Inchausti also comes to understand, under Brother Blake's tutelage, that teachers model an attitude toward life, a way of being that may turn out to be more important than any set of skills or knowledge they may initially set out to teach.

"There is another life, an inner life, a higher life, that has its own heroic dimensions" (p. 42), Brother Blake advises, and it is a life that transcends the race for grades, position, and material possessions, not only because it is ultimately more enduring and significant but also because it is a sphere where success is possible for everyone. Inchausti is learning, thanks to his mentor, just how much is at stake in a classroom for his students and for himself, and how much can be imparted and internalized in a single, fleeting educational encounter.

Brother Blake recalls the time when a student insulted him by using an obscene term for female genitalia. When Blake tells the boy to avoid words he does not understand and when the boy protests that he knows perfectly well what the word means, Blake urges him to draw one on the chalkboard. The attention of the other boys is riveted as they watch expectantly to see whether their classmate can draw a vagina and whether Brother Blake will indeed let him. The boy struggles for some time to render an accurate drawing, but upon finishing all that he shows for his effort are a few indecipherable smudges. Brother Blake approaches the drawing with a discerning tilt of his head. "You know," he gleefully offers, "I have been celibate for over forty years, and even I can draw a better one than that" (p. 47). Amused and relieved, the entire class laughs heartily, including the offending student. But Brother Blake is not satisfied. He wants to use similar profanities to put these word choices beyond the students' reach and to transform this harmless incident into an unforgettable educational experience. He moves toward the student and throws his arm around him in an affectionate manner. Then he says:

> You've really got to get your shit together, and to do that you need a good asshole. I am going to be your asshole this year. And after me, if you are lucky, you'll meet another asshole and another until your shit is packed so tight it coalesces into a fine powder. And then maybe you will be ready for the greatest asshole of them all. (p. 48)

He then motions toward the crucifix hanging on the wall, leaving the boys without doubt as to whom he means. There is a general gasp. Is this sacrilege? Or do they all have the wrong idea about what an asshole is? It is a powerful moment that makes the class question everything, while offering them a glimpse of the irrepressible weight of words and ideas. Brother Blake is enigmatic, delightful, and wise. He has a way of turning everything upside down for a while, which grants new meaning and sense to everyday experience. You never know what he will say or do, but you sense that his very next word could change your life.

With the help of Brother Blake, Robert Inchausti slowly becomes a teacher. At first, Brother Blake's influence changes only how he sees the world; Inchausti isn't yet able to teach like him. But as Inchausti also says, he is "between sanities," unable to live as he had in the past but still not able to adopt a wholly new way of being either. He can't teach like Brother Blake yet, but he also can't teach like anyone else. Remembering Mike Morton's suggestion that teaching is impossible work, he is not discouraged or daunted by it but begins to wear it as a badge of pride. It is impossible but important work, beyond the inclination or capacity of most mortals, and this makes him feel very alive and invigorated. Now he looks forward to each day and to the never-ending battle for young minds. He is in the thick of a struggle that seems unwinnable but from which both he and his students derive great satisfaction. He reaches a point at which he does not expect anything from his encounters with students, nor does he fear anything. He is a witness, "seeing everything and providing a space for spirit to express itself" (p. 69).

Humility is one of the characteristics that the protagonists in the best teacher narratives share. These teachers are themselves always learning. One sign of Inchausti's intellectual humility and his growth as a teacher is the lesson he teaches to his students about Elie Weisel's novel *Night*. Baffled and deeply disturbed by Weisel's chronicle of the Nazi death camps, the students strain to make sense of a hanging of three prisoners, one of whom is an emaciated boy who survives half dead on the gallows, his body too slight to force the snapping of his neck. Compelled to witness these horrifying events, one of the prisoners inquires, "Where is God now?" In the novel, Weisel hears a voice answering, "He is hanging here on the gallows" (p. 119).

When the students turn to their teacher for an explanation, for a key to the mystery of this haunting passage, Inchausti refuses to offer the glib but plausible explanation that this event symbolizes the death of God. Instead he responds simply that he doesn't know what it means. When one student likens this incident to the death of Christ, Inchausti objects, saying that the Nazis slaughtered a million children like this one; it can't just stand for Jesus. When another student insists that the hanging must be a symbol, Inchausti hesitates at first to disagree and then replies: "To see this child as a symbol would be to forget his humanity, his precious irreplaceability, his never-again individual character" (p. 120). A discussion ensues in which the students raise thoughtful questions and put forward some tentative answers. But when another student again attempts to characterize the entire novel as one great symbol, Inchausti brings the discussion to a close by resisting this characterization.

"No, it's a memory," Inchausti affirms. "And now, in a way, it's our memory too, so we've got to live with it, and have to live lives of substance to be worthy of it. If we live, we have obligations as survivors not to betray the humanity of those who came before us by belittling our own" (p. 121).

Eloquent and moving as these exchanges are, Inchausti, in retrospect, begins to question his right to speak in this idealistic, even heroic manner. Is it dishonest, inauthentic, even an obstacle to real learning? Brother Blake once again comes to his aid, explaining that this kind of teaching is a way of employing all the power, virtue, and possibility that surround us and that ultimately affect us in some form. From this Inchausti concludes:

> That for teachers to dramatize the ideals they teach—to impersonate the wise, if only for the space of a single lesson—is not an act of hubris or usurpation, but a natural and noble, honorable deed. Part of one's job. And if the sublime is to remain alive in education, we must dare to inspire, even if we ourselves are social outcasts with little money and less prestige. (pp. 122–23)

People learning to teach need to witness others learning as well, evolving into more thoughtful teachers and more caring human beings. One of the important things new teachers can learn is how others have coped with barriers to learning and how they have devised and carried out creative solutions to seemingly insurmountable problems. Narratives like *Spitwad Sutras* are chronicles of classroom life, of succeeding and failing, of witnessing both teachers and students arriving at new understandings. As these new understandings emerge, teachers must use them to pose still more problems and frame even more incisive questions. The narrative of apprenticeship, in particular, reminds us how much can be learned from masters of the teaching craft like Brother Blake and how important such relationships can be when forming a professional identity.

JAMES HERNDON: FREEDOM, IRONY, AND THE SEARCH FOR EDUCATIONAL RELEVANCE

As we have already seen in the case of Jonathan Kozol (in chapter 3), stories of teaching do not always end happily or follow a path of uninterrupted growth. Sometimes the idealism of beginning teachers conflicts with the entrenched practices of traditional schools. In all of his books about his experiences in schools, James Herndon wryly accepts the conservative, reform-resistant nature of most educational institutions even as he tries to put little dents in the bureaucratic armor that protects these institutions from change. Herndon is not out to transform the world or even to alter significantly the schools in which he teaches, but from the beginning of his career in teaching he endeavors to give his own students freedom and, in so doing, to set up situations for them to learn personally meaningful things.

In *The Way It Spozed To Be* (1968), his first book, Herndon tells the story of how he learned to teach at a nearly all-black, inner city school called George Washington Junior High. One of the first things he learns about the school and about many of the educators he runs into is the importance they put on classroom discipline—maintaining order and decorum. Order seems to be not only a highly important means but also the chief end of the school. Herndon expects considerable disorder and even chaos, but preventing it or even thinking about it just isn't one of his priorities.

He learns early on that sorting the students into different ability groups is another of the school's most important functions. At George Washington there are eight ability levels; based on the scores of the IQ tests they take, students are assigned to levels A through H. Sometimes only a few points separate the students in A from the students in B or C. Despite the fact that everyone accepts that these tests are not precise and that a 10- or 20-point spread between students is not a reliable indicator of whether one student enjoys more intellectual capacity than another, these tests are the sole measure for differentiating students into different levels. Herndon, newcomer that he is, wonders about this, but questioning the reliance on IQ tests is a cultural taboo.

Herndon is assigned a seventh grade B class and an eighth grade B class. From the beginning, he clicks with the seventh grade class and comes to admire them greatly. The eighth-grade class, Herndon decides, has a completely different view of teaching and learning. The students expect much from him and little from themselves; Herndon eventually characterizes them as "shallow and deceitful" (p. 23). His disappointment in them grows as the school year progresses. Despite the differences in these classes, little is said about them in Herndon's chronicle of first-year teaching. However, Herndon mentions that, in the case of 7B, whenever he tries out new ideas with them, they almost always respond positively. Some of the most curious kids he will ever meet are in this class; they allow him to remain relaxed and easygoing and to be the kind of teacher he had always hoped to be. Despite the other problems he faces, this 7B class provides him with a valuable apprenticeship in which he can not only teach his students but also teach himself.

"9D and 7H were unreasonable," begins the first sentence of Herndon's seventh chapter, and so begins the heart of this tale of learning to teach. Exciting these students about learning and giving them something to do that actually matters to them becomes his year-long challenge. Both classes are older and more rambunctious than he is prepared for. Most significantly, they lack basic skills; this is especially true of 7H. Four of the students in 7H, Herndon learns on the first day of class, cannot even read their own names.

Undaunted by the severity of the academic deficits he observes, Herndon settles on free writing as the focus of his ninth-grade class. He has hardly begun an explanation of how he wants to run the class and the kind of things he hopes his students will write when Maurice, fresh from Juvenile Hall, joins them. Herndon continues with his opening explanations about writing only to be interrupted by a brawl between Maurice and another boy. Maurice is on top of his opponent, literally pummeling him when Herndon calls for them to stop. Maurice keeps hitting his classmate and Herndon keeps insisting that it cease. Finally, desperate to bring the fight to an end and to protect the boy being beaten, Herndon grabs Maurice by the armpits and throws him backwards onto a row of desks. Ready for the worst, the class awaits the verdict that will land Maurice back in Juvenile Hall. But Herndon simply nods and retreats to his large teacher's desk while Maurice accepts the peace and takes his assigned seat.

In most teacher narratives—especially narratives turned into movies—Herndon's next move would not only be viewed as brilliant, it would be the turning point in the story. He simply announces that the students' first writing assignment is to describe what they have just seen. Instead of leaping at the chance to document these exciting events, the students resist it in every conceivable way. They exclaim: No materials to write with! Not a proper thing to write about! We never had an assignment like this before! You should be telling us the right thing to do! You can't expect us to do that! In the end, no one except Maurice finishes the assignment. This is typical of Herndon's story, for in this world of trial and error, hope and despair, there are no simple answers.

Like most novice teachers, Herndon feels overwhelmed by his new responsibilities. In an effort to cope and to improve his skills, he seeks out the help of his colleagues. He talks frequently to teachers, administrators, and a wide range of students to find out what others do to meet young people's needs and to make their teaching interesting. He also intends to observe different teachers, but most are not particularly welcoming. The exceptions are shop and art classes where students roam fairly freely and where, as a result, discipline presents less of a problem. In the course of these conversations and observations, Herndon notes two themes. One is that some techniques and methods make teaching work better. These include creative ways to group students and to evaluate them, and the supplementation of texts with media like films and recordings. Herndon finds these suggestions useful, though relatively trivial.

The second theme is more complex and more troubling. It focuses on the obsession with order that pervades his school. Although there is much talk of order as the necessary condition for getting kids to learn, Herndon sees little evidence of the learning itself. For the most part, order and discipline have not helped students to develop even the most rudimentary of skills, nor do the students grow more effective in coping with the temptations of the outside world. Students at George Washington are rarely given practice in making choices, thinking through problems, or in exploring the connections between the curriculum and their everyday lives. In short, even if the obsession with maintaining order had made it possible for students to learn, learning is defined so narrowly at George Washington that even learners regarded as accomplished would benefit little. Consequently, Herndon finds that within a few months most of his conversations with colleagues are confined to the mundane and perfunctory, rarely veering off toward the complexities of learning and teaching.

Despite being totally committed to helping his two problem classes—7H and 9D—Herndon knows that by the middle of the year little has been accomplished with them. The first and primary problem with 7H is the inability of most of the students to read even elementary material. Herndon takes the logical step of inviting his two best readers to tutor the rest of the class. This should have worked, but one of the students is impatient and easily angered and the other derives far more enjoyment from confusing the students and giving them false information than he does from seeing them succeed. These discoveries teach Herndon an important lesson. Students are assigned to H level for not just academic reasons, but also because they have uncontrollable tempers or are just plain uncooperative.

9D's problem is different. They can read fairly adequately, but they are fed up with school and not inclined to complete assignments or to do most of the work expected of them. Herndon has led them in some spirited discussions on a variety of topics, including homogeneous grouping at George Washington and, specifically, what it means to be assigned to level D. This discussion, which lasts several days, is both informed and critical, but, at the end of it, Herndon is at a loss how to follow up. He wants them to choose to write, to practice expressing their thoughts as clearly as possible, and to feel the power and the persuasive force of the written word. They resist making this transition, however, from discussion to writing, from expressing their thoughts orally to recording them on paper. But he is hopeful that something transformative will happen. He strives to be flexible and to leave room for the invigorating spontaneity that may signal real change for his students.

Because Herndon's difficulties are public knowledge in the school, he is approached by a series of veteran educators eager to offer advice and to see him through what they fear is a troublesome apprenticeship. But Herndon quickly learns that their emphasis on maintaining order conflicts with his higher purpose of getting the students to learn by allowing them to make their own educational choices.

First, the teacher who substituted for him during a long absence comes forward. She is a highly efficient teacher who is known for her no-nonsense attitude. She counsels Herndon to begin each class period by having the students copy a long paragraph from the chalkboard. She explains that it is something they all can accomplish without assistance and that it puts them in the mood for learning. Herndon sees this procedure as part of the tradition that seems to work because it tends, more or less, to promote order. It is a classic example of how a technique that is supposed to be a means becomes an educational end and results in a climate that stresses busywork and unreflective ritual.

Similar advice comes from Mrs. A, the district consultant for language and social studies. She decides that Herndon has never learned a basic truth about teaching, especially about teaching these particular children. Teaching them is like training animals, she offers matter-of-factly. If you want the child to pull the cart, you have to attach a carrot or a cube of sugar; then the work takes care of itself. An outraged Herndon wonders why the work itself can't be the carrot, but Mrs. A tut-tuts that away and reminds him that every child has his carrot or his sugar; you just have to find it. Herndon is left once again with the impression that keeping up the appearance of learning is the chief goal. Motivating students to do busywork, without any thought of the difference it makes in their lives, seems to be the energizing focus.

The principal, Mr. Grisson, is also eager to help. Although he has never observed Herndon's classes, he at least appears to know that Herndon often resorts to raising his voice to get his students' attention. Knowing that this doesn't work, Grisson suggests that Herndon take voice lessons during his daily free period to acquire "the tone of command" (p. 114). Grateful to Grisson for his concern but not looking forward to giving up his free period and skeptical that voice lessons are the answer, Herndon replies that he doesn't want to bring the students under control; he wants them to "regard self-control as a good that they freely choose." Imposing external control just isn't working, Herndon insists, not if something more than the appearance of control is desired. Grisson disagrees, reminding Herndon that control to ensure safety must be the preeminent concern. Herndon asserts that, in a school, learning should be the preeminent concern but concedes that Grisson has a point. His attempt to help is, nevertheless, useless to Herndon.

Now what? Having received professional advice from a number of "experts" and finding it worthless every time, Herndon is left to rely almost entirely on his own instincts about what works. This includes his own sense of what it means to do the right thing and, perhaps most important of all, his stubborn faith that the students themselves are the final arbiters of what is educational. He decides that he must remain open to opportunities that will make learning fun and that he must continue to honor the right of the students to make important choices about what they will learn. In his own words, he resolves simply to start "in with everything it had occurred to me to try out" (p. 126).

With these things in mind, he begins to build into his class a variety of activities and routines to help his students sharpen some basic skills while also giving them considerable latitude in how they go about it. At one point, he unearths an old tape recorder and makes it available to students who want to hear what they sound like when they read, orate, act out original dramas, or experiment with different voices. Herndon keeps this process fairly open but is pleased by how much of the tape recording time is taken up by practicing reading, writing, and speaking skills.

In another case, upon learning that "slambook" season has arrived, a time when many of the students keep detailed records of how their peers rate in such areas as appearance, athletic ability, and intelligence, Herndon encourages the students to use classroom time to keep these books updated. Unlike the other instructors in the school who spurn slambook season, Herndon seizes on such activities because the students elect to do them, and he seeks to derive from them all the educational value he can.

Although he does not make an explicit effort to correct or evaluate the content in the slambooks—he is barred from reading most of them—he notices the care devoted to this work. Absorption is total and, for the first time, an eerie quiet descends on the classroom as the students confer about possible entries and painstakingly inscribe these books with their well-considered characterizations.

Even before interest in the slambooks wane, Herndon welcomes into his classroom another naturally occurring activity and, in so doing, sanctions it as a legitimate form of learning. One afternoon, a restless ninth-grader begins listing on the chalkboard the current Top 40 rock and roll songs played on the radio every day. When Herndon assures the other students that this is an acceptable thing to do, a discussion ensues about the proper spellings and titles of the songs, and opinions are advanced about the comparative merits of the biggest hits. What begins as an entirely spontaneous event becomes 9D's ritualistic way of beginning every class. Instead of saluting the flag, the students daily acknowledge their favorite pop songs and, in so doing, effortlessly practice spelling, writing, and speaking skills. Herndon even provides a bit of historical context by showing the students that a number of the songs featured in the Top 40 are new manifestations of old blues tunes. Listing the Top 40 becomes so popular that the students challenge one another for the privilege of performing this task. Taking advantage of the power of intrinsic motivation, Herndon insists that the students figure out an orderly way to give everyone a chance. Improving negotiation skills is an unexpected boon of monitoring the Top 40.

At another point, Herndon disinters from his classroom storeroom multiple copies of the story of Cinderella in play form. Expecting nothing, he leaves the plays stacked in a corner of his room. One day, a few of his most reluctant readers find the plays and propose that the whole class act out the story. So begins another favorite pastime. The reading of Cinderella reveals dramatic talent and exhibitionist impulses among the students that have gone unrealized for years. They can shout, fume, scold, guffaw, and cower within the context of reading a class assignment, and this adds unanticipated excitement to a period that becomes crowded with important things to do.

Herndon's most difficult classes begin to take shape. They inevitably start with the posting of the Top 40, which may lead to slambook writing or to tape recording a short story and conclude with a whole-class reading of a portion of a play. Each activity reinforces the value of expressive communication and contributes to expanding the students' vocabularies and to increasing their exposure to a variety of literature. The class is hardly trouble-free, however. Lack of discipline and excessive noise remain serious problems, and few of the students do any work outside of the classroom. Nevertheless, most students enjoy coming to class and most regard the time there to be stimulating and engaging. Most gratifying of all, when the riots come, Herndon's classes carry on without change.

In May, even the most effective disciplinarians have difficulty maintaining order at George Washington Junior High. Vandalism increases, absenteeism skyrockets, and general disorder abounds. The GW riots are in season, but in Herndon's classes, business proceeds as usual. Slambooks lose their fascination, but play production goes into high gear, while the Top 40 and tape recordings continue to keep students absorbed. Also, the seventh graders discover educational movies and set aside every Friday for films and food. All of these activities are student-selected and student-generated, and they retain a meaning for the students that their other classes can't match. As Herndon says:

We were making it. Rolling. They weren't doing things the way a group of thirty-year-old teachers would do them, of course. They didn't even

do them the way everyone seemed to think that kids should do them
. . . but they were doing it, making their revolution in the class. I was
enthusiastic, pleased, proud of them. (p. 169)

In the midst of these riot-resistant classes, Herndon is called into the principal's office to be informed that he is not only unfit to be rehired for the following year, he is also unfit for employment as a junior high school teacher
anywhere. In a long interview, Mr. Grisson explains that Herndon has failed
again and again to meet the most basic expectations. Students are chronically
late, far too many appear idle and uninvolved, the classroom atmosphere does
not promote serious study, and, most of all, the students remain utterly undisciplined. When Herndon asks Mr. Grisson to explain why his students are the
only ones in the school who do not succumb to rioting, Grisson concedes that
this is true but contends it only proves his point. He explains:

> A riot meant that some order had been imposed, some control estab-
> lished, since it was against that control that the children were re-
> belling. It followed that, as I was allowing them do as they pleased it
> was unnecessary for them to riot. (p. 173)

In the end, Herndon loses his job over the very point from which he had
always dissented—that the object of school is to keep order. He steadfastly resists this notion, insisting with an unremitting consistency that freedom,
choice, and meaning are all both the means and the ends of good schooling.
Whether we agree with Herndon or not, we cannot help but admire how hard
he works to tailor his classroom to his students' interests and how deeply committed he remains to educating them to use their freedom responsibly and
wisely. It is also plain that Herndon learns to teach by thinking hard about
what he is doing, by refusing to accept what others do habitually and unreflectively, and by staying attuned to the lived experiences of his students. As
all of the narratives in this chapter show, teachers can apprentice themselves
to many mentors, but it is a rare teacher indeed who does not eventually come
to see students as the greatest mentor of all.

PATRICIA SCHMIDT: THE QUEST FOR MEANING IN LIFE AND WORK

In many ways, Patricia Schmidt's teaching apprenticeship is the most unconventional of the three. As a first-year high school English teacher in 1969, most
of her classes go reasonably well. Yet her inability to connect with one group
of high school seniors during that first year devastates her so completely that
much of the rest of her career becomes a quest to restore her professional confidence and to find new meaning in her life and work. For Schmidt, induction
into teaching continues for at least two decades. Only after she discovers a
theory and practice of interpreting and teaching literature that helps her to see

the connections between her life and her profession does she feel she has arrived as a teacher. Perhaps part of what she learns is that her identity as a professional teacher is never fully formed. Rather, it is constantly in the making through experience and reflection, through a continuing cycle of recollecting and retelling transforming tales of teaching and learning. As Schmidt points out, to conjure up these stories can be painful, but they are an integral part of the challenge to make meaning out of life "and to understand the struggle we all have to make some sense of what we're doing here and why" (p. 3).

As a lover of books and reading, Schmidt enters Fresno State University in 1966 to study English and to find a vocation that will allow her to develop further her love of language. Although satisfied at the time by the classes she takes, in retrospect she realizes that her teachers are all proponents of New Critical Analysis, which claims that literary meaning is embedded in a text and that the art of interpretation is that of unpacking that meaning through logical analysis. This means, for Schmidt, that the reader's experiences and interests are irrelevant in interpreting literature. Schmidt wholeheartedly adopts this method of reading and employs it in her first teaching position at Alhambra High School in a suburb of San Francisco. In time, however, she discovers that overreliance on the New Criticism stunts her growth both professionally and personally.

Although Schmidt has had a wonderful student teaching experience at a local Fresno high school, her first year of teaching at Alhambra is marked by an abrupt and disorienting disjuncture from which she never fully recovers. After a few weeks of teaching three classes on a part-time basis, Schmidt is offered a full-time tenure track position, which she eagerly accepts. The only drawback is that she must surrender the three classes originally assigned to her and pick up five new classes, all within the span of a weekend. This is not only a difficult adjustment for Schmidt, it is a hard transition for the students who have grown fond of their teachers. This is especially true in the case of the seniors who resent the fact that they are now saddled with an inexperienced pedagogue fresh out of college.

Despite repeated efforts to form a strong relationship with this group of seniors, Schmidt makes little progress. She first looks to the English Department chairperson for help but is simply told after one observation that she is dealing with "a bright and difficult group." She next turns to the school counselor who informs Schmidt that the students really don't like each other very much and "that there [are] a great many personality conflicts in the group" (p. 22). The counselor expresses sympathy for Schmidt's plight but claims there isn't much that can be done.

Like Herndon, Schmidt learns quickly how isolating it can feel to be a first-year teacher and how little help one can expect even from those responsible for mentoring novice educators. Indeed, there are times when the very people who are expected to be supportive quietly undermine one's efforts to improve. For instance, Schmidt later discovers that the department chair inserted a note into her personnel file, without her knowledge, indicating that she is not a competent teacher of older students and should not be assigned to seniors again. Yet the chair never exchanges more than a few words with Schmidt about this situation, nor does she make any subsequent observations. What should have been an opportunity to develop and nurture a young teacher and to use evaluation in a formative manner turns out to be still another example of thoughtless and deflating summative evaluation.

By the end of this first year, despite some good experiences in other classes, Schmidt's experience with the seniors causes her to question her ability to teach and command authority. It seems to her that she lacks the knowledge and the experience to win their respect, to maintain discipline, and to teach effectively. These feelings are exacerbated by the sense that her supervisors do not support or appreciate her. As Schmidt says, "My sense of who I was as a person and a teacher was shaky after that first year with that class" (p. 23). Similarly, the structure and culture of the school isolates Schmidt from her colleagues, leaving her feeling vulnerable and alone. Study groups for teachers are nonexistent, and professional development, like traditional teaching, follows a hierarchical model in which the professional development expert conveys new knowledge and the teacher passively receives it. The opportunities for teachers to support one another and to experience the relief of witnessing one's colleagues articulate problems and concerns similar to one's own just aren't available.

Much later, after years of journaling and reflecting on her experience as an English teacher, Schmidt discovers that her love of literature remains and her desire to foster that love in her students has not abated. However, the objectivist, New Critical thrust of her academic preparation pervades her teaching and has the effect of diminishing her students' interest in reading. She teaches as she has been taught: "Teaching literature involved doing a close reading of text, giving an authoritative lecture on the text to my students, discussing interpretations of the text, and then having students write prescriptively and formulaically about them, using Warriner's composition exercises on standard essay forms" (p. 31). The authority for what literature is chosen and how it is interpreted comes from the literary critics she has mastered in her own studies. It does not occur to her until much later that at least part of the authority for what is taught and how it is imparted can come from herself. "Why couldn't I recognize my own authority?" Schmidt asks (p. 32). The answer is that, as she herself shows, everything about her upbringing and her education discourages her from questioning authority and inclines her to depend on the established authorities in family, church, and school. Especially as a woman she is affirmed when she docilely accepts what she is told and passively receives what she is taught. To be acknowledged for being "a good girl" depends on maintaining an uncritical and unchallenging demeanor. It requires a young woman who derives her "sense of self from external authority" (p. 33).

Again in retrospect, Schmidt learns that part of the problem of that first year of teaching is that her desire to infect students with a passion for reading great literature is overwhelmed by an even stronger but far less conscious desire: to do what she can to please the people in authority so that they will regard her as good—as a woman, as an English teacher, and as an authority in her own right. Although she goes on to many years of relatively successful teaching during which she is viewed by supervisors and colleagues as good, she never feels satisfied. Only gradually does she realize that her penchant to please, so scrupulously nurtured over time, has temporarily squelched her fire for teaching young people to love language and literature. This, she realizes, must be recaptured so that every aspect of her teaching is employed to foster that love.

It takes many years for Schmidt to come to this realization. In her first year and for many years thereafter, the emphasis is on looking good in the eyes of supervisors. Thus Schmidt's greatest concerns are maintaining control and reinforcing the hierarchy between herself and her students. Furthermore, she mistakenly assumes that she must do all the work herself and that she alone is responsible for what her students achieve. For at least her first 15 years of teaching she has "no clue how to include [the students] in the process of learning" (p. 42).

Schmidt characterizes her first 15 years of teaching as a time of "searching." She searches, often in a scattered and unsystematic manner, for ways to be a better teacher, a better wife, a better mother, and a better person. But in all of these roles, she continues to struggle. How can she learn to cooperate with the other people in her life for making things come out right? Time and again Schmidt falls into the trap of assuming sole responsibility for ensuring that her students are learning, her husband is satisfied, and her daughter is flourishing. Often left out of this desperate search is time to cultivate her own well-being. In the mid-1970s, Schmidt is elected the president of the local teacher's association, a considerable honor and a sign that others regard her as an accomplished educator and effective leader. But guiding the association becomes another burden, and the group grows dependent on her advocacy and good will.

Finally, after 9 years of full-time teaching, Schmidt decides to offer herself a gift. She takes a year off to earn her master's degree at a nearby college, Holy Names. The experience is a powerful one. The instruction she receives is excellent, and for the first time in her life she establishes close relationships with her professors, many of whom are women who respond to her ideas and writing with respect and a great deal of constructive criticism. Strangely, though, this is strictly an academic experience, sealed off from her life as a teacher. It does not prompt her to reflect on her teaching or her life and, when she returns to teaching in the following year vowing to concentrate on becoming an authoritative teacher, her experience as a graduate student does not sustain her through the isolation she forces on herself. Judging wrongly that by sequestering herself from colleagues she can finally generate the time and effort to become a great teacher, she becomes so depressed that she must take an extended leave of absence.

For almost 4 years she continues searching for a meaningful calling. Gradually she is drawn back into teaching. In the midst of this return to the profession she loves so much, Schmidt is diagnosed with breast cancer. For a while she teaches part-time in the morning, relieved to focus on the caring of others, while during the afternoon she receives radiation treatments and meets regularly with a psychotherapist. Together, the combined impact of these experiences begins to change her. She becomes more introspective and more willing to face her fears, to "name them, and to begin to take risks in spite of them" (p. 87). Her teaching is also affected. She lectures less and encourages more general discussion. She substitutes a student-selected research project for the perennial five-paragraph essay and involves her students in evaluating each other and the class itself. Her teaching becomes more student-centered and collaborative, and she feels the difference in the classroom climate they create together.

All of this experience prepares Schmidt for the timely suggestion that she involve herself in the California Literature Project. The year is 1986 and in the following 4 years, thanks primarily to a series of stimulating professional development opportunities, Schmidt enjoys her most fulfilling years to date as a teacher. The links between her teaching and her humanity grow readily apparent, and her identity as a professional, authoritative yet flexible English teacher is solidified. The California Literature Project, which sets the stage for important curricular reform, introduces Schmidt first to the work of James Moffett and then, even more importantly, to the contributions of Louise Rosenblatt. More or less at a distance, they become the mentors Schmidt never had and induce a transformation in her outlook and practice that is incalculable.

Moffett, who influences her method of teaching writing, offers the transforming suggestion that she begin with reflection on her own life first, that her initial composing be autobiographical before moving herself and "her writing outward into the world" (p. 91). Moffett also encourages her to make her teaching more student-centered, to base it more substantially on the lived experience of her students. This she does, but over time she also develops a critique of Moffett in which she regards student-centered teaching as a faulty conception that reinforces the dichotomy between student and teacher. What she seeks as a teacher is not so much student-centered education as a collaborative, transactional relationship between students and teacher in which everyone contributes to the education of all.

Of all the scholars Schmidt reads during these heady years, it is Louise Rosenblatt's reader response theory that leaves the greatest and the most lasting impact on her teaching and her life. At its simplest, Rosenblatt's theory enjoins readers to approach texts conversationally and transactionally, to see reading and interpretation as processes that are enlarged and clarified by bringing in personal experience. From Rosenblatt's point of view, part of the point of reading is to shed light on personal experience and to generate meanings that are personal and unique and yet also true to a text's contents. Schmidt finds Rosenblatt's perspective liberating for herself and eventually for her teaching as well. In fact, her critique of Rosenblatt takes her one step beyond the reader response theorist. Schmidt reasons that if a text fosters an "intense personal response" (p. 109) it does not matter whether the text supports such a response or not. What she finds exciting and affirming is the process by which strong, visceral responses are engendered, regardless of their sources. She also appreciates the complexity of reader response, the wonderful, even mysterious ways in which literature and personal experience can illuminate each other. As Schmidt notes with enthusiasm, "What and how we read or write a text is a confluence of the moments we have lived, the moments we are living both inside and outside the text, and the present moment. We need to consider this when we teach literature, when we are 'reading a text' " (p. 118).

Schmidt's enthusiasm for Louise Rosenblatt and reader response theory leads to study abroad and to summers pursuing a Ph.D. in English education. The papers she writes using a reader response approach not only open literary doors but also guide her in rethinking and revising her teaching methodology. Unfazed by the postmodern confusions between reader and text, Schmidt seeks to empower her students "to read literature so that . . . the reader becomes the text" (p. 122). The more she reads and the more she studies, the more Schmidt realizes that she is dealing not so much in literary theory as she is in pedagogical theory. She adopts the view that teachers must stop teaching and "see themselves and their students as readers together" (p. 122). Her teaching reflects these insights, becoming more project oriented and more collaborative, even communal. The emphasis is less on the text or the student and more on the transaction between text and student and on the exchanges that occur among students and between teacher and students. Schmidt is achieving her goal of creating a community of readers and learners. It is a community that honors the individual as much as the group, the idiosyncratic response as much as the typical reaction. Furthermore, it is a community in which the teacher strives as earnestly to unlock the secrets of her multiple selves as do her students. The teacher's need to make sense of her life is embraced as readily as the need of the students to uncover their most authentic selves through the study of literature.

In the end, Patricia Schmidt writes a story of finding herself to find herself; the struggle for identity goes on. As a teacher and reader, as a learner and woman, Schmidt acquires an increasingly stronger sense of herself over time. She also sees more clearly the relationships between her profession and her selfhood, between her love of literacy and her place in the world. After years of doubt and questioning, she acquires the confidence and the assertiveness to declare herself an accomplished English teacher and an authoritative professional. She is also finally able to reconcile her feminism and her femininity and to offer this self-description: "multifaceted, strong, still becoming, loving, intelligent, compassionate . . . concerned with the lives of women and teachers and students, male and female, in relationship to educational literary cultures" (p. 178). Her teaching, her reading, and her life remain inextricably woven together, with each immeasurably and continuously enriching the others.

CONCLUSION

Teachers learning to teach must remain open to every opportunity to hone their craft. They should strive to make connections between their students' experiences and the subjects they love, and take time to reflect on how they ultimately acquired a difficult skill or mastered a challenging concept. They should recall, as well, the obstacles they encountered and the failures they endured while trying to learn something without success. All of these experiences and all of the pedagogical lenses available to them that the adult educator Stephen Brookfield (1995) has identified—self, students, colleagues, and theory—should be exploited to help them develop into the most resourceful and empathetic teachers they can be. This means, as Brookfield has pointed out, that teachers should take time to reflect critically on their individual autobiographies and devise strategies to get constructive feedback from their students. They should furthermore seek out colleagues eager to share different perspectives on teaching and read educational theory to enlarge their professional knowledge and to frame their pedagogical practices within a more critical and complex social context. As Eliot Wigginton (1985) notes, the best teachers keep "tearing things apart and putting them back together." They reflect constantly on their practices, boldly confront their greatest weaknesses, but also maintain a genuine humility about their abiding strengths.

The best novice teachers gradually learn the value of relentless self-criticism, yet in the process of developing this quality acquire a quiet self-confidence as well. They grow confident of their ability to go on improving and become convinced, like Robert Inchausti, that what they teach will eventually touch their students' lives and ultimately make a difference in how they choose to live. Over time, they learn, as James Herndon did, that giving students the freedom to make important choices and to practice their powers of judgment and evaluation will allow them to become, slowly but steadily, more thoughtful, discerning, and adventurous learners. Finally, like Patricia Schmidt, they recognize the links between their growth as human beings and their effectiveness as teachers, and they make every effort to renew and challenge themselves, not just for their own sake but ultimately for the sake of their students as well.

In summary we conclude that *apprenticing teachers:*

> *Do everything they can to learn from the people around them.*
> *Do everything they can to make the most of available resources.*
> *Learn constantly from their experience and from their interactions with students.*
> *Maintain a high level of resiliency, or enjoy a strong capacity to spring back from adversity.*
> *View mistakes and errors as valuable opportunities for professional growth.*
> *Believe that through observation, reflection, and renewal wonderful things can happen in classrooms.*

STUDY QUESTIONS

Inchausti

1. What views of education does Inchausti learn from Brother Blake?
2. How does Inchausti's image of himself as a teacher change over time?
3. How is Inchausti's view of education similar to or different from your own?

Herndon

1. James Herndon and Robert Inchausti have very different experiences with mentoring during their first years of teaching. Describe these differences and how they might have affected the course of their teaching careers.
2. What are Herndon's views on order and discipline in the classroom?
3. How would you describe Herndon's teaching methods?

Schmidt

1. How might Patricia Schmidt's supervisor in her teaching position at Alhambra High School have helped her improve her teaching in her first year?
2. How does Schmidt pursue her own professional development?
3. Why does a literary theory have an important effect on Schmidt's views of teaching literature? Is there a theory in your field of study that you imagine will have a significant impact on your teaching philosophy or methods?

REFERENCES

Brookfield, S. D. (1995). *Becoming a critically reflective teacher.* San Francisco: Jossey-Bass.

Greene, M. (1978). *Landscapes of learning.* New York: Teachers College Press.

Herndon, J. (1968). *The way it spozed to be.* New York: Bantam Books.

Inchausti, R. (1993). *Spitwad sutras: Classroom teaching as sublime vocation.* Westport, CT: Bergin and Garvey.

Palmer, P. (1998). *The courage to teach.* San Francisco: Jossey-Bass.

Schmidt, P. (1997). *Beginning in retrospect: Writing and reading a teacher's life.* New York: Teachers College Press.

Wigginton, E. (1985). *Sometimes a shining moment.* New York: Doubleday.

Excerpt

Spitwad Sutras

Next we read *The Martian Chronicles* by Ray Bradbury as part of our social studies unit on American history and the westward expansion. I told the boys that Ray Bradbury was doing more than just telling us fantastic stories about creatures who never existed; he was also trying to tell us, in the most literal language our "puny human brains" could comprehend, the meaning of conquest.

Just as a novel about St. Vincent's may be a warning to your friends not to come here, so Bradbury's book may be a warning as to how *not* to colonize space, how *not* to move into the future.

The progression of our reading assignments was ingenious. We had begun with "the image"—pictures, cartoons, lines from poems; moved on to symbols—the crucifix, Madonna and Child, the American flag; progressed to the fable via Aesop and to the parable via Matthew. *Lord of the Flies* advanced us to full-blown narrative and served as a bridge between the fable and the myth of *Siddhartha.* And now, with *The Martian Chronicles*, we had arrived at the novel as a criticism of myths: the myths of manifest destiny, scientific progress, capitalism, and Western cultural superiority.

The Martian Chronicles contains twenty-six stories organized around the topics of invasion and exploration, colonization, and apocalypse. Mars is the New World, the new frontier, lush virgin territory, and yet like *our* frontier already occupied, already ancient, with a culture going back a million years. The Martians are the Mayans, the Indians, subdued by the white man. And as wave after wave of settlers arrives, each wave has its own story, its own crimes, its own discoveries.

The Martian Chronicles tells the story of our future as a repetition of our past and so serves as a warning of how not to proceed. It is Ray Bradbury's sermon to technological America, a reminder that in between our fantasies of a utopian past and our dreams of a utopian future lies a very problematic present. Our tragedy as a people may come from our inability to imagine the greatness of other cultures and other worlds.

It is a book about the need for reverence, and the difficulty we have as a nation acquiring it. If our desires reach out for things that have no meaning for the growth of our spirit, if we lose ourselves in ambitions and illusions, in the end, our lives will become forces for destruction. However talented we may be or advanced in our technology, we will find ourselves aliens from ourselves and from God.

As we read the book, we began to formulate a new repertoire of class mottos and figures of speech. I would sometimes say, "I feel like I am from Mars!"

And they would immediately understand that I felt like a creature from another world—an older world with more ancient sympathies.

This incorporation of textual images into our everyday speech allowed the students to see the way literature works as an ongoing commentary on life—as a system of images, as a language in itself. If Marty "spaced out" during a class discussion, I could now signal him back to earth by saying, "Well, Marty, are you on the expedition?" The phrase would reverberate with symbolic significance.

"Yeah, Colonel," he would reply. "You want to go hunting Martians?"

The novel, in other words, became our class theme, the code through which we deciphered events, the medium through which we understood *everything*. We didn't simply read *The Martian Chronicles*—we spoke it; we thought it; we lived it. Just as we had done with *Lord of the Flies* and *Siddhartha*. Only now, we had entered into a more conscious criticism of social mythology.

Prior to reading *The Martian Chronicles* with my class, I had considered Ray Bradbury a second-rate writer, sentimental, nostalgic, the Norman Rockwell of science fiction. And I had never liked science fiction much anyway for its gimmicky, facile theorizing and its use of all those weird proper names: "Gimlack Three," "Queen Zina of Tarse," "The Moons of Platitudia."

But now, I saw things differently. *The Martian Chronicles* was not a great book, but the genre of the novel was itself a great idiom. For those who had eyes to see, there were treasures to be found here. Besides, we had poured so much of ourselves into that book that it took on second life as a cultural document in a living community and thereby became a reservoir of images that far transcended the specific intention of the author.

After *The Martian Chronicles*, we read *Night* by Elie Wiesel. And as most literature teachers will confess, sometimes when we are trying to explain a work, we are visited by a peculiar eloquence not entirely our own, and the book we are teaching not only teaches itself but lifts us up to its own heights. I remember the scene at the end of the fourth section with its chilling description of the hanging of three prisoners—one a young boy who did not immediately die because his body was too light to snap his neck. The other prisoners are forced to march by the corpses and this child's half-dead body. Someone asks, "Where is God now?" And Wiesel hears a voice within answer, "Where is He? Here He is—He is hanging here on the gallows."*

The students were puzzled by this line and wanted to know what it meant. I was a little self-conscious about presuming to "teach" this book, especially to such callow youth. But I took courage from an account I had read of Wiesel's own appearance before a high school in New York, where he answered each and every question posed to him with patience and complete

*Elie Wiesel, *Night*, trans. Marion Wiesel (New York: Summit Books, 1988), p. 209.

honesty. One of the kids had asked him to describe the looks on the faces of the guards as they committed their atrocities. Wiesel answered that he didn't look into their eyes; they were his masters. I could at least try to be as honest about my own experience. Besides, there is something about Wiesel's prose— its honesty, its refusal to "protect" the reader from the realities of life, however harsh—that immediately earned the trust of these adolescent boys. They felt elevated by his respect for them as readers. Of all the books we read that year, *Night* was the one they took most seriously. They wanted to talk about it; they needed to talk about it. But they didn't know what to say.

"What does that mean that God is hanging on the gallows?" they asked.

I could have offered some glib remark about the death of God, but I decided to be honest. "I don't know."

"Did it really happen?"

"Yes."

"This is really a weird book!" And I could see by their expressions that they meant awesome, uncanny, disturbing.

Finally, one student ventured his own version of a "Catholic" interpretation. "I think he was talking about Jesus. The three men, the suffering one in the middle—it's like Jesus on the cross."

"This is a child," I said. "A million of them were killed by the Nazis. It's not Jesus."

"But it's a Jewish boy. Isn't it a symbol?"

I was uneasy saying "no." All literature is, in some sense, symbolic, since it synthesizes the abstract and the concrete into typical representations, but *Night* was different. It was testimony and witness—an attempt not to betray those who died—and I wanted to live up as best I could to Wiesel's intentions. "No," I said finally. "It is not a symbol. At least not the kind of symbol we are used to talking about. It would be just as accurate to say Jesus is a symbol for this child than that this child is a symbol for Jesus." I could tell by their quizzical faces that they weren't getting me. I was sounding heretical. Perhaps even a bit crazy.

"Look," I continued, "it's really a question of what is most real. In this story, nothing is more real than the death of this child. I think for Wiesel, Jesus' death is not any more or less important than the death of two million Jewish children. And we are meant to experience the horror of the camps through his precise particularizations. To see this child as a *symbol* would be to forget his humanity, his precious irreplaceability, his never-again, individual character."

"But then what's it *mean?*" they asked again. "What is it supposed to mean *to us?*"

"The fact that a death like this could happen—did happen—confronts us with certain uncomfortable truths about life and what it means to be a human being, such as the vulnerability of the innocent before those who would be gods. But there isn't always a universal truth in every situation. Perhaps the point here is more particular and temporal: that death in the camps was never symbolic, that it was always personal, insufferable, beyond mythic explanation."

The class didn't say anything. I wondered if they followed me. I wondered if I followed myself. But I could tell they were thinking.

"So you mean that this death doesn't mean anything *good?*" asked Albert Perez, straining to make sense of it all. "That it's not part of some point he's trying to make, that it's a total waste and *that's* what it means?"

"Sort of," I replied. "I don't think it was a total waste, because it did affect people, change lives, forced us to examine our consciences, but these effects are never to be seen as worth any fraction of the price that was paid for them. This death is not redemptive in any Christian sense. It is one of the worst things that human beings have ever done."

"Even worse than satanic tortures and sexual mutilations?" asked Marty Shuster. I could tell by this question that the conversation had become quite real for him.

"There were tortures and mutilations in the camps. Besides, this was government-sponsored torture and mutilation aimed at an entire ethnic population, endorsed by 'good' citizens as prudent political policy. In this sense, it was the worst thing civilized man ever did."

"So what can we do about it? It's over. Most of these people are dead."

"They live in memory and conscience. Their ghosts haunt our lives. They are as real as we are, maybe even more real," I said.

"How can they be more real than we are?" Jim asked.

"They died for who they were. They died because they were Jews. We would do well to stand for so much."

"So the whole book is symbolic; the boy's death is a symbol," Jim insisted.

I attempted one last time to explain the distinction. "No, it's a memory. And now, in a way, it's our memory too, so we've got to live with it, and we have to live lives of substance to be worthy of it. If we live, we have obligations as survivors not to betray the humanity of those who came before us by belittling our own."

5

The Narrative of Reflective Practice

I
t is surely a recurring theme in this book that good teachers think a great deal about their teaching. They plan carefully without sacrificing spontaneity, and they reflect constantly on what they have tried and what they can do to improve. The best teachers teach many wonderful lessons but somehow are never satisfied. They go over these lessons in their minds again and again, until they can think of better, more satisfactory ways to engage their students' minds or stimulate their imaginations. For these people, teaching is a 24-hour commitment. It infiltrates their dreams, interrupts their reading, and creeps into their conversations. When teaching well becomes your life's mission, it is never far from your thoughts.

In *The Reflective Practitioner*, Donald Schon (1983) studies practitioners in a variety of fields and finds that highly reflective people are willing to "experience surprise, puzzlement, or confusion" (p. 68) about situations that are ambiguous or extraordinary. He claims that these individuals draw on their current knowledge and on past experience and are flexible enough to generate new categories and theories that more powerfully explain the special circumstances they now face. They do not rely on orthodoxy or convention but ask themselves hard questions that may yield new understanding. Additionally, these practitioners regard doing and thinking and means and ends as parts of the same, interactive process. Schon likens reflective practice to an ongoing "conversation with the materials of the situation" (p. 78). This means that the practitioner not only reacts to the sometimes unforeseen circumstances of the situation, but also assesses and responds to the consequences, both intended and unintended, of her own actions.

Few teachers have documented their efforts as thoughtfully or as exhaustively as Vivian Paley. In her books, Paley often seems to be playing a relatively minor role, but alert readers know that most of the marvelous things that happen in her classroom grow out of her open and reflective approach to teaching. Following Schon, her teaching style can be described as conversational or dialogic. Paley reflects on the interactions in her kindergarten classrooms, asks probing and penetrating questions about her teaching and the needs of her students, and relishes the challenge of unlocking the everyday mysteries of teaching young children. Just as she encourages rich dialogue between the children and herself, she embraces a dialogue with the totality of the classroom situation that daily confronts her.

WHITE TEACHER

Vivian Paley's *White Teacher* (1979) is a particularly good example of the narrative of reflective practice. In this book, she is teaching kindergartners in a racially integrated classroom, and she tells her story in a simple, straightforward manner. No detail is too small, no incident too mundane. Her story reminds teachers that every interaction with every child makes a difference and that the accumulation of such interactions and decisions can shape one's life. One of the themes that implicitly emerges from this story is that stereotyping and prejudice are insidious. They must be combated by subjecting everyday practices to relentless critique. Another key theme is that, by reflecting on one's actions as a teacher, progress can be made in showing deep respect and unconditional regard for every child.

Paley's Jewish identity provides her with an important frame of reference for understanding children of color in her classroom. Time and again, with uncompromising honesty, she interrogates herself about her treatment of the nonwhite children. Employing her experiences as a Jew as a backdrop for her questions, she muses: Is it possible or even beneficial to ignore the skin color of children? She recalls her own childhood and the well-meaning teachers who strove to ignore her Jewishness; she also recalls that this usually meant treating all children as Gentiles. Paley relates the story of a black mother who ridicules the teacher who claims there is no color difference in her class. This mother asserts: "My children are black. They don't look like your children. They know they're black and they want it recognized. It's a positive difference, an interesting difference, and a comfortable natural difference. At least it could be so, if you teachers learned to value differences more. What you value, you talk about" (p. 12).

On another occasion, Paley unconsciously labels a group of five girls who happen to be black and often play in the doll corner together, "the black girls." Her friend, Sonia, points out that this is an easy way to categorize them, but it nevertheless contributes to stereotyping. Knowing Paley's most vulnerable area, Sonia asks how she would respond if someone referred to a group of Jewish girls who often played together as "the Jewish kids." In her characteristically forthright manner, Paley replies that such labeling would have to be considered condescending and bigoted. How to recognize the children as individuals while honoring and respecting their color is a constant struggle. For Paley, it is a matter of avoiding the platitudes and unreflective practices that obscure differences and negate complexity.

In acknowledging her own prejudice and in reflecting on her own teaching practices in this brutally honest and humble way, Paley allows her readers to identify with her. Her example gives beginning teachers permission to probe their own practices for errors and inappropriate actions and to learn how to adopt a strategy to make these mistakes less likely to occur in the future. Paley's story is one of learning and growth, of coming to understand a few things more clearly and acting on those understandings as affirmatively as possible. But it is also a story that embraces the unfathomable complexity of teaching and assists others in seeing that even the best teachers are constantly correcting their mistakes and doing their best to grow into and to construct truer, more responsive selves.

This growth would be impossible, however, without the support and critical insights of others. For Robert Inchausti, Brother Blake stands out as the mentor, the master teacher to whom Inchausti willingly apprentices himself. Paley, the day-in-day-out practitioner, seems to learn from everyone. At various times, colleagues, parents, and former students are her teachers. But most important, perhaps, are the kindergarten children themselves. At one point, Paley worries about a black child named Kathy, whom she thinks relies too heavily on a black dialect and appears unwilling or unable to converse in white, middle-class English. But as she observes Kathy more closely and engages her in additional conversation, she discovers that Kathy is not only extremely bright but also able to employ different speech patterns in different situations with remarkable facility and grace. It is not Kathy but Paley herself who has the problem, as she is the first to acknowledge. She is reminded of her many Jewish friends who often use Yiddish expressions and inflections when they gather together to talk and reminisce. It is really no different, Paley concludes, with Kathy and many other black children like her.

On another occasion, Paley finds herself drawn to a shy but imaginative black girl named Claire who adores the story, "The Three Billy Goats Gruff." Claire carries the book with her everywhere, reading and rereading the text and pictures, often whispering to herself the words of the troll hidden under the bridge. Paley wants Claire to act out the words of the story before the rest of the children, but she is just bashful. Claire finally comes up with the idea to do the whole story in mime. Claire's version of the story is a great success, much loved by the children, and Paley learns for the first time that mime is a wonderful way to present these traditional stories from an alternative point of view. As Paley admits, Claire shows her how to "look at ordinary activities in new ways" (p. 118).

These experiences make Vivian Paley a better teacher, but an underlying theme is that they make her a better human being as well. She becomes more responsive, caring, and respectful of individual differences. She learns to love and embrace diversity and grows more committed than ever to integrated classrooms. Such classrooms are better not only for the children—teaching them how to get along and appreciate one another more and how to profit from the rich diversity of experience they find all around them—they also show Paley that "teaching children with different cultural and language experiences keeps pushing me toward the growing edge" (p. 118). Paley is a master of making much out of the ordinary and the quotidian, of finding something in every day of teaching that can aid her in honing her craft and help her in reshaping her identity. *White Teacher* is a story of a teacher who lives, grows, and flourishes in what is sometimes derisively called the unreal world of the classroom. For Paley and her children, few experiences could be more formative.

KWANZAA AND ME

From another perspective, however, Paley's idealism and her unquestioned commitment to integration reveal a surprising naiveté about the persistence of racism in American society. In *Kwanzaa and Me* (1995), a kind of sequel to *White Teacher*, Paley is genuinely surprised when a former student, now grown, asserts that, as a black woman, she would have been better off in all-black school. "I'd have been more confident," she explains. "I was an outsider here" (p. 6).

This revelation appears to take Paley entirely by surprise, yet one would think that an educator as thoughtful and as skeptical as Paley would have anticipated this kind of reaction. As the book proceeds, Paley turns to the parents of her African-American students for guidance and illumination. She also gets her black colleague, Lorraine Barnes, to participate in a dialogue with her about these issues.

During one of these sessions, Paley encourages Lorraine to talk about the strengths and weaknesses of integrated schools versus all-black or all-white schools. Lorraine says she welcomes an almost endless variety of such schools, but Paley finds herself defending integration on the grounds that "the classroom should be a family with all sorts of people learning to care about each other and respect each other's differences" (p. 33). Lorraine agrees but adds that such a spirit can be engendered in any school regardless of its racial or gender makeup.

In their next conversation, Lorraine confides in Vivian that at times she yearns to be part of an all-black school. She recalls her first years of teaching and the unwritten prohibition against any display or activity that was too self-consciously black. As in Kozol's school, it was taboo to acknowledge black history or culture. Although that has changed, her experience in a good integrated school has been characterized by mutual respect but not by the kind of kinship that comes from identification with a common color, common experience, and common culture. Lorraine describes the annual educational conference she regularly attends for educators of color. Her enthusiasm for this group's ability to create an instantaneous sense of community is powerful.

As Paley struggles with the challenging perspective offered by Lorraine and with her own commitment to integration, she recalls another black friend, Janet Albright, who was a student teacher at her school in the earlier book,

White Teacher. She urged Janet to take a permanent position at this integrated but rather privileged school, but Janet opted instead to work with those whom she claimed needed her most—inner city African American children. At the time, Janet extended a counter-invitation to Paley to come teach with her in the inner city. In her forthright way, Paley remembered that the reason she did not go with Janet is that she feared being an outsider in an alien culture. Was she asking black children to risk doing the same thing, she wondered, by being such a stubborn advocate for integration?

Over the years, Paley keeps in touch with Janet and continues to pester her about returning to the site of her student teaching experience to accept a full-time teaching position. Although disgusted with the lack of financial support for inner city schools, Janet continues to resist Paley's entreaties. "I just wouldn't be happy in a white school," (p. 43) Janet explains flatly. Inquiring whether Janet believes the school to be racist, Paley braces herself for Janet's predictable (though perhaps not to Paley) response. The school is part of a larger culture riddled with racism, Janet laments. Her all-black school may be located in an area that is so dangerous that she must warn Paley to stay away, but the school has nevertheless been able to create a rich African American environment in which the talent of the local community is woven into the innovative curriculum.

But not all of the people Paley talks to and learns from are so negative about the value of integrated education. Perhaps the three teachers from North Carolina—two black and one white—whom she meets while delivering a speech at the statewide teachers' conference are representative of the many educators and parents who voice support for integration in *Kwanzaa and Me.*

They begin by recounting their personal experiences with desegregation in the 1960s and note that the changes wrought were painful, disorienting, and disruptive. Community leadership disappeared and then reemerged, curricula were overthrown, and school cultures were transformed. But people, both black and white, learned to cope, first just by surviving these changes and then by taking advantage of the opportunities to thrive that desegregation opened. Convinced of integration's value, the three teachers assure Paley that too many good things have happened to retreat now. They also note that integration transcends issues of color and extends to questions of social class and, perhaps even more important, to the problem of ability grouping. Children and teachers have been pitted against each other for too long, they observe, over claims about who the brightest and most talented children are. Even in all-black schools, one teacher recalls, she was favored when she taught the gifted class and neglected when assigned the special ed students. True integration, they seem to be saying, will regard all such distinctions and comparisons as odious.

When she returns from her trip, she is eager to share her North Carolina experiences with Lorraine. Respectful and impressed, Lorraine points out that such an open conversation about race and integration would have been impossible 10 years earlier. Still, Lorraine goes on, worrying about whether a school is integrated or not is a waste of her time. "As long as this school has everything any other school has," she insists, "why worry about trying to change the way white people are going to be" (p. 85)?

Indignant, Paley exclaims, "But Lorraine, that can't be the meaning of all this struggle?" For Lorraine, however, the struggle has granted people like her the freedom to create and sustain all-black schools and to provide the most nurturing environment possible for coping with and combating the racism that can never be completely eradicated.

Lorraine's strong words are still echoing in Paley's mind when she arrives in Alaska to give a talk and meets a Tlingit woman named Lily. Lily favors the all-native schools that teach the rich culture and history of native peoples and provide the same sort of nurturing environment that Lorraine describes. Furthermore, she believes that only Indian teachers can effectively deliver such a curriculum. Once native children have the foundation in culture, self-knowledge, and self-esteem that they need, Lily adds, then they can decide whether to live among Anglos or to remain separate in all-Indian communities.

When Paley returns to her own school, Lorraine introduces her to some educators visiting from Ohio who offer still another view about race and integration. Paley pauses in her story to observe that teachers everywhere seem interested in expanding their knowledge base and in learning from other people's experiences. She comments with pride: "The notion that teachers are not reflective or introspective is far off the mark. Of all the people involved in educating our children, the classroom teacher is most likely to be responsive to the intimate details of the changing environment" (p. 89).

The first Ohio teacher, Sue Ann, comes from a white Catholic upbringing and has been teaching in an inner city black school for a decade. Do her children, Paley asks, suffer from the lack of an African American instructor and role model? Sue Ann doubts this, emphasizing how much she works to keep herself informed and how inadequate any teacher's knowledge is when confronted daily by the kaleidoscope of cultures increasingly found in schools. But she also concedes that it would be ideal for her to team teach with a black colleague who has a rich knowledge of African American culture and history.

The second Ohioan, John, is an African American teacher assigned to fifth-grade students in the same school as Sue Ann. He agrees that a white teacher can educate black children as effectively as a black teacher but only "if he or she conscientiously makes the effort to discover and include more of an Afrocentric curriculum . . . and to speak to the black children as black children" (pp. 92–93).

A third teacher from Ohio, Connie, is also African American and picks up where John leaves off. Paley asks her what she would do if the children she works with could attend an integrated school instead of one that's virtually all black. Her answer turns out to be a middle position between Lorraine and Lily on the one hand and the teachers from North Carolina on the other. Completely integrated or all one color, either way is okay with Connie as long as the school environment is rich and children are learning. As for how an all-black class or an all-white class can have the opportunity to learn about other races and cultures, Connie asserts confidently that there are many ways to do this: through texts, field trips, establishing relationships with other schools, guest speakers, but most of all through the "attitude of the teachers" (p. 94). Connie notes that the teacher's positive and affirming attitude must be complemented by schools that are friendly and inviting to parents and the general community. Paley recognizes that many of the black parents she knows are faced with the delicate balance between wanting to be included more in constructing the culture of the school and biding their time, watching expectantly for the "trouble signs" of marginalization and discrimination to emerge.

In still another dialogue about integration and diversity, Paley travels to a private school in Boston where she meets five white female teachers, all with a passionate interest in the topic. For a moment, Paley is disappointed that there is not a person of color among these five, but then she wisely notes: "To assume homogeneity in one race is as unfortunate an error as is the assumption of separateness and dissimilarity between races" (p. 100). She learns that two of the women are parents of adopted Korean children, that another has adopted a child who is part Puerto Rican and part African American, that still another is a lesbian mother, and that the fifth woman emigrated from Europe to America as an adult and resided for a time with a black colleague in a black neighborhood. Because of these teachers' backgrounds, there is a special commitment in this school to honoring and respecting nontraditional families, to understanding diversity not just in its racial, ethnic, or cultural senses, but in the myriad ways that can affect people when they are open to its influences. This brings Paley back to one of her original questions, which she now frames in a new way: "To what extent does the struggle to give voice to every concern make up for the absence of a 'whole mix of people?' " (p. 107). For Eileen, the mother of the child who is part Puerto Rican and part black, that struggle is a worthy one but it can never equal the richness, variety, and challenge that comes from daily encountering "a whole mix of people."

After a side trip to New Hampshire to visit Evelyn, an educator who calls herself an integrator and who, like the teachers from North Carolina, believes integration should be focused on mixing children with different abilities, Paley returns home. On the airplane, she writes in her journal and reflects on the conversations she has heard. She finds herself rethinking the meaning of "homogeneity," speculating on whether it is the attitude of the teacher that determines how willingly a class embraces differences and how enthusiastically "those who act, feel, look, think, or learn differently" (p. 112) are included in the group.

She also reflects on the unfortunate tendency toward bias. Apparently, even in classes where racial and ethnic differences are scrupulously recognized and respected, other prejudices toward other kinds of differences creep into classrooms. Avoiding such bias is an enormous challenge, but Paley is heartened by the teachers she meets who are working tirelessly for schools that strive to tolerate and to understand every sort of difference that emerges.

Finally, she finds herself agreeing with Eileen that exposure to a "whole mix of people" is one of the pillars of democracy. However, she also knows that many classrooms remain racially and ethnically homogeneous. All the more reason, she concludes, that teachers must make a special effort to prepare their children to take their place in a multicultural society. This means that teachers must listen to their students' individual stories and "try to imagine the stories that all the children who don't look or sound like us might tell if they were in our classroom" (p. 114).

Before the plane lands and before she closes her journal, Paley adds a remarkable note: every viewpoint she hears and every conversation she witnesses seems to contain a piece of the truth and to have applicability in her classroom. This is the statement of a wonderfully alive and deeply mindful teacher who learns constantly and remains open to the value of each new perspective she encounters. Her colleague and friend, Lorraine, testifies to this openness when she notes appreciatively that Vivian is less judgmental, less likely to accept absolutes, and more willing to rethink some of her most cherished assumptions and beliefs.

The more Paley rethinks her ideas about integration and diversity and the more she converses with her colleague Lorraine, the more she comes to see that diversity in schools means creating a "safe harbor [in which] every child finds a ship that fits and is taught how to sail" (p. 126). For her, it follows that children must be taught to confront their fears and to seek out help, wherever possible, in having those fears allayed. Her beliefs and practices collide one day when a student of hers named Michael admits that sometimes he gets hungry in the morning and is afraid to ask Paley when lunch is going to be. Paley urges him to talk more about this and, as they do, they are joined by another boy who admits to being afraid of being scolded in music class for not knowing the answer when the teacher calls on him. This leads to an all-class discussion in which many of the children share their fears. One Jewish girl recalls being scared when Paley quieted her for saying that there is no Santa Claus. Almost literally cringing from the pain of this little girl's charge, Paley applauds her children for talking so openly about what they fear. She tells them: "You've been talking about what embarrasses you. Very few people will do that. Even grown-ups are afraid to do that. I feel I am with brave people" (p. 129). Revisiting the notion of safe harbor, Paley realizes what it means to her: "a place where you are able to tell the truth about yourself and not feel ashamed" (p. 130). Furthermore, Paley continues, the safe harbor must make possible a "safe passage" from home to school in which, with the help of parents and other community members, the individual family can "see itself reflected in the school culture" (p. 131).

At the conclusion of *Kwanzaa and Me*, Paley returns to her conversation with Lorraine. She asks Lorraine how she feels about the book she is writing. Lorraine sagely replies: "It's all about dialogue, isn't it? To me, colleagues can read your book and see that they can sit down and talk to each other and to the parents. And parents can read the book and see that it is a good thing to talk to the teachers. You are encouraging the dialogue, not necessarily the answers, but the dialogue. This points to the need for more people of color in the schools. So there can be the dialogue" (p. 140).

Perhaps Vivian Paley's greatest contribution to the literature of education and of reform is the stimulus for dialogue and deep reflection that she provides. Few writers or teachers are as skilled as she at putting readers in situations that stimulate them to think about what good education is and how a good life is lived. Nor are there many teachers or writers who write narratives that so compellingly link our missions as teachers and our missions as human beings.

THE BOY WHO WOULD BE A HELICOPTER

Even before *Kwanzaa and Me* was written, Paley had already begun exploring her commitment to creating classrooms that are safe places for children. In *The Boy Who Would Be a Helicopter*, Paley introduces Jason, a troubled boy who keeps people at a distance by constantly whirring his imaginary helicopter blades or by warning others that, because his blades are broken and so delicate, they must not be touched by anyone. Paley refuses to categorize or label him. Despite his insistence on separating himself from his classmates, she says, "he is the one we must learn to include in our school culture if it is to be an island of safety and sensibility for everyone" (p. xi). Paley sees that Jason is an invaluable class member because it is only in teaching children like Jason, with all their differences and uniquenesses, that a "style of teaching is best illuminated" (p. 11).

A second interesting theme of her book is that one child's story or, for that matter, one teacher's story never stands alone. Each story is always best understood in relation to other stories. In fact, Paley thinks that part of her function as a teacher is to help the children see the relationships among their own stories, the stories of their classmates, and the stories of their teachers. She believes that children should also understand their own stories in the context of the stories of their families, their neighbors, and even the stories of the larger society.

This theme is related to still another. It is essential to chart over time one's own growth as a teacher and to understand how that growth is triggered and sustained by the close observation of one's students. In Paley's case, she tells us briefly that, as a novice teacher, she was not a good listener, a good observer, or a good storyteller. In time, she came to believe that her chief function as a teacher was to help the children think about and solve the problems they faced. After a few more years, she realized that by observing the play of children she could draw out their problems and their questions and use this knowledge to ask her own questions of them more pointedly and effectually. Still later, she realized that the problems and questions that emerged from their play could be put in story form by the children themselves and that these stories could then be used to build connections between classmates, enhance their ability to listen to one another, and create a stronger sense of community and shared purpose.

The teaching process that Paley has evolved for herself is a deceptively simple one. First, she listens to the stories and repeats each word for the benefit of all the children in attendance and for the benefit of the storyteller who may want to revise what has been contributed. Then she records the story to make it permanent and to have a record of the story when it is time to act it out. Next, she rereads the story to make sure she hasn't misinterpreted anything, to ask questions of the storyteller about parts of the story that may require clarification or elaboration, and to ensure that the story makes good sense to everyone else. Finally, like a good discussion facilitator, Paley makes connections among the stories she hears by pointing out similarities and differences between the story she is recording and the many other stories she has recorded during the course of the day. In this way, she creates a classroom culture that is steeped in the narrative experience of the children and that emerges from the web of experience that the children's stories represent.

She describes all of this in *The Boy Who Would Be a Helicopter*, but the focus of this book is on Jason and his classmates and on how the classroom culture that is constructed through stories helps Jason to grow. For Paley, growth depends on providing opportunities to participate as fully as possible in classroom life while also honoring the distinct and creative contribution each child makes to the whole. This means that the teacher must develop the ability and the discipline to observe, listen, question, appreciate, reflect and then observe, listen, and question some more. Nothing is more important for such a teacher than to remain alert to everything that is happening around her. Although this may entail confirming what is already expected or understood, it is more often a consideration of "what we don't understand and what has not worked out according to expectations" (p. 47). For Paley this kind of reflection often works best when it is at least partly carried out in concert with others. In *Helicopter*, her assistants are Gail and Trish, who often help her to think more deeply about teaching and learning. For all of them the key question is: "What did we find out today that we didn't know yesterday and for which we have no answer" (p. 47)?

One of the issues that the three of them discuss, sometimes rather heatedly, is discipline. Both Trish and Gail take the view that Paley is too permissive. For instance, early in the year, Jason constantly interrupts the efforts of other children to compose and tell their stories. Trish and Gail wonder why Paley allows Jason to do this. Paley contends she is merely avoiding a power struggle with Jason. When Gail expresses fear that this only encourages the other children to act inappropriately, Paley advises that what the other children are really interested in is whether Jason, whom they regard as unsettled, "is safe from harm" (p. 53). Both Gail and Trish doubt Paley's judgment on this point, leading her to concede that, when they have their own classrooms, they will have to figure out for themselves what works best for them and their children. But, she continues, if you intervene in the group by punishing the offending child, you are admitting "to a lack of faith in the power of reason and good will to solve our problems" (p. 53). Trish wonders whether reason and good will are enough and then notes, drawing on her university studies, that perhaps Jason's tendency to "perseverate" is really the problem that must be addressed. Paley urges her to note the similarities between perseverate and persevere—one pathological and negative, the other a synonym for "a sense of strength and self-direction" (p. 54). Trish immediately begins to doubt the value of the terminology she's learning, but Paley quickly returns to the heart of the issue. These terms and labels just aren't relevant, she explains, when children are viewed as storytellers. She goes on: "A storyteller is always in the strongest position; to be known by his or her stories puts the child in the most favorable light" (p. 54). As she says later, stories are very simply "the most reliable structure for ever thinking about anything" (p. 93).

In another exchange, Gail and Trish express concern that, without the option of punishing children through the use of a time-out chair, a practice that Paley dispensed with years earlier, they feel that their authority as teachers is undermined. They admit it seems to work for Paley but argue that, as inexperienced teachers, they feel powerless. Paley explains that, once you rely on threats and punishments, difficult situations become the province of the teacher rather than problems that the whole group must work on. Punishment is counterproductive, Paley insists. And then, with emphasis, she adds: "It creates no useful dialogue" (p. 87).

Through dialogue and a process of careful reflection, Paley and her protégées gain new insight into how their students learn and how best to teach them. Just as important, perhaps, they learn a great deal about themselves. They learn that how one decides to teach and relate to children grows out of one's most deeply held beliefs. For Paley, participation, dialogue, collaboration, and the social construction of the classroom culture are paramount, but these processes and values cannot be separated from the things that give everyday life its meaning and purpose. Reflective teachers are also the ones who are most earnestly in quest of their own truest selves, their own sturdiest convictions about how to live our lives together as fully as possible.

To make the classroom a place where Jason can contribute freely and substantively, he must first feel safe. Paley does not spend time worrying about the significance of the helicopter for Jason, but she does struggle to understand how the helicopter as a symbol can be used to "carry him to safety in our classroom" (p. 57). Part of the answer is found in the wisdom of the children themselves. They do not find Jason's imitation of a helicopter to be nearly as strange as the adults around him do. In another interesting exchange with her assistants, Trish accuses Paley of encouraging the unorthodox fantasy play of children like Jason over the more ordinary play of some of the other children. Paley denies this but insists that there must be a place in her classroom for many different forms of play. The children, on the other hand, ardently defend Jason's right not to conform. According to Paley, fairness for these young children has nothing to do with sameness but everything to do with the equal opportunity to "demand special treatment" (p. 62). She quickly dismisses the adults' concern that, in time, every child will want to imitate a helicopter and insist on building his own heliport. The children know this will not happen and, even if it does, "the true pretenders" are the only ones who will finally last.

So Paley watches, listens to the children, and takes advantage of every exchange to bring Jason more fully into the discourse of the classroom. It is not the strangeness of his helicopter fantasy that holds him back, Paley finds; it is the fact that "he seldom watches the other children." As he slowly picks up on how much they have to teach him, he begins observing them for the "best ways to fix his moods and misgivings within the context of play" (p. 111). Paley watches as Samantha strives to turn Jason into her baby and thereby give him a greater variety of roles to play in the classroom. She witnesses the way Jason eases himself into Lilly's doll corner game and gracefully plays the role of a boy who brings stolen bears back for Eli's birthday. And she listens closely to Simon as he explains Jason's desire to act out a story without writing it down as Simon had done only a few days before. In all of these situations and many others, Paley learns that "children adapt best to school through the culture they themselves invent" (p. 112).

In reflecting on Jason's efforts to adapt to the strangeness of the classroom, she recalls her own early attempts to adapt to classroom life as a teacher. She remembers how much the approval of the principal, the other teachers, and the children meant to her and how reluctant she was to take risks that might threaten her relationships with them. She sees Jason in a similar light, using his imaginary helicopter to keep other children at a distance until he gains enough confidence to enter into their stories and fantasies. As Paley and her assistants continue their dialogues about Jason and the other children, Trish blurts out in exasperation that it isn't possible to spend all her time as a teacher analyzing the fantasies of every child in her classroom. In response, Paley is quick to pick up on one of her favorite themes. When children have the freedom to play, work, talk, and act out each other's stories, they teach, guide, and support one another, leaving time for the teacher to focus on the most difficult cases. It is only "when a classroom is set up to isolate children that the teacher is required to make all the connections" (p. 126). As Paley says at another point, "Children are able to teach one another best if they are permitted to interact socially and playfully throughout the day" (p. 136).

Like many of the other teachers in this book, Vivian Paley has a knack for putting a positive frame on even the most difficult problems. Rather than seeing Jason as a slow learner, she calls him a "cautious researcher" who takes each new idea and "collects data on its application until he is satisfied that he knows every response and reaction it might receive in the outside world" (p. 135). As she so often does, Paley points out the similarities between her own work as a teacher and Jason's fantasy play. They both take errors and mistakes seriously, think often and deeply about them, and then practice them repeatedly so that they can recognize them when they come along (p. 140). Although Jason is probably not conscious of the role these mistakes play in his own education, Paley recognizes that such errors are, as Mike Rose has said, important signs of growth for both of them.

In the end, Jason remains the boy who would be a helicopter, but his private fantasy no longer keeps him from playing with others. Indeed, it becomes the vehicle by which he makes connections to his classmates. As Paley concludes most satisfyingly: "He has in a real sense, come home. Which is to say, school is starting to feel like home. He can breathe deeply and open the doors of his helicopter house to others" (p. 146).

Why is it so important for Paley to keep the conversation going, to continue "useful dialogue," to immerse children like Jason in the culture of the classroom? These experiences lead to everything that she considers to be fundamental educationally, including:

- learning to appreciate differences
- collaborating on the construction of shared classroom norms
- bringing children closer together and helping them to form important friendships
- learning to speak, listen, and observe more effectively
- creating a safe, nurturing environment for all children
- acknowledging and appreciating more fully the many approaches available to explore any topic
- learning to address problems more deliberatively and addressing the variety of solutions over a long period of time more patiently
- developing practice in the ability to think
- teaching "social responsibility and logical thought" (p. 98)
- constructing sites for promoting affection and respect

YOU CAN'T SAY YOU CAN'T PLAY

These educational fundamentals may have led Paley to write a book about an educational rule outlawing all social exclusions. After all, such exclusions limit the scope of the children's experience, limit the exploration of many topics, curtail useful dialogue, diminish the sense that the classroom is a safe place for all, and endanger the development of healthy self-esteem. In *You Can't Say You Can't Play* (1992), Paley has grown painfully aware of how ready even kindergartners are to exclude certain children from their play. For Paley, the feelings of hurt and rejection among the children who are left out are almost unbearable. She believes that "the children who are told they can't play don't learn as well. They might become too sad to pay attention" (p. 28). She is eager to implement the new rule that will eventually become the title of her 1992 book.

But being the thoughtful, reflective teacher that she is, Paley first wants to know what various children think of such a rule. She begins by engaging her own kindergartners in dialogue about the fairness of the rule, you can't say you can't play. Angelo and Clara, two children who are often excluded from the play of others, argue strongly for the fairness of such a rule. They seem to contend there is no experience more disheartening than being rejected by another child. But Lisa maintains just as persistently that an important part of playing is being able to choose the people you most want to spend time with. She claims that it is just as sad to be required to play with certain children as it is to be left out of the game altogether.

As Paley considers what the children have said, she returns to one of her original premises about classroom life: It should provide an opportunity for all children to participate as fully and as equally as possible. It is taken for granted that most activities in classrooms, particularly early childhood classrooms, are shared equally; in this early experience with sharing public space, everyone should have equal access to teachers, materials, and other children. The exception, as Paley points out, is free play. In the case of free play, most of us accept that choosing one's playmates is largely a private issue, even in the public space of the classroom. But as Paley emphasizes, "free acceptance in play, partnerships, and teams is what matters most to any child" (p. 21).

In a brief exchange with a fifth grader, Paley reveals her vision for education. The fifth grader notes that, since exclusions and rejections are part of everyday life outside the school, allowing them to happen in school is a way of preparing for the outside world. Paley responds that perhaps school can be more humane than the outside world. The fifth grader contends that rejection in school teaches us to deal with the inevitability of rejection outside the school. But the sting of exclusion is much on Paley's mind when she answers that, too often, the burden of rejection falls on the same few children year after year. "They are made to feel like strangers," Paley concludes (p. 22).

However fair and just she believes her proposed rule to be, she is still reluctant to impose it. Although she does not say so, she seems to hesitate because, like the time-out chair or other imposed disciplinary measures, such rules deprive the children of the opportunity to work things out for themselves. If developing the ability to solve problems is one of the most important objectives of schooling, then telling the children how they must deal with each other diminishes their individual and collective agency. On the other hand, if rejection prevents some children from learning and harms their self-esteem, then imposing a rule against all rejections would seem a relatively small price to pay. Still not satisfied, Paley prepares to do more research on the topic by consulting groups of children in grades one through five.

Each group of children greets the problem with enthusiasm and high emotion. Although each grade level has different reactions, each is similarly passionate about the topic. Paley asks each group two questions. "Is the new rule fair? Can it work?" When the first graders struggle with these questions, the result is an animated discussion in which no easy answers are put forward. They express their concerns about the possibility that the rule might alienate a best friend, that the rule would require them to include a person with a reputation for meanness, or that it could foment more conflict rather than less. They also think that, even if the rule were put into effect, it should not require girls to include a boy or boys to include girls. Paley is sympathetic to all of these concerns but, in an effort to balance the discussion, offers a brief story about her assistant's neighborhood where the expectation is that everyone can play. The children find this anecdote appealing but doubt that it can happen under most circumstances. As one child says, "people aren't that fair as the rule is" (p. 36).

The second graders also have a spirited discussion and conclude that, although letting everyone play is probably a good rule for kindergartners, it wouldn't be effective with older children. The second-grade children, for the most part, operate under the boss system in which one child, designated the leader, tells the other children who is entitled to play and who is not. Although many of them agree that this system has its flaws, they also maintain it is more humane to have one person doing the rejecting rather than an entire group of children. When Paley reports back to the kindergartners about what the second graders have said, they are surprised that bosses are so important. Although the kindergartners occasionally use the boss system themselves, they find that the bosses become, well, too bossy after a while. They vow not to have bosses until they are in the second grade—when presumably it will become necessary.

The third graders immediately launch into a lengthy and detailed discussion about Shirley, the girl in their class who is consistently the most frequent victim of rejection. When Paley expresses concern that this may be unfair to single out one child, Shirley interjects that she is actually pleased to be the focus of the discussion. Another boy named John chimes in that he is also regularly excluded. Both Shirley and John defend the rule "You can't say you can't play," but many of the other children view it as counterproductive, believing that forcing children to include others only leads to greater hostility among the children who are required to play together. Hope that the rule can work hangs in the air, but many of the children can't help believing that, in the end, kids just want to play with the kids whom they have voluntarily chosen as their friends. Paley summarizes what many of the older children tell her: "Friendship comes first, with fairness off somewhere in the distance" (p. 57).

The fourth graders seem even more pessimistic about the workability of such a rule. They claim that, by the time they have reached fourth grade, they have grown so accustomed to being mean to one another that there is very little that can be done to counteract it. The girls contend they are especially hostile toward each other, but the boys deny this, saying they are just as disagreeable. By the end of the discussion, they have concluded that "everyone can play" is a good rule, but that it must be carried out and enforced in the earliest grades for it to have an impact on the later age groups. It is too late for them, the fourth graders lament.

When the discussion with the fifth graders is postponed, Paley finally decides to display publicly the "You can't say you can't play" rule and to have the children act on it. What cannot escape the reader of this story, however, is how thoughtfully Paley has reinforced for her kindergartners, and even herself, the importance of dialogue, group problem solving, and inviting multiple perspectives. She reminds us that learning how to reflect and deliberate are invaluable skills and can never be developed too early or practiced too frequently.

Once the rule is in effect, the children seem to follow it dutifully. Although lapses into the old patterns of excluding some children still occur, when the children are reminded of the new expectation, differences are easily resolved. Paley likens the implementation of this rule to an escape route from a trap—the trap being the agonizing process of trying to decide who can play and who must be excluded. With the rule in place, there appears to be less interpersonal tension between children. Lisa, one of the original opponents of the rule, worries that the rule may be causing her to lose ground with her best friends. She proposes to Paley that the rule be adjusted slightly to make allowances for established role-playing games and to give the "boss" of the game more discretion in assigning roles to new children. But Paley is adamantly against all exclusions and concludes, with satisfaction, that the new rule eliminates much of the uncertainty and vulnerability associated with more traditional classrooms. As she says, by discouraging all hurtful exclusions, "another classroom trap has been eliminated" (p. 95).

Later, however, Lisa is embroiled in a stark inconsistency about how the rule is applied. The children in Paley's class write stories and then are given the prerogative to choose the children who will act out the stories in front of their classmates. When Cynthia does not choose Lisa to be one of her actors, Lisa is desolate. Disaster is averted when Paley leans over and quietly urges Cynthia to make Lisa a sister in her story. She adds, however, that the whole class will need to have a talk about how to deal with story acting in the future. Never quite comfortable with the process for choosing actors, Paley wonders if this is the last vestige of the boss system in her classroom.

The enthusiastic and active discussion that ensues shows that choosing actors for stories is a real sore spot for many children and a vivid exception to the rule "You can't say you can't play." A number of the children point out that they are tired of being passed over again and again, while others, like Lisa, can't even see the point of telling stories without the power to choose the children who will act them out. Despite these opposing sentiments, Paley concludes that the rule must be extended to story acting as well as general play. After all, she explains, "if we're going to learn to stop rejecting people in school we can't have one activity in which children are still told they are not wanted" (p. 129). She adds, however, that if good things don't come out of it, they can reconsider the whole idea. Lisa and another boy threaten to stop doing stories altogether, a threat which they are able to keep up for about two days.

But, of course, even Lisa quickly comes to accept a more open and democratic process for choosing story actors. This more inclusive process has some surprising residual benefits. Not only are all the children now given opportunities to act out stories, the variety of roles that are written for them increases and their willingness to play any role regardless of peer expectations—boys playing girls, girls playing boys, quiet children playing bad guys, tall children playing babies—also increases. Paley harbors a hunch that the stories may be getting better as a result, but she is certain that the level of participation and satisfaction among all the children is on the upswing.

As valuable as the new rule has become, Paley reflects on the process that the children underwent in arriving at it. "The real excitement," she notes, "has been in the process of discovery" (p. 129). And no matter how effective it may seem to be, the instructor cannot simply impose the rule because she has found from experience that it works. Each new year brings a new group of children who must think about and appreciate the value of such a rule for them. The rule must be rediscovered and refined by each new group. Talking about it, experiencing it, and reflecting on it is the only way by which it becomes real for the children and for Paley herself.

THE GIRL WITH THE BROWN CRAYON

The Girl With the Brown Crayon may be the book in which Paley most explicitly explores the connection between her lifelong work as a teacher and her growth as a person. Like so many of her books, this one focuses on a single special child, a black girl named Reeny whose love of life, her classmates, and the children's author Leo Lionni converge in touching and revealing ways. But it is also about Vivian Paley and the manner in which Leo Lionni's books and Reeny's precocious wisdom help her to uncover new aspects of herself.

Paley introduces Reeny as a confident, loving, and independent child. She is the sort of girl who "refuses to blend in yet has everyone for a friend" (p. 14). Reeny's strong sense of self is something Paley especially admires as her own search for self has been such a long, drawn-out, and continuous process. For Paley, knowing oneself is not a static, stable state; it is nurtured and renewed constantly, particularly through the act of teaching. As she says, "I still cannot take my measure without a classroom of children to give me clues" (p. 4).

What gives this narrative of Reeny and Vivian Paley its spark is the advent of Leo Lionni. When his story *Frederick* accidentally turns up in the kindergarten curriculum, it completely captures Reeny's imagination and provides the basis for much of what transpires in Paley's class during the school year.

The story Reeny loves is about a brown mouse named Frederick who appears to be idle while the other mice diligently prepare for the winter. When the other mice protest, Frederick calmly replies with eyes shut that he is expending energy gathering sunlight, color, and words for the long winter. Reproachful but patient, they leave Frederick alone. Finally, during the darkest and coldest part of the season, after most of the food has been eaten, the mice inquire about Frederick's "supplies." They are amazed and delighted when he warms them with the sun rays he has collected, showers them with the colors he has gathered, and soothes them with the words he has stored. He is celebrated as the poet of the group.

Reeny falls in love with Frederick, in part because of his brown color, which matches her own, but most of all because he is appreciated by his peers for being a thinker. The other mice end up treating Frederick well, Reeny points out, " 'cause they know thinking's not being mean. You hasta be quiet for thinking" (p. 7). Reeny instinctively identifies with Frederick for his ability to think and for his ability to share his love of beauty. Paley notes: "Who is Reeny if not Frederick? Her imagery lifts our spirits in the way Frederick's poetry cheers his friends when the food supply is gone" (p. 8). But, for Paley, Reeny is even more. Reeny is her agent of reawakening, of rediscovering her true self. Each year, she yearns for a Reeny to give her work as a teacher new meaning and new vitality, just as Reeny now discovers Frederick, "as something to ponder deeply and expand upon extravagantly" (p. 10).

The next Leo Lionni story that the class reads and studies together disturbs Paley because it seems to challenge her commitment to honoring each child's distinctiveness. The story is *Tico and the Golden Wings*. Tico is a little bird who has no wings and cannot fly. The other birds look after him by bringing him food from the nearby trees. One night Tico wishes for golden wings so he can fly high above the tallest trees. His wish is granted and he soars over the land. When his friends see Tico, though, they call him a show-off and fly away. Saddened, Tico goes off on his own and gives away his valuable golden wings to the people he meets. When all his golden wings are gone, he flies back to his home and is greeted with enthusiasm by his friends because he is once again like them.

Most of the children in Paley's class identify with the other birds and are relieved when Tico can once again "fit in" with his friends. Paley desperately wants to know what Reeny thinks. Philosopher that she is, Reeny defends both Tico and his friends. Tico, she insists, never thought he was better than the other birds, but as long as his current friends see the golden wings as a mark of privilege, he will have to give them up to regain the love of his friends. When asked to compare Frederick with Tico and explain why Frederick was permitted to be so distinctive while Tico wasn't, Reeny answers simply, "they's just different friends" (p. 14). Paley marvels at Reeny's insights and notes that, instead of seeing Tico as the martyr she always thought he was, Reeny shows her that Tico "is a perceptive friend who values the flock and empathizes with its feelings" (p. 18).

The next day, sensing that Mrs. Paley is still not satisfied, Reeny asks her teacher whether Tico's story makes her sad. After chatting a bit about the differences between Tico and Frederick, Reeny gets up to leave to play with her friends. She hesitates, though, before departing and looks Paley squarely in the eye to tell her that she must love Tico. Later in the day, Reeny recalls a dream about Leo Lionni and comments that he looks just like Frederick. The children discuss their various dreams and then Reeny returns to her own and says, looking again straight at Paley, that the next time Leo Lionni enters her dream she will ask him about Tico. Paley is dumbfounded. "Who is this Reeny girl?" she marvels. "How does she know that Tico's dilemma and mine are intertwined and must be resolved" (p. 19)?

After assessing the impact that the first two Leo Lionni stories have had on her classroom, Paley decides that the entire year must be devoted to reading all of Leo Lionni's stories. She asks her assistant, Nisha, what she thinks of the idea of spending so much time on Leo Lionni. Nisha, who is from India, says that much of her childhood was spent in reading the epic Hindu poem, the *Ramayana*, and that it was only because she read it so regularly that it had such a profound effect on her thinking. Returning to Leo Lionni, she comments that the stories are abstract and puzzling, especially when only one or two are read. To read them all could be very illuminating. Most of all, she notes, "I want to see how it can be done" (p. 20). Paley concurs. She wants to see how it can be done, too. Somehow, as readers, we are also aware that Paley wants the children to read all of Leo Lionni because their insights and their questions help her to uncover important parts of herself as well. She thrives on classrooms full of curious children because, it seems, without them she cannot, as she says, "identify my own voice and imagine my own questions" (p. 43).

As the year proceeds, the intensity and passion that is invested in reading these stories is amazing. Each story is read again and again until the children know the lines almost by heart. Then they write stories about the characters, paint pictures of the most telling incidents, discuss the most interesting parts, and eventually reenact each scene. Comparisons are made from one Leo Lionni story to another. As Paley says, "the characters enter our stories, our play, and our ordinary conversations" (p. 49). This process of reading, studying, and building on each story can take as long as 2 weeks. Although there are many other activities going on during this time, for Paley and her students Leo Lionni is the focus, the center of all things. There is nothing half-hearted or moderate about this obsession with Leo Lionni; no apologies are to be made as far as Paley is concerned. Like her 5-year-old mentor Reeny, Paley seeks passion, "the intense preoccupation of a group of children and teachers inventing new worlds as they learn to know each other's dreams." Recalling the theme of wide-awakeness, Paley exclaims, "To invent is to come alive. Even more than the unexamined classroom, I resist the uninvented classroom" (p. 50).

As the Leo Lionni stories are each read and studied, Reeny points out something that no one, not even the teachers, had noticed. All of the main characters are boys, she offers. Her discovery leads to a long discussion about whether certain characters must be boys or girls. With their awareness heightened, the children search for more Leo Lionni stories about girls. One of the most important and revealing they find is called *Geraldine, The Music Mouse.* In this story Geraldine locates the biggest block of cheese she has ever seen. With the help of her friends, the cheese is lugged back to Geraldine's home. After the other mice take away their pieces of cheese as a reward for helping Geraldine, she remains alone with the cheese block and begins to nibble away at it. As she eats, a miraculous thing occurs. An image of a mouse holding a flute to his lips emerges from the block of cheese. In awe of what is revealed but also exhausted from all the nibbling and gnawing she has done, Geraldine falls asleep. She is suddenly awakened by beautiful flute music coming from the block of cheese. The cheese flutist plays the beautiful music every night, and every night Geraldine listens intently until she falls asleep with the music still echoing in her ears. Then, one day, the other mice tell Geraldine that she must share her cheese because they have run out of food. Geraldine tells them this is impossible because the cheese is music. The other mice have never heard music before, so Geraldine lifts her tail to her lips and strains valiantly to reproduce the music she has heard nightly. Finally, she emits the same beautiful sounds as the cheese flutist. The other mice are spellbound by Geraldine's music and agree that the cheese must not be eaten. But Geraldine reassures them that the cheese can be eaten because now the music is *in* her.

At first the children and their teacher are puzzled by the story, though they have a good discussion about its possible meanings. Suddenly, though, Paley thinks she has the answer. With thoughts of selfhood and identity much on her mind, she excitedly proclaims to the children: "All of us are like Geraldine! We all have, inside of us, something only we can see and hear. It comes out in our stories, our play, everything we say and do!" (p. 73). With Paley leading the way, the children dance around the room chanting their newfound insight. It is not long before Paley thinks of Reeny and her link to the story of Geraldine. Reeny also makes a kind of beautiful music, one that helps the children and the adults better understand who they are and how they are connected to one another. Later, as Paley prepares to conclude her final year of teaching, she thinks again of Reeny and the other children and of what good friends they have been. "They know my real name," she rejoices. But then she adds mournfully, "And what if the mirror that holds my truest reflection is the one that hangs on the classroom wall? When I no longer hear the name 'teacher,' will I be left with no name at all" (p. 89)?

Finally, the last day of school arrives, perhaps the last day of Vivian Paley's remarkable teaching career. Paley and her assistant Nisha, who will teach the kindergarten class next year, begin to remove the Leo Lionni posters that the children have made during the year. Nisha wants to remove these posters so that next year's children are free to construct posters of their own choosing. Reeny intervenes then and, with a remarkably precocious sense of history, implores the teachers to leave the posters intact. "Otherwise," she explains, "they won't know what we did. The new children, they'll say, like, 'Who was in this room? We have to know who lived here!' That's what they're going to say. 'Oh, what's this one called,' like that, and 'Tell us all the names of the children that did this fine work.' Okay, then, after that, let them paint their own posters. Because, see, how do we know? They might decide to do Leo Lionni!" With a laugh, Nisha agrees and decides that the first day of next year's class will be devoted to the "story of the year of Leo Lionni" (p. 98).

Amazingly, at what must have been a moment of intense nostalgia, joy, and sadness for Paley, Reeny tells Nisha to recount the story of Tico, only to do so with a new twist, a new birth of understanding. Tell the children, Reeny says speaking directly to Paley, that Tico "could keep his gold wings." But how would his friends respond, Paley asks. They probably wouldn't like it at first,

Reeny answers, but then Tico would say in Reeny's new version of the story: "Yes, you could too be my friend. I just don't want to give up my wings because I like them, because they look pretty. I'm not saying I look prettier than you. But I'm thinking, why don't you stay and we'll talk about it. Don't fly away. See we can keep talking about it, okay?" (p. 99).

CONCLUSION

There simply can be no more fitting ending to the works of Vivian Paley than the injunction "to keep talking about it." To find ways to include everyone in useful, respectful, and thought-filled dialogue is one of Paley's greatest legacies as a learner, educator, and human being. Throughout her books, her reflective talks with children, with colleagues, with parents, and with herself have yielded new insights and new understanding that cannot have come about any other way. As teachers, we must ask again and again how can we get useful dialogue going in our classrooms and how can we sustain it despite all the pressures and challenges of teaching too many children under often unfavorable conditions. Keeping the conversation going in constructive, stimulating, and boundary-crossing directions must remain one of the highest priorities in education.

Finding time for meaningful reflection is the other great contribution of Vivian Paley's work. In her teaching and writing, Paley remains unflaggingly committed to thinking profoundly about the quality of her interactions with children. How the classroom she runs can make children feel safe, how the rules she proposes can raise everyone's self-esteem, how the lessons she plans can honor each child's uniqueness, how the activities she encourages can foster authentic collaboration, how the books she reads can stimulate wonderful thoughts and creative reenactments—all of these considerations and many more are constantly running through her mind. Her ability, year after year, to make her class an inviting and exciting place for children and adults alike is attributable in large part to this marvelous and complex habit of reflection. Without it, teaching can never be great. With it, the possibilities are boundless.

In summary, we conclude that *reflective teachers:*

> *Think continuously about their practices.*
> *Document carefully the growth of learners with whom they work.*
> *Encourage learners to engage in dialogue with each other and the teacher.*
> *Use dialogue and storytelling to construct understanding collaboratively and to give students control over their own learning.*
> *Create a "safe harbor" for learners to gain confidence in themselves and to flourish intellectually and emotionally.*
> *Learn constantly from the people around them—especially their students.*

STUDY QUESTIONS

1. How does Vivian Paley exemplify the reflective practitioner?
2. How does Paley allow herself to learn from her students? Why is dialogue so important in her teaching?
3. How does Paley demonstrate her ability to learn from her colleagues? From parents? From children?
4. How does Paley make use of storytelling in the classroom? Why is this so important to her?
5. What is Paley's view of children as learners? Of ways of knowing?
6. How are Paley's views on classroom management similar to or different from your own?
7. Do Paley's views on early childhood education have any applicability to teaching in elementary school? In middle school? In high school?

REFERENCES

Lionni, L. (1985). *Frederick's fables: A Leo Lionni treasury of favorite stories.* New York: Pantheon.

Paley, V. (1979). *White teacher.* Cambridge, MA: Harvard University Press.

Paley, V. (1990). *The boy who would be a helicopter.* Cambridge, MA: Harvard University Press.

Paley, V. (1992). *You can't say you can't play.* Cambridge, MA: Harvard University Press.

Paley, V. (1995). *Kwanzaa and me.* Cambridge, MA: Harvard University Press.

Paley, V. (1997). *The girl with the brown crayon.* Cambridge, MA: Harvard University Press.

Schon, D. (1983). *The reflective practitioner.* New York: Basic Books.

You Can't Say You Can't Play

My voice has improved only a little but I have a speaking commitment in Arizona that cannot be canceled. This will definitely be my last trip until the hoarseness clears up. Before I leave, the children and I talk again about the question that persists in my mind. I tape the discussion in order to listen to it on the plane. The replay of children's voices often helps clarify a problem for me. I cannot hear everything the first time around.

Teacher: Should one child be allowed to keep another child from joining a group? A good rule might be: "You can't say you can't play."

Ben: If you cry people should let you in.

Teacher: What if someone is not crying but feels sad? Should the teacher force children to say yes?

Many voices: No, no.

Sheila: If they don't want you to play they should just go their own way and you should say, "Clara, let's find someone who likes you better."

Angelo: Lisa and her should let Clara in because they like Clara sometimes but not all the time so they should let her in.

Nelson: They don't play with her too much so they should let her in.

Teacher: Angelo and Nelson think that even if you don't like someone all the time or play with her very much, she should have a chance to play. Shall we insist upon it? I can see you don't think so.

Charlie: If I was playing, I'd let Clara in.

Teacher: When you play with Ben do you always let others in?

Charlie: Not if it's too special I might not.

Ben: Like when we was Transformers and Nelson he wanted to come in—he always has to, that's the problem—but we couldn't stop playing so I said Charlie has to decide because I didn't care and he was the boss.

Nelson: Both people can decide.

Angelo: They always like someone else better.

Waka: I say let two people whoever wants to play. But who they don't want has to find someone else. My brother says that. He's in fourth grade.

> *Teacher:* We should ask the older children about this.
> *Angelo:* Let anybody play if someone asks.
> *Lisa:* But then what's the whole point of playing?
> *Nelson:* You just want Cynthia.
> *Lisa:* I could play alone. Why can't Clara play alone?
> *Angelo:* I think that's pretty sad. People that is alone they has water in their eyes.
> *Lisa:* I'm more sad if someone comes that I don't want to play with.
> *Teacher:* Who is sadder, the one who isn't allowed to play or the one who has to play with someone he or she doesn't want to play with?
> *Clara:* It's more sadder if you can't play.
> *Lisa:* The other one is the same sadder.
> *Angelo:* It has to be Clara because she puts herself away in her cubby. And Lisa can still play every time.
> *Lisa:* I can't play every time if I'm sad.

How clearly the issue is stated. Later when I read this part of the transcript to some older children, they all agree with Angelo and Clara. However, in practice, they admit, they follow the course set by Lisa.

No one wants to force the issue. And so Clara will continue to find solace in her cubby and Angelo will stare at us as if we were strangers. Furthermore, Charlie will get used to being the boss and Lisa can push Clara out one day and Smita the next and Cynthia after that. The way we do it, exclusion is written into the game of play. And play, as we know, will soon be the game of life.

Listening to the tape on the plane, I hear Lisa's plaintive "But then what's the whole point of playing?" and Nelson's knowing response, "You just want Cynthia." Is the primary purpose of play to have and to hold a best friend? Or to establish who's the boss? If, indeed, possessiveness comes first, then how can any plan work that attempts to eradicate exclusive ownership?

The next morning at sunrise, as I run past tall cactus plants tipped in orange flowers, I try to pin down a few premises. First of all, play, in and of itself, gives pleasure. It is certainly attached to friendship but the equation is a tricky one. Play flows out of friendship and friendship flows out of play. The relationship works both ways and equally well, but the children are not convinced that this is so, a suspicion that grows stronger as they grow older.

The children I teach are just emerging from life's deep wells of private perspective: babyhood and family. Possessiveness and jealousy are inescapable concomitants of both conditions. Then along comes school. It is the first real exposure to the public arena. Children are required to share materials and teachers in a space that belongs to everyone. Within this public space a new concept of open access can develop if we choose to make this a goal. Here will be found not only the strong ties of intimate friendship but, in addition, the habit of full and equal participation, upon request.

Equal participation is, of course, the cornerstone of most classrooms. This notion usually involves everything *except* free play, which is generally considered a private matter. Yet, in truth, free acceptance in play, partnerships, and teams is what matters most to any child.

We vote about nearly everything in our democratic classrooms, but we permit the children to empower bosses and reject classmates. Just when the old-fashioned city bosses have all but disappeared and the once exclusive dining clubs are opening their doors to strangers, we still allow children to build domains of exclusivity in classrooms and playgrounds.

"In your whole life you're not going to go through life never being excluded," a fifth grade boy will tell me. "So you may as well learn it now."

"Maybe our classrooms can be nicer than the outside world," I suggest.

"But then," he argues, "you won't be so down on yourself when you do get excluded."

I don't give up. He looks as if he has known rejection. "Here's what troubles me, as a teacher," I tell the fifth graders. "Too often, the same children are rejected year after year. The burden of being rejected falls on a few children. They are made to feel like strangers."

6

The Narrative of Journey

There comes a time in the life of a teacher when it is especially fitting to reflect on the arc of one's development, to recall the events that culminated in choosing teaching as a career and to remember the experiences and actions that, over time, transformed the job of educating others into an authentic calling. The narrative of journey is the ideal medium for just such reflection.

As defined here, the narrative of journey encompasses at least half a lifetime of teaching and learning. Ordinarily told autobiographically by a veteran teacher/protagonist, it documents the development of this central character into both a purposeful and committed adult and an effective, thoughtful educator. The most ambitious and comprehensive form of teacher narrative, it usually incorporates the other narrative forms, including the narrative of social criticism, the narrative of apprenticeship, and the narrative of reflective practice. By virtue of both its breadth and depth, the narrative of journey might be the narrative structure that has the greatest intellectual and emotional impact on the reader.

The journey narrative usually opens with the autobiographer's birth and formative family experiences, followed by accounts of schooling and adolescence. It highlights important educational turning points and culminates with the discovery of a vocation or calling that makes the fullest possible use of his talents and interests. In responding to this calling, the autobiographer generates a distinct personal and professional vision that guides subsequent action and underscores the obligation to help others develop their own potentials more completely. As with all of the teacher narratives, the narrative of journey emphasizes searching and questing. Especially in this case, the reader witnesses emerging ideas and transforming experiences that direct and nurture the protagonist's quest and lead from tentativeness and uncertainty to finding a more secure and meaningful place in the world.

All of the journey narratives that are explored in this chapter are autobiographical, and they devote nearly as much space to recounting early developmental milestones in family, school, and community as they do to reporting professional activities and accomplishments. In fact, in all of these books the authors assert that readers cannot understand how they became teachers or fully comprehend how their philosophies of education emerged unless a great deal is known about the other aspects of their lives. These authors are saying that the professional cannot be separated from the personal. Furthermore, in all of these autobiographical accounts, these authors show that their growth as educators continuously influences the kinds of people they are becoming and profoundly shapes the political and moral principles they come to espouse.

MIKE ROSE: A LIFETIME OF TEACHING, LEARNING, AND CROSSING BOUNDARIES

Perhaps more than any other teacher narrative, the story Mike Rose tells in *Lives on the Boundary* (1989) brings together all of the elements that make these stories such powerful and useful guides for both novice and experienced teachers. This book is not simply a series of anecdotes about teaching but a full-fledged autobiography of struggle, growth, and high professional accomplishment. Rose recounts his early years in an inner city Los Angeles home where his mother worked long hours for little money and his father was chronically ill. He writes about his first years in school and the difficulties he encountered finding both success and meaning. He recalls the educational transformation he experiences near the end of high school and then during college, thanks largely to the intervention of his remarkable teacher, Jack MacFarland. His long post-graduate search and eventual discovery of a career allow him to both educate and support the lives of students like himself. Rose writes this story so that we can watch him grow, first as a reader, student, and thinker and later as a teacher of young children, as an instructor for returning Vietnam veterans, and finally as director of a writing center at UCLA. In describing all of these experiences, Rose vividly conveys the evolution of his intellectual and professional identity and the ways in which his successes as a teacher gradually mold his sense of self.

The early passages of *Lives on the Boundary* describe a young Mike Rose who seems aimless, with no abiding interests or controlling passions. The son of poor immigrant parents, Rose appears destined to reproduce his parents' precarious working class existence. Raised in a Los Angeles neighborhood just a mile or so from Watts, Rose's life offers little intellectual stimulation. His early schooling is indifferent and directionless, and his time out of school is consumed gazing at TV westerns, hanging out at the bowling alley, and trying to grow vegetables in the infertile soil of his Vermont Avenue neighborhood. He receives a chemistry set one Christmas and wiles away the hours trying to concoct a solution that will blow his dilapidated house off its foundations. As he approaches adolescence, the habit of reading takes hold, though his preferences do not extend much beyond comic books or *Confidential* magazine.

His beleaguered parents retain faith in the American dream, somehow scraping together enough money to send their son to a private, Catholic boys high school called Our Lady of Mercy. Despite his parents' high hopes, Mike enters high school feeling bored and neglected, and these feelings are exacerbated when a mix-up over standardized test scores lands him in a vocational track, noteworthy for its lack of academic challenge. Destined for a working class job, Rose later comments that he found the "voc ed" boys to be both likable and bright, but once they are branded "slow" they defensively take on the characteristics of that label. Like Paul Willis's (1977) "lads," the voc ed boys grow contemptuous of school, cultivating an anti-intellectual identity that only confirms the original diagnosis that puts them in vocational education.

Mike Rose's story turns out differently from most of his voc ed peers, however, when an alert biology teacher discovers the test score mix-up and restores Mike to the college-prep program in his junior year in high school. Because he is so far behind, young Rose struggles to earn passing grades. Luckily for Rose, a teacher named Jack MacFarland comes into his life, changing his whole attitude toward education.

MacFarland loves to teach, to share exciting ideas through his well-crafted lectures, and to argue late into the night with the handful of students—which soon includes Rose—who are entranced by his observations on literature, philosophy, and the meaning of life. Seemingly knowledgeable about everything, with a knack for teaching that makes even the most difficult ideas accessible, MacFarland opens up a new world to Rose that revolves around words and books, artistry and wonder. Although not aware of it at the time, Rose learns that teaching can be a kind of romance. "You wooed kids . . . invited a relationship of sorts, the terms of connection being the narrative, the historical event . . . Knowledge gained its meaning, at least initially, through a touch of the shoulder, through a conversation . . ." (p. 102). Teachers use whatever they can to draw their students in, Rose discovers, and then they hold them by encouraging close reading, lots of open dialogue, and plenty of questioning. By making connections again and again across texts and disciplines, teachers make it possible for a broader and deeper understanding to emerge.

The dynamic of encountering great intellectual difficulty and overcoming it with the help of a wise and experienced mentor is repeated frequently in Rose's early academic life. Despite MacFarland's marvelous tutelage, the lost time in high school is not easily made up; Rose has few post-high school prospects. With MacFarland's help, though, Rose is admitted on academic probation to MacFarland's alma mater, Loyola College in Los Angeles. Poorly prepared for the rigors of the classical curriculum, he flounders in his first year and is close to flunking out. MacFarland again intervenes by requesting that his old professors give Rose and a few of his classmates some tutoring and academic support. They don't just teach Rose and his friends; they lavish attention on these needy young men. They read and reread difficult texts together until they are sure that Rose and his peers understand the most important points. They invite the boys home for barbecue, beer, and talk into the night about poetry, fiction, and the value of great literature. Together they read poems and stories, savoring each carefully chosen word, and they use what they read as models for the lean, precise prose the students are expected to produce. Finally, they relate everything learned to other ideas, other texts, and other perspectives until these young men can identify and explain many of the recurring themes that underlie the Western tradition.

By the time he graduates from college, Rose has acquired most of the skills and habits of mind that have been so lovingly taught to him. He receives a prestigious scholarship to do graduate work in English literature, but the significance of this work quickly gets lost in what Rose sees as a sea of irrelevant citations and arcane dissertation topics. Although eligible to go on for the Ph.D., he stops after earning the M.A. and studies psychology for a year in search of some kind of scholastic meaning. When this too proves unsatisfying, he joins the National Teacher Corps (NTC) to work with underprivileged fourth and fifth graders and to find out if elementary school teaching is for him.

The two-year program of the NTC teaches him a great deal about the economic and social roots of the children's educational disadvantages and even more about the limits and the promise of good teaching. With the help of instructors in the NTC and some excellent veteran teachers, Rose discovers that he can work well with young children. He invents some imaginative lessons to sharpen the students' reading and writing and, when he receives some positive responses, slowly learns that perhaps he is called to teach. It is as a tutor for the National Teacher Corps that Rose discovers the power of invitation, about how much can be accomplished with children unaccustomed to success when they are offered the right kind of encouragement. Recollecting his own experiences in vocational education, he also discovers that, for some unfortunate children, certain educational judgments can be frighteningly stigmatizing and final, and he laments how poorly standardized tests and other numerical measures capture what children can actually do. Although he ends up working primarily with adults, he learns much about how often children are stunted by the sorting and limiting that goes on in grade school and decides to devote his life to counteracting the worst effects of such practices.

Mike Rose really comes into his own as a teacher and as a human being when he starts to teach in the Returning Veterans' Program. Here he encounters Vietnam veterans and many others with long experience in the military who have enjoyed little success in school and are utterly lacking in scholastic confidence. Many of them, however, have slowly acquired a grudging respect not only for the economic opportunities that school provides but also for some of education's intrinsic satisfactions. Rose takes advantage of the veterans' motivation to learn by developing a rigorous and carefully sequenced curriculum that both stimulates them to think for themselves and assists them in mastering the tools needed to write and solve problems with clarity and critical insight. By teaching them to summarize, classify, compare, and analyze through close reading and frequent writing, Rose seeks to make up, in a relatively short period of time, for the missed opportunities of their youth. In this methodical and detailed manner, Rose uncovers academic ability in his students that few had previously discerned.

"But give them time," Rose learns, "provide some context, break them into groups and work with the whole class . . . let them see what, collectively, they do know, and students will, together, begin to generate meaning and make connections." The teacher's role in this view is a highly active one, darting "in and out of the conversation, classifying, questioning, repeating, looping back to link one student's observation to another's. And so it is that the students, labeled remedial, read and talk and write their way toward understanding" (pp. 145–146).

While teaching in the veterans' program, Rose also comes to appreciate and understand the power of error, just as Marva Collins does during the course of her own education. Instead of error being a sign of a deficit, a handicap, or a difficulty, Rose notes that often error is a sign of a student straining to try things linguistically, to move from the relatively simple to the complex and abstract. It is, in short, "a valuable kind of error, a sign of growth" (p. 151). But Rose is also increasingly comfortable with errors in his own teaching. As he progresses toward more daring pedagogical moves, as he attempts to experiment with challenging even the most poorly prepared student, he also becomes more tolerant of his own mistakes, more self-critical about his own performance. This comfort with error is not a smug, carefree response but an admission of his own fallibility and a commitment to strive to do better. It is, ironically, both a humble acknowledgment of the unending complexity of teaching and an assertion of confidence that experience, in this most difficult of professions, can increase practical wisdom and enhance effectiveness. Again, novices and veterans alike can benefit a great deal from Mike Rose's observations about the power of error: It means different things in different contexts, and it frequently represents a confused yearning after something higher, which is a crucial sign of growth and development.

While teaching in the veterans' program, Rose branches out, looking for other ways to serve his community. He does some counseling and finds that he is very good at helping troubled people. He works at the Suicide Prevention Hotline in Los Angeles, learning how to respond to callers in crisis, and, before long, orienting new volunteers and supervising their work. Rose also tutors in a community college writing center and teaches writing courses by telephone conference call to people who cannot leave their homes. In all of this work, Rose becomes an expert at uncovering ability and finding ways to nurture it further. He also observes how fragile people can be and how important it is for teachers to maintain a human connection. While teaching and reading poetry with elderly people by phone, a number of students send him their own verse. Rose finds it sentimental and maudlin, little better than greeting card rhymes. He is about to offer his frank assessment when it dawns on him that his students don't want his opinion; they simply want to share something, to participate more fully. As a result of this experience, Rose wisely and humbly notes: "There are times when it's better to let all that schooling slide" (p. 163). What an important lesson for teachers at all levels! Sometimes it's just better to join in with admiration or to express a kind of uncritical awe. Wise discretion such as this comes only with experience and with the time and effort it takes to see one's students whole.

From the Returning Veterans' Program, Mike Rose goes on to become a successful director of tutoring through UCLA's Equal Opportunity Program. His job is to train and organize other tutors and occasionally to work directly with undergraduates who find themselves a little overwhelmed by the rigors of a major university. Drawing on all of his experiences as a struggling, young undergraduate, disillusioned graduate student, instructor of young children, and teacher of adults, Rose fashions a program based on his democratic faith that all students possess academic promise. The trick is to find the method or strategy that will tap that undisclosed ability. Impatient with those who charge the university with admitting too many unqualified students and skeptical of the claim that attrition is a benign process that eliminates the academic chaff, Rose insists that these attitudes force you to "limit your definition of achievement—blunt your sense of wonder. What you'll have to do, finally, is narrow your vision of the society you want to foster" (p. 204).

As Rose comes into his own as a teacher and person, he develops new respect for the wonder of teaching and learning, and he increasingly appreciates that our vision of education is, and has always been, an important reflection of who we are as a people. Too often, our tendency has been to tally up deficiencies, unnecessarily handicapping millions of academically promising children. Despite all of the tragic misjudgments of students' ability, despite all of the tendencies to track, herd, differentiate, and stigmatize, Rose retains his simple faith in teachers and learners. He insists: "That if you set up the right conditions, try as best you can to cross class and cultural boundaries, figure out what's needed to encourage performance, that if you watch and listen, again and again there will emerge evidence of ability that escapes those who dwell on differences" (p. 222).

Rose recalls a friend who defines education as one culture embracing another. Such an image can, on the one hand, suggest a smothering, disrespectful encounter in which the one does not really acknowledge the distinctiveness, the uniqueness of the other. Too often, education is conducted in this thoughtless, desperate manner. But education, Rose continues, can also be an "encouraging, communal embrace—at its best an invitation, an opening." Or, as Rose offers, education can be thought of as a relationship "in which the terms of endearment [are] the image in a poem, a play's dialogue, the winding journey of a novel" (p. 225). What is clear is that for teachers to form these pedagogical relationships, to extend themselves to their students openly and generously, they must acquire a strong and keen sense of themselves, a renewed self that puts the interests of the students in their classroom on a par with their own continuing growth. This emerging and rejuvenating self should help shape the vision and purpose of education. Unless teachers possess a democratic faith in their students' capacities, unless they believe that what they do with students makes an important difference in their lives, then hopes for the future, both educationally and otherwise, are dim. But if the sense of self that a teacher cultivates includes a vision of students who are achieving, self-creating people, then new possibilities abound. One of Rose's greatest discoveries and contributions is his concrete and detailed description of his understanding of the role humane, thoughtful, and generous teachers can play in shaping the educational futures of their students.

As *Lives on the Boundary* comes to a close, Rose explores the vision of education necessary to foster the intellectual, artistic, and social capacities of America's most marginalized populations. He writes:

> Finally, we'll need a revised store of images of educational excellence, ones closer to egalitarian ideals—ones that embody the reward and turmoil of education in a democracy, that celebrate the plural, messy human reality of it. At heart, we'll need a guiding set of principles that do not encourage us to retreat from, but move closer to an understanding of the rich mix of speech and ritual and story that is America. (p. 238)

These are the words of a wise teacher with vast experience and a clear sense of self, a teacher who knows his own strengths and limitations, but who also knows how much can be accomplished by hopeful pedagogues who employ their understanding of history, culture, and language to highlight the special gifts each learner enjoys. They are also the words of a teacher who seeks to collaborate with other like-minded educators in making the promise of democracy a powerful reality.

HOWARD GARDNER: THE TEACHER AS SCHOLAR OF LEARNING

An educator no less interested in the promise and power of American democracy is Howard Gardner. A renowned developmental psychologist, he has written widely about education and creativity and has propounded the influential theory of multiple intelligences in his best known book, *Frames of Mind* (1983). Gardner has also contended for many years that the vast majority of students have more academic ability and a greater range of capacities than public education is structured to reveal. Much of his recent scholarship shows how education can be organized to tap individual potential more effectively and to substantiate the claim that talent is much more widely distributed among people than generally recognized. But it is particularly in *To Open Minds* (1989), published in the same year as Rose's *Lives on the Boundary*, that Gardner explores the personal and autobiographical roots of this research and these beliefs. Like Rose, he argues that one cannot fully understand his views on creativity and education without a glimpse of the events that shaped his scholarly perspective. Indeed, Gardner asserts that these views are:

> inseparable from who I am, where I came from, which values are most fundamental to me. Moreover, I think that they are most effectively

conveyed and convincingly justified in terms of pivotal events of my own childhood, the educational course I followed, and certain formative experiences I have had along the way—as a young pianist, a dutiful scholar, a schoolteacher, a family member, and, most recently, a visitor to China. (pp. 15–16)

Gardner begins the account of his early life by recalling himself as a youngster seated at the piano laboriously practicing musical exercises. He learns quickly and is soon playing intricate classical sonatas with impressive fluidity. Having begun to study piano at age 7, Gardner's next 5 years are dominated by the practices and recitals that constitute the regimen of any young, talented musician. Indeed, the residents of Scranton, Pennsylvania, the town of his youth, shower him with acclaim for his accomplished playing. But when Howard's piano teacher informs him at age 12 that he must greatly increase the amount of practicing he is doing to become a concert pianist, he balks. Although he continues to play informally, his formal lessons cease and he never again thinks of himself as a serious musician.

These early events leave their mark in at least two ways. First, through these experiences Gardner has his first direct experience with excellence in a particular domain. He learns first-hand what it is like to be perceived to be musically talented and he sees how these talents must be nurtured and developed through long hours of drill and practice. Second, he is coming to understand something his German immigrant parents do not yet fully grasp. As a dutiful but typically headstrong American youth of the late 1950s, he enjoys a power to say "no" that is granted few children in other cultures. Even at this young age, he controls his own destiny with a simple refusal that his parents seem powerless to deny. This early experience with the power of choice will, in some way, shape his later attitudes as a student and leave an impact on the brand of neo-progressive education he eventually advances.

His musical precocity is matched by a remarkable and early facility for reading and writing. Having taught himself to read, young Howard spends most of his spare time poring over a wide range of texts, including both fiction and nonfiction. He also writes prolifically and begins producing his own newspaper as early as age 7. From that time on, Howard is always associated with some sort of student publication that uses his increasingly sophisticated skills as a writer.

Eventually, Gardner's musical and linguistic gifts motivate his parents to have him tested at the Stevens Institute of Technology in New Jersey. After enduring a 5-day battery of tests at considerable cost to his parents, the testing expert reports that Howard will make an excellent bookkeeper. This anticlimactic experience has a profound impact on Gardner. Much of his subsequent professional work amounts to a careful and systematic critique of the kind of standardized tests that are administered to him in New Jersey. Arguing that they miss more than they capture, Gardner claims:

that they fail to pick up the most important human capacities and attributes; that they favor the glib and the conventional rather than the profound and the creative; and that people who do not understand these instruments attribute to them much more merit than they actually warrant. (p. 30)

In the absence of help from the Stevens Institute, Howard's parents hope that Scranton Central High School can offer an exciting intellectual challenge for their son. But when the opposite proves to be true, they enroll him in a reputable local preparatory school. Surrounded for the first time in his life by scholastically serious students and excellent, knowledgeable teachers, Gardner flourishes. Academically, he is a first-rate student, especially in science and math, despite being drawn toward history and the humanities. But more than that, this school bolsters his confidence and encourages his love of writing. As coeditor of a publication that serves as both school newspaper and literary magazine, Howard hones his writing, learns valuable organizational skills, and figures out how to work with peers and adults to secure their cooperation and exploit their talents. It is an early experience in making the most of his own and others' abilities that serves him well in his later professional life.

Gardner's introduction to Harvard University as an undergraduate in 1961 launches the intellectual and interdisciplinary adventure in which he still revels as a scholar today. At Harvard, Gardner is exposed to world-class thinkers in a variety of fields and learns how to use his newly found freedom to seek out additional experiences that complement and enhance the academic foundation he is laying. From the beginning, Gardner avoids any particular undergraduate major or specialization and endeavors to use the vast resources of Harvard to expand his horizons and challenge his intellectual preconceptions. He studies history, philosophy, political theory, and the visual arts. He intentionally seeks out the best minds to teach him literary theory, social psychology, economic history, and the roots of theatrical drama. It is only a slight exaggeration to state that the man who becomes Gardner's undergraduate tutor, the distinguished psychoanalyst Erik Erikson, brilliantly combines most of these disciplines to produce a view of the human life cycle and a slant on the study of personality that strikes Gardner as irresistible and compelling. Erikson's brilliance in employing biography and history to illuminate and revise key psychoanalytic concepts is especially influential, as is his emphasis on close observation and on the value of qualitative methods. All of this leaves an incalculable impact on Gardner's scholarly outlook. In all, Harvard represents an academic feast from which Gardner still draws intellectual nourishment. And it is an experience he recalls repeatedly in arguing against premature specialization and in making a claim for both interdisciplinary study and for giving students an active role in shaping their own education.

Upon graduating from Harvard, Gardner encounters still another intellectual mentor who combines expertise in cognitive and developmental psychology with a marvelous assortment of insights and understandings from fields as wide ranging as history, philosophy, anthropology, and literature. This mentor is the brilliant cognitive psychologist Jerome Bruner. In 1965, Bruner is in the midst of directing a very ambitious curriculum project called Man: A Course of Study (MACOS), designed to engage 10- and 11-year-olds in exploring three "mind-opening questions: What makes human beings human? How did they get that way? How could they be made more so?" (p. 50). Bruner and his talented team of associates labor diligently to translate the latest insights and discoveries of professional social science into language and ideas accessible to young children. This project is, in a sense, a test case of Bruner's famous claim from *The Process of Education* (1960) that anything can be taught to anyone, regardless of age or level of intellectual development, as long as the content is appropriately adapted and sequenced. The intellectual atmosphere created and sustained by Bruner to study and pursue such issues is a highly stimulating one, and when Gardner accepts Bruner's generous offer to join this project, the course of his professional career is forever altered.

One of the keystones of MACOS is the role played by the Underwood Elementary School in Newton, Massachusetts, as a site for trying out and refining the emerging curriculum. Gardner joins other researchers in helping to teach the curriculum there, and he learns much during this experience about the look and feel of education at its most challenging and engaging. While trying out MACOS, the children at Underwood School hold passionate and informed debates about parallels between Eskimo culture and a typical middle-class community as they painstakingly investigate the complexities of family relationships within many traditional societies. This exciting and liberating academic climate convinces Gardner of the desirability of progressive methods that are "open, exploratory, nondirective, but intellectually rich." It also inspires him to spend many subsequent years searching for underlying theories and powerful instructional practices that can form the basis for a better education for all American children.

Although MACOS ultimately loses favor with parents and legislators alike (see Dow, 1991, for an interesting discussion of how this came about), Gardner discovers his professional calling under the nurturing hand of Jerome Bruner. Like Bruner, Gardner invests his scholarly energies in research that combines interests in cognitive and developmental psychology, creativity, the arts, and education. In finding a career and life for himself that draws on many different perspectives and diverse ways of knowing, Gardner begins building a view of education and of teaching that is similarly rich, diverse, and multifaceted.

These varied interests lead Gardner to many lands and cultures, but it is his encounter with Chinese ways and schooling, particularly schooling in the arts, that has the most profound impact on his educational philosophy and on the proposals he advances for restructuring American education. While investigating the nature of intelligence and the many problems associated with conventional instruments for measuring cognitive ability—work that leads to *Frames of Mind* (1983)—Gardner receives an invitation to study education in China. Although initially appalled by the poverty and ignorance he witnesses, he is also charmed and fascinated by the people. His work in intelligence begins to intersect with his research on creativity, leaving him wondering whether China is a fruitful place to extend these investigations and give his findings a cross-cultural context. After an initial $3\frac{1}{2}$-week sojourn in China, he finds that he develops an almost irresistible affinity for things Chinese and concludes:

> As Henry Adams had been drawn to the Middle Ages, Margaret Mead to the South Seas, Erik Erikson to India, and Claude Levi-Strauss to the Indians of Brazil, I was now being drawn to China as a source of illumination on the questions central to my chosen profession and important to my life. (p. 138)

Gardner devotes most of the second half of *To Open Minds* to painting a detailed portrait of Chinese arts education and to showing how his experiences in China shape his thinking about creativity and educational excellence. In almost every Chinese classroom he visits, Gardner is struck by how much control and structure the teacher imposes. The typical Chinese instructor serves as a conduit of knowledge, conveying to the students in strict didactic fashion the proper way to paint, sculpt, sing, or perform. As a result, arts classes vary little from school to school and city to city. It is as though all arts classes in China resembled "exquisitely executed performances," Gardner points out. In comparing China to the United States, Gardner frequently comments that the Chinese very effectively bring a large number of students to a high level of technical proficiency as artists, while sacrificing a certain amount of individual creativity. Americans, on the other hand, successfully educate a few students to be highly imaginative and technically adept but, lacking the structure and instructional discipline of the Chinese, allow the vast majority of students to leave school with little proficiency in or appreciation for the arts.

Gardner's goal is to combine the best aspects of both of these outcomes in a single system of education. He believes there is much to be learned from Chinese education, particularly in enabling many more students to achieve, without attempting a wholesale transfer of the Chinese system to the United States. Since much of Chinese education reflects its culture just as American education does, any attempt by American teachers to simply mimic Chinese ways is almost certainly doomed to failure. But one pillar of Chinese education that especially impresses Gardner is the emphasis on artistic apprenticeships, in which an older person guides a child as young as six or seven through the rudiments of an art or craft. These apprenticeships, which are carried out daily and sustained over many years, help students acquire "an understanding in their bones of what it is like to gain gradual mastery of a valued area or skill" (p. 293). Under these conditions, Gardner writes, students can track their own progress, gauge an appropriate future direction, and take note of how they are doing compared to others at a similar level of mastery.

To adapt this process successfully to an American school, Gardner contends, uniformity must be de-emphasized to make room for tailoring activities to the specific needs and interests of students. Gardner calls such a school the "individual-centered school" and articulates two assumptions that form its educational foundation. First, educators should acknowledge that students have different strengths. These capacities should be carefully assessed, monitored, and developed, even as students are challenged to grapple with difficult and unfamiliar material outside of an area of strength. Second, educators should learn to sacrifice educational breadth for educational depth. Every learner is entitled to a challenging education, but, Gardner maintains, that does not necessarily mean every learner should be exposed to all of the arts and sciences. Rather, an ongoing intellectual apprenticeship with an acknowledged expert in the arts, history, literature, mathematics, or science might be substituted for at least some of the content that is currently imparted in highly traditional ways.

The individualized instruction Gardner endorses does not constitute an effort to deprive some students of instruction that teaches critical thinking or valuable problem-solving skills. It is, on the contrary, a plan for schooling that allows fairly wide latitude as to what content students might study but requires that all students probe deeply enough into at least a few disciplines to acquire lasting and significant understanding of how knowledge is derived and advanced.

In generating these proposals for educational change, Gardner learns a great deal from psychology and other disciplines. However, these proposals are also a reflection of his own educational and social history and the deep satisfaction he has derived from academic climates respecting his drive to know and enthusiastically encouraging his intrinsic love of learning. Gardner (1991) has since written extensively about the problems and limitations of older students and adults who, despite exposure to extensive instruction in a variety of fields such as physics and astronomy, often retain naive understandings of key concepts from these disciplines. Although the reasons for this are complex and attributable to many factors, one problem is that most schools treat subjects in a cursory, superficial manner. Encompassing the subject by reading the textbook from cover to cover remains a standard approach, yet so much is missed when teaching and learning are reduced simply to retaining the material within the pages of a textbook. The unanswered questions, the enigmatic paradoxes, the elegant formulae, the fascinating interdisciplinary connections tend to get swept under the rug of coverage, turning potentially exciting and provocative content into dry-as-dust facts with little or no meaning for students. Gardner's educational autobiography is a reminder of how thrilling and adventurous learning can be when students are allowed to follow their passion to know and when knowledgeable and caring teachers are on hand both to fuel this enthusiasm and to find constructive ways to nurture it.

JANE TOMPKINS: TEACHING FOR TRANSFORMATION AND WHOLENESS

For many years a distinguished professor of American literature at Duke University, Jane Tompkins writes her fiercely honest autobiography *A Life In School: What the Teacher Learned* (1996) as the story of her quest for personal growth and understanding and her search for meaning and purpose. Her critique of her own experiences in school as both student and teacher serves as an especially vivid reminder that one of the most devalued purposes of teaching is the enhancement of self-knowledge. Teachers and learners must be granted the freedom to explore their inner lives, with all the risks that process entails, for education to be truly transforming. Educational institutions generally confine their mission to building disciplinary knowledge and cultivating the intellect. Tompkins notes, "What my teaching has been aiming for is not the empowering discipline itself but the wisdom to know what that might be when it comes along" (p. 160). When students are invited to inquire into the reasons for studying a subject, then school can begin the hard work of educating the whole person for living a fuller and more satisfying life.

In Tompkins' experience, fear is what keeps teachers and students from this hard work. In a chapter titled Ash Wednesday, after the T. S. Eliot poem, she describes with great intensity and poignancy the fear that pervaded the intellectual lives of first her own teachers and then her life as a university professor. She uses the poem as a framework for describing the spiritual death and suffering of "unhappy intellectuals." Her own introduction to the poem, which involved dutifully annotating each stanza with dry classical references meted out by the teacher, was, she writes, like eating dog kibble. She claims "it is possible to understand the poetry at another level without knowing what the references mean. It's possible to interrogate your soul and learn from its cries and whispers what the poet might be saying" (p. 129). But, she continues, "the reality was too much to bear for my teachers, for me, so we lost ourselves in explication" (p. 129). The fact that students and teachers have "bodies that are mortal, hearts that can be broken, and spirits that need to be fed" (p. xiii) is one that is too frightening for most teachers to contemplate.

Fear, boredom, and humiliation are the feelings she associates most strongly with her early schooling. In first grade, she yearns for recognition. "Here I am, I cried inwardly . . . Here we all are, raring to go, dying to be off on the great voyage of exploration" (p. 16). But at P.S. 98 in Manhattan, "the three basics were not reading, writing, and arithmetic but standing in line, not moving, and staying absolutely quiet" (p. 18). As in James Herndon's junior high school, deportment, demeanor, and order were stressed. She thought that school was to be a voyage of discovery, requiring everything she had "but would be worth it, for in the end, I would get to see what adults saw: the great world itself" (p. 19). But *My Weekly Reader*, which Jane finds so dry that she thinks something must be wrong with her, offers the only window leading to the outside world. In fact, the prospect of another day in school often makes her feel ill in the mornings. She arrives early, in fear of punishment for tardiness, but the loneliness of the dark forbidding hallways symbolizes her own inner fear of still another day of no learning, no illumination.

Repetition is the chief pedagogical method. She recounts with astonishment ("What did they think, that we had amnesia?") that a little book about how Peter Minuit bought Manhattan Island from the Indians for $24 and some glass beads is read over and over, each time presented as if it had never been seen before. In spite of her boredom, she is an excellent student who performs well on tests, but she soon realizes that school is chiefly about avoiding shame. If you are good, you get perfect scores; if you are bad, you make mistakes and are humiliated.

A girl with a taste for adventure, she leaps at the chance to join the Camp Fire Girls. It turns out that they meet in the basement of the school and their activities mainly consist of doing screen paintings. What is worse is that their leader, Miss Ann, who never raises her voice above a whisper, is not a likely candidate for leading girls on risky expeditions. The hope remains in Jane that somewhere are the real Camp Fire Girls doing the things that Camp Fire Girls are supposed to do. Risky expeditions must await Jane's higher education.

The long line of dreary teachers that Tompkins faces is interrupted only rarely. The first is Rose Higgins, her third and fourth grade teacher. Typical of young children, what Jane loves most about Mrs. Higgins is her physical appearance. She is immaculately groomed and wears chic suits. Although Jane knew even then that appearances aren't supposed to be what school is about, she appreciates the fact that "it was as though she dressed and groomed and primped for all of us" (p. 26). The other reason every child in the school loves Mrs. Higgins is her kindness. She calls the students her darlings, her chickadees, and tells the principal how wonderful they are. She doesn't shout, rant, or rave like the other teachers do. Jane's memories of the activities in Mrs. Higgins's room include the time each student is invited to recount what they want to be when they grow up. "We whispered our dreams in her ear" (p. 28). Jane's is to be a bareback rider in the circus. Reading her autobiography, one often gets the sense that this wish comes true in ways she never expected. In fact, it may have been in Mrs. Higgins's class that Jane discovers who she really is, as it's clear that Mrs. Higgins teaches the "whole child."

Two other memorable teachers are Mr. Bowler, her high school geometry teacher, and Mrs. Hay, who teaches English to a class of gifted students in another high school Jane attends. Mr. Bowler is trained as a history teacher, but agrees to teach geometry because there is a need. Jane knows from the first day of class when she sits at a desk with no books or papers that "it was clear that something real was afoot" (p. 55). Mr. Bowler's method is to pose questions to the students who, in answering them, derive the proofs of plane geometry for themselves. She writes, "We worked in the pure ether where only logic reigned, and by its strenuous process we were purified and invigorated" (p. 56). Mr. Bowler takes geometry seriously, takes the students seriously, and shows them their mental strength. The thinking of the class is a joint effort in which the "virtuosity of one reflected the virtuosity of all" (p. 56). Not being a mathematician by training himself, he appreciates the need for clear explanations. And there is more. Mr. Bowler's classroom feels like one awash in fresh air. "There was no staleness or tension, no emotion or expectation emanating from him to sully the atmosphere. We walked in with no balance sheet appended to our names; and just as we produced the proof of the day out of nothing, so we ourselves came into being as if for the first time" (p. 57). What a marvelous description of the power of a teacher to elicit his students' own brilliance.

Mrs. Hay, the English teacher of gifted students, is another remarkable exception. Jane describes her personality as a combination of powerful intellect, moral idealism, and strength of will. She loves her subject, knows it well, and demands much of her students, including reading the equivalent of a book a week. She puts a great deal of stock in discussion and is Tompkins's first teacher to arrange the students in a circle so that they can talk to each other. As in Mr. Bowler's class, the students strive to do well individually but are especially encouraged to work collaboratively and to view text interpretation as a cooperative project. Furthermore, Mrs. Hay doesn't just want her students to study great literature, she urges them to relate their reading to the issues of the day and to use it to make sense of their own lives. As Tompkins proudly recalls: "She aroused our moral outrage, dared us to think harder, challenged our comfortable assumptions" (p. 59). Mrs. Hay not only gives Tompkins the life-changing advice to matriculate at Bryn Mawr instead of Bennington College, she provides the initial inspiration to make the study of literature Tompkins's life work. Above all, Mrs. Hay avers, literature is not remote from life but a guide to living well. To reveal one's passion for a lyric poem or enthusiasm for an epic novel is nothing to be ashamed of; it is one of the most important reasons for reading literature in the first place.

When Tompkins enrolls at Bryn Mawr College, it is the first time in her life that she becomes a member of a genuine community. Although it is an important academic community for her where she deepens her understanding and love of literature, it is probably even more so a social community. Here she establishes lasting relationships, learns as much outside the classroom as she does in, and feels affirmed in becoming a more well-rounded and integrated person. It is also the place, however, where she learns that the sort of romantic awe and wonder she feels for certain poems and stories is something to be outgrown, something one avoids in interpreting serious literature.

After Bryn Mawr, Jane Tompkins enters the graduate English program at Yale University to study American literature. She does it out of her love of reading and writing and expects to find an intellectual community "like Bryn Mawr, only better" (p. 73). It is also a safer choice than a career in acting, her favorite extracurricular activity in college. She hopes that "When I reached the goal, a Ph.D., I'd get a job. There would be no need to sleep with strange men" (p. 72). It isn't until a bit later in her academic career that she realizes she has "no political sense" (p. 96). She does, however, quickly learn that at Yale the point is "to show the professor and other students how much you knew and how smart you were; it had nothing to do with loving poetry" (p. 78). "People led with their defenses, everyone afraid of everyone else" (p. 77). Mike Rose found the same thing in his graduate school and, after earning his M.A., dropped out. Tompkins stays with it, though every moment seems grueling and painful. She eventually writes her dissertation on Melville's *Moby Dick* under the direction of the one professor she encounters who is passionate about his specialty. But the general rule is that intellectual development depends on the suppression of passion for one's subject, not its cultivation. For a time, Tompkins bends to this expectation but eventually sees it as antithetical to education at its best and does everything she can in her own teaching to bring passion, emotion, and the inner life back into the classroom.

The years after her graduation from Yale are difficult ones both personally and professionally. She loves teaching at Connecticut College, but quits that position to stay home for a year trying to get pregnant while her husband teaches at another university and finishes his dissertation. After a year of "no book, no baby, no job," she takes a position at a community college where she falls in love with another teacher, for whom she leaves her husband. Unfortunately, her lover turns out to be an alcoholic who denounces her to the school when she finally leaves him. She finds another job at Temple University, where she battles blatant sexism in a successful effort to get on the tenure track. At Temple, she finally realizes that "woman does not advance by merit alone" (p. 98).

It is in the middle of a crumbling second marriage that she discovers and falls in love with one of the leading proponents of new literary theory, Stanley Fish. Her professional life takes a turn for the better. Tompkins admits to having difficulty sorting out her love for the theory versus her love for Fish versus her desire to "enter the literary profession as a player" (p. 104). They eventually marry and secure tenured positions at Duke University.

Tompkins realizes that, with a secure job at a prestigious university, she is free to do as she wants. Thus begins her adventure in experimental teaching methods. At last, risky expeditions await, and her courage does not fail her. As she tells it, one day Tompkins finds herself reflecting on the kind of teacher she is trying to be. It astounds her to realize that for her, like her fellow graduate students at Yale, her primary goal at Duke is not so much to help her students to learn but to impress them with how much she knows.

She responds by radically altering the way she organizes her classes. Instead of taking all the responsibility for its content, instead of taking up all of the class time with the sound of her own voice, she invites her students to choose topics of interest and to give presentations to the class. Almost immediately the classes become alive with the sounds of many student voices. The discussions that take place are rich and thoughtful, and the presentations students give are often surprising and challenging. Most interesting of all, as Tompkins takes a less active role in these classes, she observes the students exchanging ideas with one another directly, without constantly looking to her as the pedagogical mediator. Additionally, the more Tompkins defers to the students, the more she can pay attention to "what was being said, to who was talking, to how things felt in class" (p. 120). She confesses that the desire "not to be alone" in her classes and the "longing to be free from fear" (p. 124) propel her efforts. "I taught from places inside me that needed healing" (p. 177) seems one of the truest and bravest of her confessions in this remarkable autobiography. One wonders how many other teachers have felt the same loneliness and fear in their own classrooms but lack the courage, or encouragement, to find ways to overcome it.

As she finds herself yearning for more chances to hear what her students think and feel about the literature they are reading, she imposes less and less on them. There are fewer prearranged assignments, fewer formal evaluations, almost no prepared lectures. Instead of teaching for validation of her own intellectual achievements, she now teaches to engage the students on their own terms, to relate the assigned material to their everyday lives, and to make the reading not an end but the means to help them discover and reconstruct themselves. One of Tompkins's classes evolves into a highly student-centered experience in which students take turns presenting interpretations of works of literature that have special meaning for them. Part of the point of these presentations is to have students consider the source and depth of their attachments to these topics and to explore what these attachments reveal about them as people. As a follow-up to each presentation, the remaining students then write a letter to the presenter to ask questions or make comments and to deepen the class dialogue even more.

As this class proceeds, students take complete responsibility for course content, leaving Tompkins with little more to do than furnish the refreshments. Although she questions whether she has taken her experiment too far, she also notices that the discussions just keep getting better: Everyone participates, contributions are rarely forced or artificial, and the ties between the content and discussion topics are strong. She also observes that the atmosphere of the class is almost like a family—safe and secure, even caring. She comes to see that perhaps this kind of safety is one of the necessary requirements for sound education:

> I believe that school should be a safe place, the way home is supposed to be. A place where you belong, where you can grow and express yourself freely, where you know and care for other people and are known and cared for by them, a place where people come before information and ideas. School needs to comprehend the relationship between the subject matter and the lives of students, between teaching and the lives of students, between school and home. (p. 127)

Over the next few years, she continues these kinds of educational experiments with her classes, finding them both exhilarating and disorienting. The hardest part is, as Tompkins says, "letting the chaos in, not knowing, not being in control" (p. 132). But she also discovers that the only way for people to find themselves is first to get lost. You must be stripped of all the habits, conventions, and preconceptions that get in the way of self-reflection and take time to weave into learning "the memory and desire of every person" in attendance. It is dangerous, uncertain, and initially directionless, but such experiments can lead to classroom encounters that are truly transforming.

Sometimes, though, it takes a long time to gauge the extent of the transformation. In one class, Tompkins organizes an overnight trip to one of the barrier islands of North Carolina. The idea is to create a bonding experience for the class and to set the stage for reading *Moby Dick*. While on the island they do a number of things to bring the class closer together, though reading Melville aloud is a highlight. Back on the mainland the class continues. Tompkins encourages the students to analyze and savor Melville's language carefully—this was actually the topic of her dissertation—but the students continue to be free to set the agenda for most of the class. Other field trips follow, at least one of which launches the best discussion Tompkins has ever participated in about oppression. Later they read Toni Morrison's *Beloved* and again pay especially close attention to the language and the images the author employs. By the end of the class, Tompkins is sure that it has been a life-transforming experience for every single student. But when the final, open discussion is held about how the class went, Tompkins can hear only the criticisms that come tumbling all too frequently out of her students' mouths. Too little structure, too much discussion about this and not enough about that, too much consensus, not enough willingness to confront one another, etc. What Tompkins is certain will be viewed as a resounding success turns out to be a near-failure, or at best a middling success.

Or is it? Over time most of this class's 15 students stay in touch with Tompkins, even seek her out, to recall the glory of this unique educational experience they shared together. Part of the problem with this kind of experimental teaching is that you are never really sure when you are successful. It seeps in over time, takes hold only after a long period, and gradually reveals its meaning in the light of further reflection and subsequent experience. Teachers who do this kind of work must take solace in the experiences of others and in the faith that organizing classes for maximum student participation and agency can make an enormous difference for participants in the long run. As Tompkins writes, "When you teach like this you don't know what failure is anyway, or success. What looks like victory could turn out to be defeat, as well as the other way around. You just do it, as the Nike ad says, and hope for the best" (p. 180).

Although the extremes to which Tompkins goes to honor her students' experiences and to help them rediscover their individual and collective identities may seem egocentric or selfish and ultimately too removed from subject matter, there is nevertheless a gnawing sense that, for Tompkins herself and especially for her students, the novel way in which she organizes these classes is more transformative and more life-enhancing than any of their previous experiences in school. Whether teachers should follow Tompkins' example in putting the lives of one's students at the center of the educational enterprise is an open question. But there is little doubt that, when as teachers we open ourselves up to our students, making room for the diversity of their experiences, for the full range of their knowledge and emotion, and for all the spontaneity and unexpectedness such openness represents, then remarkable, even magical things happen.

For Tompkins, there is nothing anti-intellectual or counter-cognitive about her approach. It is a quest for education for wholeness. Near the conclusion of *A Life in School*, she writes:

Human beings, no matter what their background, need to feel that they are safe in order to open themselves to transformation. They need to feel a connection between a given subject matter and who they are in order for knowledge to take root. That security and that connectedness are seldom present in a classroom that recognizes the students' cognitive capacities alone. (p. 213)

CONCLUSION

The journeys these three people have traveled remind us that great teachers begin as curious and persistent students and then continuously draw on their past and present experiences as learners to improve and refine their teaching. Their lifelong penchant for learning fuels their commitment to education and prepares them for the lessons their students provide daily. Their stories also show that, when students have opportunities to explore and understand themselves and to relate what they are studying to their own self-development, what they learn is more striking and meaningful. In the end, the content they learn and the self-knowledge they gain become inseparable.

Teachers whose lives are devoted to learning and teaching are especially sensitive to the nuances of emerging understanding, the subtle errors that signify growth, and the powerful insights that connect theory and practice. These are the things that experienced teachers like Rose, Gardner, and Tompkins strive to cultivate and are quick to affirm. These teachers also know that, unless attention is paid to the human side of learning, unless you occasionally "let all that schooling slide," opportunities to make an enduring difference will be missed again and again. Veteran teachers have learned from long experience that every diverse group of people has riveting stories to share, impressive talents to display, and untapped abilities to discover. Setting aside the space, finding the time, and exerting the will to allow these gifts to be revealed is a sacred trust for teachers. For when students are freed to realize and even exceed their individual and collective potential, the sense of affirmation that is enjoyed and the communal bond that is formed make the experience of learning truly memorable. Such experiences can spur individuals to seek out similar opportunities to learn and grow with others in the future. For educators who trigger this kind of transformation, teaching becomes much more than a process of introducing a new subject matter to unknowing students. It is, like John Dewey's notion of democracy, a way of life that has the potential to influence every facet of human experience.

In summary, we conclude that *journeying teachers:*

Begin as learners questing for connection, understanding, and meaning.

Continue to see themselves primarily as learners who engage in an ongoing struggle to construct understanding, make meaning, and connect with other learners.

> *Recall their past experiences as learners and use these experiences to ground their teaching.*
>
> *Emphasize that their accumulated experiences as learners and as human beings are an important part of who they are and what they teach.*
>
> *Affirm that each learner has gifts that should be recognized and exploited for the benefit of all.*

STUDY QUESTIONS

Rose

1. What were the two or three most important influences in Mike Rose's education?
2. What does Rose mean by the "power of invitation"? Have you ever had an experience in school that exemplified that?
3. Why is Rose successful with students who have previously done poorly in school?
4. What is Rose's attitude toward students' mistakes?

Gardner

1. Why is Howard Gardner interested in expanding our views of what counts as intelligence?
2. What is Gardner's view of children as learners?
3. Why does Gardner advocate apprenticeships as a method of teaching and learning? What effect did his own apprenticeships have on him?

Tompkins

1. Why does Jane Tompkins advocate educating the whole person? Do you agree or disagree with this philosophy?
2. Tompkins states that fear is a barrier to the kind of education she wants school to offer. What does she mean by this?
3. Why did Tompkins change her methods of teaching? How would you describe her methods?

REFERENCES

Bruner, J. (1960). *The process of education.* New York: Vintage.

Dow, P. (1991). *Schoolhouse politics: Lessons from the Sputnik era.* Cambridge, MA: Harvard University Press.

Gardner, H. (1983). *Frames of mind.* New York: Basic Books.

Gardner, H. (1989). *To open minds.* New York: Basic Books.

Gardner, H. (1991). *The unschooled mind.* New York: Basic Books.

Rose, M. (1989). *Lives on the boundary.* New York: Free Press.

Tompkins, J. (1996). *A life in school: What the teacher learned.* Reading, MA: Addison Wesley Longman.

Willis, P. (1977). *Learning to labor.* New York: Columbia University Press.

Lives on the Boundary

Students will float to the mark you set. I and the others in the vocational classes were bobbing in pretty shallow water. Vocational education has aimed at increasing the economic opportunities of students who do not do well in our schools. Some serious programs succeed in doing that, and through exceptional teachers—like Mr. Gross in *Horace's Compromise*—students learn to develop hypotheses and troubleshoot, reason through a problem, and communicate effectively—the true job skills. The vocational track, however, is most often a place for those who are just not making it, a dumping ground for the disaffected. There were a few teachers who worked hard at education; young Brother Slattery, for example, combined a stern voice with weekly quizzes to try to pass along to us a skeletal outline of world history. But mostly the teachers had no idea of how to engage the imaginations of us kids who were scuttling along the bottom of the pond.

And the teachers would have needed some inventiveness, for none of us was groomed for the classroom. It wasn't just that I didn't know things—didn't know how to simplify algebraic fractions, couldn't identify different kinds of clauses, bungled Spanish translations—but that I had developed various faulty and inadequate ways of doing algebra and making sense of Spanish. Worse yet, the years of defensive tuning out in elementary school had given me a way to escape quickly while seeming at least half alert. During my time in Voc. Ed., I developed further into a mediocre student and a somnambulant problem solver, and that affected the subjects I did have the wherewithal to handle; I detested Shakespeare; I got bored with history. My attention flitted here and there. I fooled around in class and read my books indifferently—the intellectual equivalent of playing with your food. I did what I had to do to get by and I did it with half a mind.

But I did learn things about people and eventually came into my own socially. I liked the guys in Voc. Ed. Growing up where I did, I understood and admired physical prowess, and there was an abundance of muscle here. There was Dave Snyder, a sprinter and halfback of true quality. Dave's ability and his quick wit gave him a natural appeal, and he was welcome in any clique, though he always kept a little independent. He enjoyed acting the fool and could care less about studies, but he possessed a certain maturity and never caused the faculty much trouble. It was a testament to his independence that he included me among his friends—I eventually went out for track, but I was no jock. Owing to the Latin alphabet and a dearth of *R*s and *S*s, Snyder sat behind Rose, and we started exchanging one-liners and became friends.

129

There was Ted Richard, a much-touted Little League pitcher. He was chunky and had a baby face and came to Our Lady of Mercy as a seasoned street fighter. Ted was quick to laugh and he had a loud, jolly laugh but when he got angry he'd smile a little smile, the kind that simply raises the corner of the mouth a quarter of an inch. For those who knew, it was an eerie signal. Those who didn't found themselves in big trouble, for Ted was very quick. He loved to carry on what we would come to call philosophical discussions: What is courage? Does God exist? He also loved words, enjoyed picking up big ones like *salubrious* and *equivocal* and using them in our conversations—laughing at himself as the word hit a chuckhole rolling off his tongue. Ted didn't do all that well in school—baseball and parties and testing the courage he'd speculated about took up his time. His textbooks were *Argosy* and *Field and Stream*, whatever newspapers he'd find on the bus stop—from the *Daily Worker* to pornography—conversations with uncles or hobos or businessmen he'd meet in a coffee shop, *The Old Man and the Sea*. With hindsight, I can see that Ted was developing into one of those rough-hewn intellectuals whose sources are a mix of the learned and the apocryphal, whose discussions are both assured and sad.

And then there was Ken Harvey. Ken was good-looking in a puffy way and had a full and oily ducktail and was a car enthusiast, a hodad. One day in religion class, he said the sentence that turned out to be one of the most memorable of the hundreds of thousands I heard in those Voc. Ed. years. We were talking about the parable of the talents, about achievement, working hard, doing the best you can, blah-blah-blah, when the teacher called on the restive Ken Harvey for an opinion. Ken thought about it, but just for a second, and said (with studied, minimal affect), "I just wanna be average." That woke me up. Average?! Who wants to be average? Then the athletes chimed in with the clichés that made you want to laryngectomize them, and the exchange became a platitudinous melee. At the time, I thought Ken's assertion was stupid, and I wrote him off. But his sentence has stayed with me all these years, and I think I am finally coming to understand it.

Ken Harvey was gasping for air. School can be a tremendously disorienting place. No matter how bad the school, you're going to encounter notions that don't fit with the assumptions and beliefs that you grew up with—maybe you'll hear these dissonant notions from teachers, maybe from the other students, and maybe you'll read them. You'll also be thrown in with all kinds of kids from all kinds of backgrounds, and that can be unsettling—this is especially true in places of rich ethnic and linguistic mix, like the L.A. basin. You'll see a handful of students far excel you in courses that sound exotic and that are only in the curriculum of the elite: French, physics, trigonometry. And all this is happening while you're trying to shape an identity; your body is changing, and your emotions are running wild. If you're a working-class kid in the vocational track, the options you'll have to deal with this will be constrained in certain ways: You're defined by your school as "slow"; you're placed in a curriculum that isn't designed to liberate you but to occupy you, or, if you're lucky, train you, though the training is for work the society does not esteem; other kids are picking up the cues from your school and your curriculum and interacting with you in particular ways. If you're a kid like Ted Richard, you turn your back on all this and let your mind roam where it may. But youngsters like Ted are rare. What Ken and so many others do is protect themselves from such suffocating madness by taking on with a vengeance the identity implied in the vocational track. Reject the confusion and frustration by openly defining yourself as the Common Joe. Champion the average. Rely on your own good sense. Fuck this bullshit. Bullshit, of course, is everything you—and the others—fear is beyond you: books, essays, tests, academic scrambling, complexity, scientific reasoning, philosophical inquiry.

The tragedy is that you have to twist the knife in your own gray matter to make this defense work. You'll have to shut down, have to reject intellectual stimuli or diffuse them with sarcasm, have to cultivate stupidity, have to convert boredom from a malady into a way of confronting the world. Keep your vocabulary simple, act stoned when you're not or act more stoned than you are, flaunt ignorance, materialize your dreams. It is a powerful and effective defense—it neutralizes the insult and the frustration of being a vocational kid and, when perfected, it drives teachers up the wall, a delightful secondary effect. But, like all strong magic, it exacts a price.

Excerpt

A Life in School

I'm not going to tell about the second half of the course. Its structure was the same as the first. Dominated by a fantastic trip, student-conceived and organized, to Somerset Place Plantation near Edenton, North Carolina, where we spent time doing work that slaves had done and wrote about it afterward. (I won't forget the gritty-salty taste of the corn bread we fried in fatback or how Erin looked, her blonde hair wrapped in a cotton turban.) Later in the motel we had a discussion about our own experiences of oppression that was as good a discussion as I've ever participated in. One student found it so uncomfortably intense, she had to leave the room twice; another burst out at the end: "It's a privilege to be in the same room with you guys!" and then he dove out the door. Talking it over later, the first student, the one who'd had to leave, said: "There were sixteen rooms in that room"—meaning there were sixteen different experiences of that discussion. At the time, though, the only one I wanted to acknowledge was mine.

And that, as Melville would have said, was the key to it all—my refusal to admit that there were sixteen different stories going on simultaneously. I was happy, so that was the only story I wanted to hear. Can you blame me? The course fulfilled old longings that were bound up with my love of Melville, and of *Moby-Dick*. The novel is a protest against cosmic injustice, a defiance of all constituted authority; it played into my ancient sense of victimization at the hands of power. *Beloved* did too, for that matter. So I loved our rebellion against grades and rules and conventional procedures, and I loved the group ethos. For both novels are also celebrations of communion and spoke to my longing to be rid of loneliness.

The student presentations on *Beloved* were antic, inventive. I saw no signs of disaffection, though they must have been there. We watched Alvin Ailey dance videos, listened to recordings of call-and-response songs like those the slaves had sung; some of us joined in. Michael sang "Every Time I Feel the Spirit" a capella, sitting on the floor with his back against the wall, and it was as if his voice was coming straight out of his chest. We read aloud passages from a flail made of paper strips that was passed around the room, each strip with a quote from the novel or a related text. We drew pictures of the box in Georgia where Paul D. had been incarcerated, no two pictures the same. And squeezed ourselves under the table and talked about what it was like to feel trapped, closed in. (Do you see what I mean? Do you see how great it was?) On another day, the students pulled down all the shades, pushed the table over to one side of the room, turned off the lights, lit candles, and we sat on the floor in a circle, reading aloud quotes from *Beloved* that had been passed out to us in advance.

I would like to stop writing right here. For now my throat clenches, and I have trouble focussing my attention. On the last two days of the course, the students read aloud their evaluations. I had no idea. I'd expected celebration, mutual congratulation, fond remembrance. What they did was criticize. Lack of structure, said New York Sarah. Unfocussed discussions, said Hilary; too much time spent planning and arranging things, said Bernard; too much time spent talking about evaluation, said two or three others; not enough disagreement, said someone else; it was utopian to think we could become a real community, said Sonya. There was tension between the norms of the institution and what we'd been trying to do, deliberated Erin. A few students said only positive things, but I barely heard them. I was devastated. For me the course had been a wondrous series of events; I began to wonder if I'd been living in a dreamworld. When it came my turn—last—with tears in my eyes and a quavery voice, I read my evaluation, full of pride and joy in the accomplishments of the class, and of my own happiness at what we'd been able to do together. And called for a vote. There was no time to talk about what happened. It was time for the grade. The students from the class after ours had been standing in the hall for ten minutes. The class split between an E (in our system, the equivalent of an A), and an E–. For an awful moment I thought I'd have to break the tie, but then Zarena switched her vote to an E, and it was over.

Another person might have taken it better, not been so sensitive. But the students had unknowingly found me out. Criticism was what I'd been trying to avoid all along, criticism of any kind—literary criticism, criticism of myself as a teacher, my having to criticize them. Why else go to the beach, work as slaves, light candles, and put on little plays if not to escape the steel trap of judgment? With creativity and imagination, I thought we could sidestep the need to measure and find fault, either with ourselves or with the texts we read. I wanted to be safe, "safe from the wolf's black jaw and the dull ass's hoof," as Ben Jonson said. I'd been criticized too early in my life and for too long. Now I wanted to be free from judgments and from judging, and I was offering that freedom to the students. But they were still learning how to criticize, and I had been trying to take that opportunity away from them.

They got me, all right, maybe in the deepest place. Taking criticism too much to heart, wanting to be free from it entirely. All along I'd known in the abstract that I taught from places inside me that needed healing. Well, here was my chance, in the aftermath of their evaluations, to forgive myself for fearing judgment so much, to forgive myself for wanting to escape. For wanting to be in school and out of school at the same time.

7

The Narrative of Hope

Many educators agree that humane, exciting, and liberating schooling cannot be achieved unless teachers maintain a profoundly optimistic and hopeful point of view. Hope is never enough, but transformation without hope, they insist, is doomed to failure. Stories that focus on hope emphasize that, although the barriers to reform are daunting and the unjust social conditions outside the school seem overpowering, part of the art and craft of teaching is creating open, critical, and participatory learning that leads to authentic change. As Herb Kohl points out, hope is a discipline. This discipline entails "the refusal to accept limits on what your students can learn and on what you, as a teacher, can do to facilitate learning" (p. 9). Disciplined, creative teachers embody hope when they stay in constant quest of a better way to teach, a more ingenious way to engage their students. Teachers who embody hope are in agreement with Paulo Freire when he says he cannot understand human existence "and the struggle needed to improve it, apart from hope and dream" (p. 8). It is in the acts of teaching and learning that those hopes and dreams are made meaningful and are at least partially realized.

Hope, in the narratives described here, is not a soft, mild, unobtrusive hope. It is a hope fueled by passion, rage, and indignation. It is a hope stimulated, ironically, by negligence, incompetence, and pervasive despair. These stories of hope acknowledge the many lives that have been tragically sacrificed on the altars of authoritarianism and institutional neglect. They also recall and honor the small ways in which great teaching and powerful human connections have contributed to the lives of children. Teaching and learning are a way to gain an informed, critical perspective on social and economic injustice and to hasten the process of extrication. Furthermore, as Garret Keizer notes, teachers who are hopeful take their craft seriously with their "eyes fixed on heaven" (p. 139). They hold the trivial aspects of their jobs in contempt. They are not called to form committees, organize bake sales, or line up buses. They are called to teach and to learn with their students. Their conviction that these things are meaningful and life enhancing is deepened when given their proper place in school. For Keizer, the bottom line is simple and nonnegotiable: "If it has to do with learning, I'm for it; if it's anything else, I want it dead" (p. 140). The narratives of Kohl, Freire, and Keizer emphasize learning and mutual growth. From this focus, more than anything else, they derive their undiminished hope.

HERB KOHL AND THE DISCIPLINE OF HOPE

The themes of shaping a new or reinvented self, of establishing a distinctive identity through teaching, of being open to what others have to teach, and of remaining stubbornly hopeful despite little evidence that progress is being made are all sensitively and eloquently explored in Herbert Kohl's book *I Won't Learn From You*. Three of the five essays in this book draw on Kohl's life; together they offer a rich perspective on the narrative of hope. These essays are "I won't learn from you," "The tattooed man: Confessions of a hopemonger," and "Creative maladjustment and the struggle for public education." They deal with three educational concepts that Kohl has coined and are much on his mind: not-learning, hopemongering, and creative maladjustment. Not-learning and creative maladjustment are similar in that they involve refusing to learn things or follow rules, or to persist in behaviors that are personally repugnant or are, in the estimation of the individual, in conflict with what it means to be human. Hopemongering, on the other hand, entails doing what one can to disseminate hopefulness and to act assertively for an improved tomorrow. All three of these notions are alike in that they are weapons in the struggle to be true to oneself and to communicate to the world what it means to be alive as fully as possible for oneself and for others. Arguably, only those in pursuit of self-renewal, of composing a distinctive personal identity, possess the confidence and conviction to act so boldly on behalf of their beliefs. Kohl's powerful sense of self dominates these essays and appears to be the result of many stimulating years of teaching, learning, and reflecting on the meaning and purpose of these experiences.

One of the great narratives of hope is Kohl's "The tattooed man: Confessions of a hopemonger." In this essay, Kohl argues that one of the chief functions of education is to teach students to imagine other possible worlds and to acquire the tools to act on those imaginings. Like John Dewey (see especially Dewey's 1939 essay titled "Creative democracy—The task before us"), Kohl retains a democratic faith in the capacity of all people to learn and to flourish when the right conditions are established and the right pedagogies employed.

Kohl's memories of growing up in the Bronx of the 1940s are similar in some ways to Mike Rose's recollections of his childhood in South Los Angeles. School offers no encouragement to dream, to imagine, or to fantasize. On their own and with the help of a few mentors, each boy discovers the ideas, books, and works of art that open up new worlds for them. For Kohl, finding an adventure story titled "The Tattooed Man" symbolizes his entry into a world "bigger, more valuable, and more accessible" than any he had ever imagined.

It is also the beginning of his realization that he can change his life "and live in different ways and in different places" (p. 36). Everything about this story—its language, exotic locales, mysterious names, and improbable plot developments—seizes Kohl's imagination, transforming him almost overnight into a young man with an unshakable ambition to create his own such tales. Reading, Kohl discovers, gives him access to other possible and more humane worlds, while storytelling empowers him to carve out spaces for children to follow their dreams. He comes to view his writing and his storytelling as gifts he can offer children to enable them to escape the everyday demands and unfulfilled promises of ordinary living. In other words, Kohl values writing as a means to engender and sustain hope.

Writing stimulates teachers to reflect on their own practices and envision teaching that is more inclusive, caring, and respectful. It nurtures hope that humane, thoughtful teaching can produce a positive difference in the world. Teachers who regularly record their thoughts to envision a more compassionate and empowering school for children are also the teachers likely to develop that strong sense of self, that sturdy professional identity, that is the first step toward educational transformation.

Like all of the protagonists of these narratives, Kohl's growth is helped by a few influential mentors. One of the most important is his Great Uncle Julius. A political radical in his native country of Austria, Julius escapes the oppression of his homeland to settle in the United States where he becomes a waiter in a delicatessen and a union organizer. Kohl fondly recalls his uncle selecting music for him to listen to in a backroom of the restaurant and taking time between customers to impart lessons about art, civil rights, and the promise of a more democratic society. Julius lends Herb a copy of Max Eastman's abridgment of Karl Marx's *Capital*, teaches him to play chess, and relates everything he shares to some higher moral vision. Kohl never forgets his uncle's teachings, cherishing particularly the memory of how joyfully he learned everything and how unwavering his uncle's faith was in his nephew's ability to master even the most difficult material. This faith instills in Kohl the confidence he will need later on to take risks in his own teaching and writing and sustains him through troubling periods of self-doubt. The example set by Uncle Julius undoubtedly inspires Kohl to become the committed hopemonger that he is today.

Another early teacher is also Kohl's first student. Robert has cerebral palsy, and virtually everyone believes him to be illiterate. Even Robert's father is unaware of his son's gifts and asks Kohl, when he is still in high school, to teach Robert how to read. Kohl quickly learns that Robert is an avid reader who is knowledgeable about many things, but his ability to communicate with others is badly hampered by his disability. Over time, Kohl learns far more from Robert than Robert learns from him. While Robert teaches Kohl many things he has learned from books, he also imparts lessons about character, perseverance, and maintaining a sense of humor even in the face of great challenges. The experience with Robert persists in Kohl's memory, reminding him that we are often too impatient to take the time to discern ability and wisdom hiding just below the surface of outward appearance.

As teachers, we must look closely and observe carefully, and when we do, we discover capacities to learn that have eluded us. Gradually, Kohl learns that "teaching well means encouraging the widest diversity and greatest depth of learning possible, and always being open to adding a new dimension or theme to what one is doing in order to tease the genius out of one more child. It consists, among all of its other roles, in providing students with opportunities to have encounters with learning that might transform their lives" (p. 04). Teaching, in this view, is nothing short of giving students space to discover their gifts and pursue their passions, to quest for the self that will bring meaning and value to their everyday experiences. It is predicated on the idea that everyone has something rich and vital to contribute to the community and that the real present is less important than the possible future ushered in by the "untapped brilliance and boundless energy of our students" (p. 86).

In the essay "I won't learn from you," Kohl recalls that, among his Jewish family living in the Bronx, most of his relatives spoke Yiddish. He resisted learning it, however, because his mother could not speak it, and he was reluctant to learn a language that would exclude his mother from conversations. He actively not-learned Yiddish, and despite the regrets he may harbor about this, he did so out of respect for his mother and because learning Yiddish at the time violated his sense of who he wanted to be. He has since developed the view that what we often interpret as failure or inability is in actuality a manifestation of not-learning. Unlike failure, not-learning "tends to strengthen the will, clarify one's definition of self, reinforce self-discipline and provide inner satisfaction" (p. 6). It is indeed an act of defiance, but almost never just for the sake of defiance but to maintain or more fully realize one's self-image or identity. Sometimes not-learning is a response to something regarded as pernicious or inhumane; at other times it is practiced to promote a cause or achieve a goal.

In the same essay, Kohl relates the story of Akmir. He is a classic not-learner who Kohl encounters while teaching at Columbia in the mid-1960s. He is also a student who becomes, like Robert, an important teacher for Kohl. Angry and defiant, Akmir disrupts a class Kohl is coteaching on Freud and immediately dismisses the lecture material as white man's psychology. Despite his abrasiveness, he is invited to join the class, which turns out to be a broad survey of counseling psychology. In subsequent class sessions, he criticizes the reading assignments, which he has painstakingly read and analyzed, for their racist language and white, middle-class interpretations of history and culture. Although at first offended by Akmir's attack, Kohl quickly learns that unlike himself and the other students, Akmir has actively not-learned a whole array of ideas and linguistic expressions that are widely accepted and practiced but that have powerful racist overtones. Akmir has also aggressively not-learned standard historical interpretations that underestimate the role of African Americans in history or de-emphasize their moral and political agency. Akmir's not-learning is far more than late-adolescent defiance; it is an expression of black pride and his own distinctive identity.

Although he dies at a tragically young age of a drug overdose, triggered perhaps by an insulting encounter with a school guidance counselor, Akmir's example provides an important opening for Kohl's growth as a teacher and human being. Never again does he underestimate the power of language to denigrate and discount the marginalized and disenfranchised. Nor does he ignore the depth of anger that often seethes below the surface of acts of not-learning.

Similarly, Kohl discovers that creative maladjustment, the refusal to adjust to racist practices or dehumanizing treatment, is usually carried out by people, like Akmir, who possess a principled moral vision and an unwavering commitment to a more compassionate world. Kohl adapts this concept from a speech that Martin Luther King, Jr., gave in 1958 in which he called upon people never to adjust themselves to injustice. King said in part: "I never intend to adjust myself to segregation and discrimination. I never intend to adjust myself to mob rule. I never intend to adjust myself to the tragic effects of the methods of physical violence and to tragic militarism. I call upon you to be maladjusted to such things" (1992, p. 33). Following King, Kohl admires those with the courage to creatively maladjust, because they are responding to injustice with an honesty and integrity that emerges from a deep knowledge of self. Creative maladjusters have a clear sense of purpose and confident understanding of their role in righting wrongs that strengthens them to act with a minimum of compromise and emboldens them to engage in conflict when there is no other way to realize their vision.

One way in which Kohl has observed teachers creatively maladjust is in rejecting hierarchical practices that sort, slot, or stigmatize students. These practices personalize student failures, rather than seeing them as, at least in part, the fault of an unjust system. The flip side of creative maladjustment is hopemongering, retaining faith in children and doing everything possible to help them develop their abilities and enjoy their gifts.

Together, hopemongering, not-learning, and creative maladjustment can be applied imaginatively by teachers to help their students become happier, more accomplished, and more fulfilled human beings. Children must be given the freedom to make a meaningful life for themselves, and teachers must use every tool at their disposal to keep this goal at the top of the educational agenda. But if teachers themselves have not been actively engaged in composing their own lives, in molding a distinctive and satisfying reinvented self, then they will probably not recognize the value in creating space for students to do so. As Kohl says, "Teaching, to come from the heart, must connect with the teacher's inner life and learning adventures. It is from that stance that one can develop judgment and sort through all of the programs and theories that 'experts' throw at teachers" (pp. 82–83). It is also out of the teacher's inner life that the essential purposes of education are distilled. Without a clear sense of purpose about oneself, attempts to identify and articulate education's mission will be greatly constrained. The quest for educational renewal is, in part, a quest for educational meaning, purpose, and hope. It is hard to say which comes first, but without one, the others are very hard to come by.

Recently, Herb Kohl has reflected again on the value of hopefulness in education by writing an ambitious autobiographical narrative of teaching that accentuates hope. In *The Discipline of Hope* (1998), Kohl argues that hope is the foundation for all good education, especially when the least privileged children are involved. He explains that promoting hope is less a form of imagining or reflecting and more a discipline, a craft that calls for careful planning and concrete action on the part of the teacher. Students who have been miseducated and neglected need to learn basic skills. They must learn history, literature, science, and mathematics, and they must be motivated to read, write, compute, and think. This means that activities must be devised that capture their imaginations and engage their minds, and a curriculum must be structured to build on their everyday experiences, giving them real chances for opportunities in later life.

When Kohl taught sixth-grade students in East Harlem, he found that career exploration was an essential way to raise his students' aspirations and spur their achievement. He invited adults from a wide range of occupations and professions to speak to his class and to share their paths to success. This simple innovation worked beautifully, but teachers who are hopeful cannot rely on any one strategy or any single methodology. They must provide a rich mix of activities and opportunities that respond to their students' particular needs and that build on their cognitive and emotional strengths. As Kohl indicates, "the source of hope lies in teaching itself, hard work requiring ingenuity, patience and a focus on what is effective with children." Thinking of himself as a craftsperson of learning, Kohl works at his teaching and collaborates with his students until what they are doing together is "both free and structured, spontaneous and planned, innovative and classical, fun and very difficult" (p. 10).

The first long section of *The Discipline of Hope* recounts Kohl's experiences teaching sixth-grade students in East Harlem in the early 1960s. His students are poorly prepared academically, but they are smart and wise to those with the insight to discern their ability. Kohl admits that he is poorly prepared to respond to his students and to teach them well. But he is open and flexible and eager to learn from them. He combines an interest in Greek mythology with a passion for writing, and, with the stories from his students' everyday lives in mind, he slowly builds a curriculum that is meaningful for them. Despite his students' lack of basic skills, he never doubts their capacity to learn and never puts limits on what they can do. The only limitations he acknowledges are his own—in his ability to teach and to keep their hearts and minds engaged. He is unrelentingly hopeful that, by arranging the learning environment effectively, there is no limit on his students' capacity to grow and learn.

The hope that Kohl imparts is not just faith in the ability of everyone to learn the most challenging material. It is founded on the conviction that even the most dilapidated neighborhood can be revitalized through thought and effort. By teaching the history of early civilizations and by exposing his students to the history of the American civil rights movement, Kohl communicates the message that people construct culture and that they can reconstruct it, too. He endeavors to help the children "imagine different, better worlds, to think about the city and their block as temporary, as made by people who could also remake them." He seeks to create a curriculum that teases his students' imaginations "into hope for themselves and for the communities in which they would later live" (p. 34).

Inspired by a variety of powerful teaching narratives, Kohl slowly grasps that learning, once unleashed, knows no bounds. Learning is, in some sense, a dangerous enterprise because it can lead to challenging the status quo and questioning widely accepted beliefs. It can channel destructive impulses in creative directions, but it also can raise individual and collective consciousness and fuel community rage over the entrenched injustices of the larger society. Kohl comes to appreciate that learning can also turn "defiant behavior into democratic self-governance" (p. 56) and can make angry, rejected children newly alert, incisive, and compassionate. Just as learning would have this kind of impact on many of his students, it would have a similar impact on Kohl himself, transforming him into an activist teacher who practices his calling as much on the streets as he does in the classroom.

In the mid-1960s, Kohl becomes disillusioned with classroom teaching in highly bureaucratized school systems. To lessen the grip of the bureaucracy, he establishes the Teachers and Writers Collaborative, which allows professional writers, poets, and artists to go into schools in New York City and to engage students in a wide variety of creative projects. Two great teacher narratives, Philip Lopate's *Being with Children* (1976) and Stephen O'Connor's *Will My Name Be Shouted Out?* (1996), are memoirs of these two writers' experiences in the Teachers and Writers Collaborative.

Despite his successes in New York, Kohl seeks work in a city with similar but more manageable problems and under freer, less inflexible conditions. Now a published author—his books *36 Children* (1967) and *The Open Classroom* (1969) are issued to much acclaim—Kohl looks for new venues and new possibilities. With the help of a generous grant from the Carnegie Foundation, he settles in Berkeley, California, and in tandem with Allen Kaprow, an eccentric stager of outlandish public events called "happenings," starts a storefront school named Other Ways. This name conveys the idea that the school is committed to exploring the widest possible variety of teaching and learning strategies. As Kohl notes, it is an acknowledgment that "if you follow a single rigid path in education you are going to lose too many students, have a long, lonely, boring journey, and end up on the margins of hope, wondering about the value of your work" (p. 180).

Although Kaprow is an enigma in that many of the events he stages seem to border on the ridiculous, he helps Kohl to stretch his understanding of teaching as "semi-improvisational performance" and to see education and learning in the broadest possible context. Rejecting all packaged curricula, Kohl embraces the notion that what is taught must emerge from the hopes and dreams of teachers and learners and that the materials used must be indigenous to the local community or integral to large cultural traditions and thus in the public domain. Kohl likens what he and Kaprow are trying to do to "messing about," in which no set program is promoted but in which the exploration of many different sources and materials is emphasized and the search for fresh, invigorating, productive questions is paramount (p. 182).

Kohl's use of "map poetry" is a good example of the sort of creative "messing about" he is intent upon. To investigate and almost literally get a "feel" for the geography and sociology of the city of Berkeley, Kohl and his students, most of whom are disillusioned enrollees from Berkeley High School, pore over maps of the area, cut them up into pieces, draw pictures on them, inscribe poetic lines over heavily traveled streets, and reconnect them into new and imaginative configurations. They analyze residential patterns on the maps using socio-economic, ethnic, and political criteria. They draw in public transportation routes and identify the areas most frequently used by pedestrians. They even make map sculptures and eventually turn the maps into aerodynamically sound paper airplanes. They take the maps in as many creative directions as they can until they are unable even to look at another map. But in the process they come to know Berkeley and each other in surprisingly profound ways.

Kohl enjoys many successes at Other Ways, but it is the semi-improvisational experiences with drop-in students like the ones doing the map poetry that give him the greatest satisfaction. Subsequently, a group of junior high school students who come to the storefront for a writing class especially challenge Kohl to make his teaching even more concrete, alive, and flexible. Choosing garbage as a first writing subject, the students produce poems in which Berkeley's enveloping debris is the central image. One gifted student named Jena writes an inventive poem that the other students are encouraged to critique. Jena is open to this criticism, though she objects to attacks on her personally. At first, her peers offer very general evaluative comments. Kohl pushes them, however, to translate these observations into specific constructive criticism that will help Jena revise her poem. In the ensuing discussion, one student notes that the ending of the poem is too abstract and predictable. Other students agree, which leads to a thoughtful exchange about Jena's original intentions and the kinds of words and images that make a poem powerful. Gradually, this group of students grows more comfortable in sharing their poetry and inviting critique, especially with those they trust. The students also become increasingly more daring with their poetry and discover ways to match verse to music.

The writing class leads to many other learning projects involving Super-8 film, photography, other forms of creative writing, and even philosophical study groups that focus especially on Jean-Paul Sartre's brand of existentialism. As Kohl notes, Other Ways becomes a substitute for public school, "a learning community in which everyone was a willing participant, where the lines between required curriculum and personal interest and between teachers, students, and community resources were blurred" (p. 193).

These experiments in teaching and learning lead to other wonderful experiences using theater as a means to motivate students and to excite them about reading, writing, and imaginative recreations of fictional and real events. Theater gives the students an opportunity to put their most outlandish ideas on stage. Kohl fondly recalls a girl named Rebecca who insists that she turn the role of Susan in a production of *Alice in Wonderland* into a major character who leads Alice through her many adventures. More significantly, Rebecca re-envisions Susan as a blues singer who wears high heels, is draped in an elegant dress, and croons a few songs at various points in the production. At first flabbergasted by Rebecca's suggestions, in the end Kohl encourages her ideas but also requires her to make her own arrangements for the blues band and for the proposed songs. Rebecca follows through resourcefully and ingeniously, resulting not only in a wonderful musical production but also in a more confident student who accepts few limits on her ability to innovate and achieve.

Perhaps Kohl's most important experience at Other Ways is the basic reading class he organizes for nine African American and Latino students. Building on everything he has learned about reading instruction from books and direct experience, Kohl begins by emulating Ashton-Warner's (1964) emphasis on key words. Each week, he invites each of the nine students to choose five key words that he or she wants all of the students to learn. This amounts to over 200 new words that all the students are expected to master each month. They take walks in the neighborhood, jotting down words from billboards and street signs and then using these lists to create still more words with similar prefixes or with rhyming endings. They write poetry, create crossword puzzles, analyze the texts they are assigned for evidence of racist language or discriminatory perspectives, and spend a great deal of time teaching each other. They do all of this inspired by Kohl's infectious enthusiasm and spurred on by his unwavering belief that there is no limit to how much they can learn. Kohl's overall approach is straightforward and common-sensical: treat the students with respect, never talk down to them, avoid the language and practices of remediation, be patient with these first-time readers, and regard all past failure as irrelevant. Although some of the students do not progress as far as Kohl hoped, many do quite well and a few perform spectacularly given their previous experience. In the final analysis, Kohl finds, teachers must learn to uncover the love of learning that is hidden in everyone. His experience shows again and again that "a teacher who has respect, a sense of humor, well-crafted material, and passion for the students' learning can free that love" (p. 215).

The work with the sixth graders and with the students and teachers of Other Ways is really only the beginning of a long career that Herb Kohl has pursued as teacher, learner, and writer. Many of his experiences are documented in *The Discipline of Hope*, and many others may be found in other books or are yet to be recorded. At the heart of all this work is the notion of hope and the idea that schools based on hope hold the promise for the future. Near the end of *The Discipline of Hope*, Kohl explains what he means by schools of hope:

[They are] places where children are honored and well served . . . They are safe and welcome places, comfortable environments that have a homey feel. They are places where children can work hard without being harassed, but also places where the joy of learning is expressed in the work of the children and in their sense of being part of a convivial learning community. They are places where the teachers and staff are delighted to work and are free to innovate while at the same time they are willing to take responsibility for their students' achievement. If you talk to children in schools like these, they express a pride of place and a sense of ownership that are also manifest in how the rest of the community regards the school. Parents feel welcome and often have a role in school governance. Community volunteers are abundant. (p. 332)

Safety, joy, learning, responsibility, and community are the themes that emerge most strongly from this discussion of schools of hope, and they are within reach of every school possessing the talent and the will to practice them. Perhaps most important of all is the notion that there are no limits: to what students can learn, to what teachers can teach, to how much we can grow together. At the conclusion of his book, Kohl says it best:

There's no end to the delights and joys of teaching, no limit to the challenges we will continue to face in order to serve children well, and no limit to the creativity and love adults can and should bring to helping children grow through teaching, which is at its heart the discipline of hope. (p. 337)

PAULO FREIRE AND THE PEDAGOGY OF HOPE

Another teacher narrative that emphasizes mutual growth, accentuates faith in the ability of people to overcome their apparent limits, and promotes hope as the foundation for all transforming education is Paulo Freire's *Pedagogy of Hope* (1994). The autobiographical reflections in this book focus on the events that lead up to and then follow from the writing of his classic 1970 work, *Pedagogy of the Oppressed*. Indeed, the subtitle of *Pedagogy of Hope* is "Reliving Pedagogy of the Oppressed." It is an opportunity for him to remember some of the defining events of his early life, to explore some of the essential elements of *Pedagogy of the Oppressed*, to revisit a few regrettable errors, and to consider for our own time, some 30 years after its initial publication, the continuing value and relevance of the theory he so painstakingly propounded in 1970.

Freire begins *Pedagogy of Hope* with a kind of meditation on both the power and limits of hope. He writes that part of the responsibility of the progressive educator is "to unveil opportunities for hope, no matter what the obstacles may be" (p. 9) and to envision a better tomorrow dedicated to the humanization of all people. At the same time, hope is not enough; action and struggle must accompany it. Although hope is a necessary foundation upon which human liberation and social transformation are achieved, they can never be fully realized until educators are willing to work actively for social change. Hope is essential. Without hope, there simply is no motivation to begin the process of praxis—reflecting and acting—that ultimately leads to emancipation.

Freire begins his story in 1947, the year he forgoes a career in law to pursue work in education and social science. He joins SESI, a Brazilian social service organization established after World War II to alleviate some of the worst social and economic problems facing postwar Brazil. Assigned to the Division of Education and Culture, Freire spends much of his time investigating relationships between schools and families in the area around the city of Recife. One of the things he discovers is that inner city parents are far more likely to use harsh, corporal punishment to discipline their children than are parents living on the fishing coast. The parents on the fishing coast clearly enjoy a more wide-open, less constraining physical environment than their urban counterparts. At one point, Freire even speculates that the coast's physical challenges may impose all of the discipline these parents feel they need. The harsh punishments employed by inner city parents to discipline their children, on the other hand, Freire attributes to the economic and social injustices that weigh so oppressively on everyday urban life. He even suggests that these parents feel "so completely subjected to the greater context of global society that they could do nothing but reproduce the authoritarian ideology" (p. 20). For these urban parents, in other words, there seems to be virtually no hope.

While working for SESI, Freire spends much of his time speaking to groups of working-class parents about the results and implications of his study regarding the different ways in which families discipline their children. He presents long, involved speeches to these groups, filled with the vocabulary familiar to academics. Rarely does he leave much time for interaction with his audience. At one of these sessions, some time is left for discussion and what one parent has to say leaves an indelible impression. He comments first somewhat sarcastically on the fine words Freire has spoken and then inquires whether Freire has ever visited any of their homes. He describes the overcrowded conditions, the lack of decent facilities, and the absence of the most basic resources that are taken for granted by middle-class observers like Freire. He then goes on to offer what he imagines is an accurate description of Freire's own comfortable domicile: the separate bedroom for his three daughters and two sons, the bathroom with indoor plumbing, the kitchen with up-to-date appliances, even a room for a live-in maid. Everything, as it turns out, is perfectly consistent with Freire's own reality. The parent concludes by noting that, although Freire is tired at the end of the day from mental exertion, the working-class people before him are so physically exhausted when their 12-hour workday ends, they lack the energy to act on the mounting rage and pain they feel. Although they labor all day and are good, reliable workers, their compensation is not nearly enough to sustain a healthy family.

For Freire this is a transformative experience. He learns volumes from a modest member of the working class who has mastered what Freire calls class knowledge. It is an experience that remains vivid as he writes *Pedagogy of the Oppressed*. It teaches him that educators must have a deep knowledge of the working class world, and that it is only through a concrete knowledge of this world that hope for changing it can be engendered.

Another way in which Freire learns to engender hope is through intense reflection on the origins of his own moods and feelings. As a young man, he finds that he falls into deep depressions for long periods. To alleviate these feelings or to lighten their effects, he reflects on the events that seem to precipitate them. As Freire says, he begins to take his depression "as an object of curiosity and investigation" (p. 28). His depressions tend to come on, it turns out, during extended periods of rain, accompanied by dark, leaden clouds and wet, muddy ground. He returns to the home of his youth on such a day and remembers how often the rain and clouds hovered over his neighborhood and how closely he associates them with the death of his father, the encroaching senility of his mother, the breakdown of the family of his boyhood. This is a hard realization, but by probing the archeology of his pain, Freire frees himself of these feelings of despair. In a very real sense, he can say of himself, "I was educating my hope" (p. 29).

In 1964, in the wake of a brutal coup d'état imposed by a military dictatorship, Freire is exiled from Brazil for his political activism. He loves Brazil, which makes the adjustment to a new land—in this case Chile—especially difficult. But he also knows that his longing for Brazil and all the things he associates with his homeland must be balanced against the opportunities presented by his new situation. He must not let his longing to return blunt his critical view of Brazil's adverse conditions, the very conditions that caused him to be an activist in the first place. He thus arrives in Chile with his whole self intact—passionate, longing, sad, dreaming, critical, and very hopeful—eager to understand class conditions in Chile and to have some sort of impact on them.

He witnesses and participates in many political discussions during the late 1960s in Chile and is often impressed by the active involvement of the peasants and the working class in analyzing their political and social situation. The dialogues they engage in seem to signal a radical shift from silence to shared, constructed knowing and express a new appreciation for the ways in which critical discourse about their world can lead to a remaking of that world. Freire sees these dialogues as nothing less than one of the central tasks of democratic popular education, of a pedagogy of hope:

> "that of enabling popular classes to develop their language: not the authoritarian, sectarian gobbledygook of 'educators,' but their own language—which, emerging from and returning upon their reality, sketches out the conjectures, the designs, the anticipations of their new world" (p. 39).

It is in Chile, in exile from his native land, that Freire comes to understand and to practice respect and appreciation for other cultures, other languages, and other ways. Here he articulates the importance of creating educational projects that build on indigenous cultural elements and that avoid, at all costs, "cultural invasion"—a concept he explores at length in *Pedagogy of the Oppressed* (see Chapter 4) and by which he means imposing, without dialogue, outside, alien perspectives. In Chile Freire also recognizes, probably for the first time, that learners, or what he calls *educands*, must see themselves as active inquirers, eager truth-seekers, not passive recipients of the educator's knowledge. From these experiences and realizations emerge his critique of what he calls "banking education." Freire ingeniously likens traditional didactic education to teaching that is nothing more than making knowledge deposits in the brains of inert, mindless students. In banking education, there is no interaction between educators and educands. "The teacher knows everything and the students know nothing; the teacher talks and the students listen—meekly; the teacher is the Subject of the learning process while the pupils are mere objects" (1970, p. 59). This critique leads to the creation of an alternative educational process in which Freire envisions teachers and students learning dialogically and collaboratively to foster emancipation and humanization. Conceptualizing this alternative process is the focus of Freire's great work, *Pedagogy of the Oppressed.*

Freire recalls that, for at least a year preceding the writing of *Pedagogy of the Oppressed,* he talked through most of its key ideas. He refers to this, revealingly, as the "oral period" of *Pedagogy of the Oppressed.* Greeting virtually everyone he encounters with a barrage of issues, concepts, and questions, Freire finds that by speaking about these ideas with friends, colleagues, visiting scholars, and interested audiences, he can test his ideas, recreate them, give "them second birth" (p. 53). He carries a notebook with him everywhere and jots down phrases, scraps of information, important vocabulary to be recorded subsequently on the note cards that are the chief organizing device for this text. In the summer of 1967 at his adopted home in Santiago, Chile, in a great flurry of activity and inspiration, Freire writes the first three chapters of his book. Then, following the advice of a friend, he locks the manuscript away in a drawer and does not return to it again for more than 2 months. Upon rereading it, he revises what he has written only slightly, but now has the perspective to see more clearly that a final, fourth chapter must be written to reemphasize leading themes and to draw a stronger contrast between dialogical and anti-dialogical education. With the four chapters intact, *Pedagogy of the Oppressed,* which Freire wrote in Portuguese, is first published in English in 1970 and, within a short period of time, is translated and published in many other languages. It is not, however, issued in politically torn Brazil in the original Portuguese until 1975.

To develop further the theme of hopefulness, Freire takes up some of the early criticisms of his original text and his responses to them. North American women, even those who find the book transforming, almost immediately criticize Freire for his sexist language, for his tendency to rely exclusively on male pronouns or to use masculine references such as "men" to stand for both "men and women." His first reaction is defensive and then to attribute such linguistic practices to his "conditioning by an authoritarian, sexist ideology" (p. 66). But the more he reflects on these linguistic habits, the more he realizes how excluding they must feel to women, particularly when he observes how resistant male audiences are to language use that is explicitly feminine. In *Pedagogy of Hope*, Freire condemns all sexist language and practice, declaring sexism a remnant of colonialism, incompatible with the goal of humanization, and antithetical to the practices of progressive pedagogy. Growing out of his claim that speaking the truth and transforming the world are part of the same unified process, Freire affirms that "The rejection of a sexist ideology, which necessarily involves the re-creation of language, is part of the possible dream of a change of the world" (p. 67).

Freire also takes up the criticism that his writing is too inaccessible to the ordinary reader, too alien to the popular mind. Although he enthusiastically embraces the notion that even the most scholarly writing should strive to be aesthetically pleasing and theoretically rigorous, he rejects the charge that his rhetoric is excessively difficult. He argues instead that reading, especially reading on serious subjects, should be difficult, should require effort. Like learning in general, Freire affirms, reading is an exacting, even painful activity, and the only way to make future reading somewhat less daunting is to keep reading deeply and conscientiously extracting defensible meanings.

One of the most important pedagogical themes that Freire repeats is the responsibility of educators both to honor the lived experience of their students and to move beyond it, methodically using that lived experience as a springboard for a deeper and more critical perspective on the world. Just as he argues that reflection without action and action without reflection are both flawed and limited, so Freire argues that popular knowledge must be both respected and subject to criticism. Through this process, teachers learn what students already know and thereby establish a foundation for greater theoretical sophistication and more generalizable accounts of the ways in which the system operates. Freire dwells on this point because it is one of the least understood in his entire theory. But, like so many of his theoretical claims, his position can best be described as a golden mean between two extremes. He summarily rejects the notion of putting popular knowledge and experience on a pedestal, where it remains untouched by critique and theoretical inquiry. But he is just as adamant about not bypassing the lived experience of learners to accelerate their education and so to expedite the process of informing their ignorance.

At times, even Freire's view seems simplistically linear. A caricature of what he sometimes seems to be saying is first determine what the learners know and then use this information to broaden their horizons. But a more nuanced view would be that popular knowledge and erudite knowledge, local knowledge and holistic knowledge, are constantly intermingled and woven together into an increasingly complex and multifaceted spiral. As Freire writes in *Pedagogy of Hope*: "Just as it is a mistake to get stuck in the local, losing our vision of the whole, so also it is a mistake to waft above the whole, renouncing any reference to the local whence the whole has emerged" (p. 87). It turns out, not surprisingly, that although this commitment to staking out a position between two extremes has resulted in frequent misinterpretation, it is in striving to honor both the popular and scholarly, the part and whole, that Freire makes one of his most lasting and hopeful contributions to pedagogical theory. While he follows in a long line of distinguished educators, including Dewey and Piaget, his assertion that the lives of ordinary people must form the basis for transformation and growth is a particularly powerful reminder of the deepening tension between an unworthy present and a more hopeful future to be erected on the foundation of everyday, lived experience.

In mediating between lived experience and academic knowledge, in appreciating the value of both concrete reality and abstract theorizing, Freire embraces dialogue as the activity and the standpoint most likely to bridge extremes and produce a new synthesis. As Freire says, dialogue can "mark the democratic position" between teachers and students, between scholars and practitioners. Dialogue does not make these conversational partners the same. Rather it allows each to "not only retain their identity, but actively defend it, and thus grow together" (p. 117). Dialogue, at its best, is a challenging, rigorous, content-rich exchange of positions and ideas. It does not preclude an occasional lecture by the teacher, nor does it disallow an extended discourse by anyone in the group with knowledge and passion to share about the subject matter. Nevertheless, dialogue must be an opportunity for everyone "to open up to the thinking of others" (p. 119), to explore new understandings and new possibilities, and to see every person in the group as both a potential learner and a potential teacher. Such opportunities fuel hope, because all are seen as partners in conceptualizing and bringing about a better tomorrow.

Dialogue also can produce the unity in diversity that Freire has often claimed must precede social transformation. In *Pedagogy of Hope*, he tells the story of the first time he spoke before a group about this issue. Attending a seminar in Chicago, he had just suffered the most humiliating kind of discrimination in a local restaurant. Blatantly ignored by every waiter in the place, he finally exits in a blind fury, feeling helpless and hungry as he prepares hurriedly for the seminar, which is about to begin. The large group assembled is extremely diverse and when it comes time to divide into smaller groups, African Americans, Indians, Chicanos, and others request that they be permitted to form groups according to ethnicity. Noting that the white group says nothing, Freire is struck by how guilt strains the relations of whites with all of the other groups. Rejecting such guilt, such paternalism, as counter-productive and anti-dialogic, Freire calls instead for discussion and debate. Part of the process of finding new allies, he insists, is in openly disagreeing with people of all different kinds, and in so doing, expressing warmth, solidarity, and even love for one another. It is not a weak, sentimental love, however, but an "armed," embattled, challenging love. Most important of all, Freire concludes:

> The so-called minorities, for example, need to realize that, when all is said and done, they are the majority. The path to their self-acceptance as the majority lies in concentrating on the similarities among them-

selves, and not only the differences, and thus creating unity in diversity, apart from which I fail to see how they can improve themselves, or even build themselves a substantial, radical democracy. (p. 153)

That task of creating unity in diversity, of marking out similarities along with differences, is most effectively achieved, affirms Freire, through a form of dialogue that gratefully includes every point of view and every diverse perspective, but in the process also creates a bond between people that transcends individual differences. Each culture must be respected for being true to itself, as long as no one culture promotes itself as being superior to any other. But opportunities for these cultures to grow together must also be protected. Open, rich, even fierce dialogue is a powerful way to foster such mutual growth. In the end, dialogue is an irreplaceable way to give birth to new possibilities and new hope.

In the last analysis, Freire's story, his *Pedagogy of Hope*, honors the give and take of wonderful ideas, underscores the drive to become more fully human by forging closer ties with others, and emphasizes the obligation to make a better world through collective thought and action. That better world, that utopian vision, cannot be imagined without a foundation of hope, but it also cannot be fostered without great teachers who respect their students and the knowledge they have acquired. These great teachers burn to take their students still higher, even as they remain open to all that these students also have to teach. This eternal interplay of learning and teaching, practice and theory, experience and scholarship goes to the heart of great education, perhaps even to the heart of making a great life. It certainly underlies much of the power of Paulo Freire's story. Without a pedagogy of hope, there is no educational renewal, no chance for either individual or social transformation. With it, humanization and liberation are possible. It takes vision and courage, knowledge and will to make it so. To be a great teacher is to be, first of all, an unembarrassed peddler of hope.

GARRET KEIZER AND THE IMPERATIVE OF HOPE

Still another narrative of hope is Garret Keizer's *No Place but Here*. Keizer's tale is a modest one of his 7 years teaching high school English in rural Vermont. It is the only place he has ever practiced this most difficult of crafts. Over time he has learned it well, but he remains humble enough to appreciate how much more he must master and how much more he will never know, despite his best efforts.

The region in which he teaches is called the Northeast Kingdom, bordered by New Hampshire to the east and Quebec, Canada, to the north. It is a cold, beautiful, and solitary land. According to Keizer, its population is quite diverse. It is inhabited not just by native farmers, but also by French Canadian immigrants who often maintain bilingual households, counterculture types escaping the rush of big city living, professionals willing to forgo six-figure salaries for the pleasures of a simpler, more communal existence, and an assortment of others who yearn for the serenity and space that the Northeast Kingdom affords.

Because it is so isolated, Keizer insists that one of his first priorities as a teacher is to expose his students to the wider world and to give them the confidence they will need to negotiate that world successfully, if that is what they choose to do. He learns quickly, however, not to assume that spurring students to escape the Northeast Kingdom of Vermont is necessarily part of the purpose of the education he provides. Although this may be an outcome, he is just as open to the possibility that, in learning about the wider world, the students may acquire a more profound, even reverent relationship to their native land that convinces them that staying put is a fine, even honorable choice.

As a teacher, Keizer is nothing if not hopeful and confident that he can make a difference and that his students can learn and appreciate even the most challenging literature. Their first reaction to a new challenge may be to complain and protest, but as Keizer notes: "they are only reacting as they have been taught to react by a few moronic TV sitcoms which they themselves but half enjoy" (p. 9).

He regularly assigns *Antigone*, the *Odyssey*, *Macbeth*, and Thomas Hardy's *Return of the Native*. He knows that the language is difficult for his students, that the settings of these works are strange and disorienting, and that the distance between then and now gapes before them. But almost invariably the excellence of this literature wins the students over, producing in them "mature commitment, unfeigned enjoyment and surprising insight" (p. 9).

Even his most academically limited students benefit when genuine challenges are posed to them. Keizer works with a small group of boys who have special problems in reading and writing. Rather than resorting to remediation, Keizer, like Herb Kohl, raises the academic bar even higher and proposes that they all write a book together. The result is *Born to Run*, a tale of high schoolers and their souped-up cars that wins acclaim from the student body and the local newspaper. The boys even win an all-school award at the end of the year. For Keizer, the moral is to have high hopes, to give students something challenging, meaningful, and purposeful to do, preferably something for which they can receive affirmation and recognition. When these conditions are in place, limits of course remain, but surprises also abound. Students thought to be unable will reach heights never predicted for them.

Keizer also writes admiringly of the remarkable sacrifices adolescents are prepared to make, despite their unearned reputation for apathy and selfishness, to help members of their own community. With a colleague, Keizer founds SALT, Students and Adults Learning Together, an organization designed to capitalize on the students' energy and skills to assist adults in overcoming illiteracy. Although the group runs into unavoidable resistance and is unable to follow through on its plans, Keizer is impressed that so many students are willing to spend large blocks of leisure time tutoring their neighbors without a hint of the usual incentives: grades, glory, or greenbacks. Certain that most young people are more compassionate and honorable than anyone gives them credit for, Keizer asserts: "They believe in a promised land. And if we are not inclined to believe in something like the same thing our every effort to help them amounts to a betrayal" (p. 16).

Although the story Keizer tells is sometimes tinged with sadness, it is almost always brimming with hope as well. It is a hope that stands proudly in opposition to conventionality and holds firm against social conformity. It is also a hope that reaches out to the little noted and rarely courted.

Take the FFA, the Future Farmers of America, a group that would ordinarily be a prime target for ridicule and derision. Keizer will not tolerate such scorn. Instead he finds reasons to acclaim and applaud the FFA. He recalls with emotion the night he served as judge of the FFA's Creed Speaking Contest, an important competition in which young people recite the FFA creed from memory with as much expression and poise as they can muster. One of the competitors that night is a boy with severe cerebral palsy who bravely recites the creed but does so with enormous difficulty and limited articulation. Although the judges choose not to award the boy with a prize, Keizer subsequently marvels not only at the boy's amazing courage, but also at the FFA's capacity to create an atmosphere in their meetings that is so respectful and encouraging that the boy feels invited to attempt a task most others would have regarded as hopeless. Apparently, for the FFA, hope really does spring eternal.

Keizer goes on to praise the FFA as the school activity that Socrates, if he visited the school, would most readily understand and appreciate. Not only would he recognize and feel at home with the symbolism of the FFA, much of it harking back to the mythology of ancient Greece, he would have regarded its well-run meetings that make strict use of parliamentary procedure as a model of self-governance. He also would have admired the FFA's refusal to dichotomize the academic and the vocational, or the scholastic and the athletic, and "he would have found it worthy of a philosopher's contemplation that the same organization was devoted to arm wrestling, declaiming speeches, pressing cider, and mowing the town cemeteries with equal enthusiasm" (p. 22). Keizer writes that agriculture made civilization possible and that, if its decline is allowed to go unchecked, it could spell disaster for the country. The FFA not only stands for a hopeful future in which farmers continue to support the national economy and steer national policy, it also represents a vision of integrated, holistic education that can serve ably as a model for many of our contemporary schools.

Keizer also embraces courtesy, despite its unpopularity and outdatedness, as a necessary foundation for sound education. By courtesy, though, he does not primarily mean etiquette, which he associates with aesthetics. Courtesy, for him, is chiefly a moral concern that affirms everyone's right to be and to follow her or his own path. In the main, he thinks his students are courteous people and is heartened when they reach out to help him and others in simple but meaningful ways. Such acts reinforce his hope for the future and restore his faith—a faith that he believes all teachers must have—in his students' fundamental decency.

He worries, however, about two areas in which his students seem to fall short with respect to courtesy. The first has to do with failing to respect the privacy of others. Too often, Keizer finds that students insist on knowing everything about the background of a peer who has been misbehaving or is having difficulty maintaining an adequate academic record. At other times, they seem almost obsessed with the private lives of their teachers and are willing to do anything to pry further. Keizer attributes this attitude to a society that seems to know no limits in protecting the so-called right to know, but does little to protect the equally important and rapidly eroding right of privacy.

The second area in which students can show more courtesy concerns the public space that people share. Keizer is especially indignant about students who pollute public silence with excessive noise, undermine the beauty of the natural landscape with litter, and diminish the human-made environment through vandalism. He recalls visiting a beautiful public park where an attractive fountain at the park's center is stuffed with garbage and debris. Ashamed of such senseless desecration, Keizer, in a somewhat unexpected way, uses the fountain as a metaphor for two ways that teachers regard their students. Teachers may view their students as the very culprits who mindlessly spoil public space, but they also can see them as the fountain itself, daily victims of small acts of desecration, slowly but steadily stripped of their self-esteem and identity.

What does all this imply for students, schools, the practice of courtesy, and the maintenance of hope? Keizer writes that as educators:

> We need to tell ourselves over and over that school is the first place where many students will encounter both a sense of public domain and a sense of personal worth. We need to tell our students . . . that each of them is sacred and that they have just walked into a sacred place. That means that no one is mocked, no one is ignored, no one's right to learn or to work fruitfully and with dignity is violated or abridged. It means that there are no nerds, no queers, and no retards . . . no untouchable people. We don't 'make an effort' to be courteous; we simply are. (pp. 48–49)

Even when it comes to articulating and practicing a philosophy of education, Keizer's position is unconventional. In the chapter titled "Skylla and Kharybdis," he begins by admitting that most students and parents in his Vermont community see school chiefly as preparation for getting a good job. He does not disparage this view. Rather, he understands and appreciates it as the claim of people who often lack education and who, as a result, have worked tirelessly throughout their lives with little to show for it monetarily. They have a right to expect that a good education will enhance their children's vocational and financial prospects.

But Keizer also warns, "if the real world is as full of injustice, waste, and woe as it appears to be, and school has no other purpose than to prepare young people to man or woman the machinery of the real world, then schools are pernicious institutions. They serve to perpetuate rather than remedy evils" (p. 68). This is strong stuff. Keizer raises in a razor sharp manner an age-old educational dilemma: how to prepare students for the world as it is and, at the same time, prepare them just as avidly to change the world into something far more worthy of human beings at their best. As Keizer says, a really good school is "realistic and utopian. It prepares students to survive the real world, and it prepares them to make a more humane world" (p. 69).

As that chapter unfolds, Keizer engages in a kind of running conversation with himself. The real world is important and necessary, and we do our students a disservice when we do not prepare them effectively to perform well in it. But the utopian Keizer, the hopemongering Keizer, the Keizer who dreams of a society whose citizens embrace complexity and appreciate ambiguity and strive to make a more just and loving community, this Keizer must also have his due. In achieving a reasonable balance between the real and ideal, the present and a more hopeful and creative future, teachers can reclaim schools that matter, now and for a very long time to come.

Striving to honor both the real and the ideal is an ongoing struggle. For Keizer, striving to find places in his teaching for both criticism and wonder is a joy and goes to the heart of transformative learning. Keizer opens the chapter titled "Criticism and Wonder" by describing how he remembers learning the facts of life—a story he often tells to introduce his students to a unit on mythology. In 1955 when Garret was 3 years old and he and his father were sitting in a 1955 Chevrolet anticipating the birth of Garret's brother, Garret asks his father where babies come from. Preoccupied with the condition of his wife and new child, his father answers that angels bring babies down from heaven. Satisfied for a while, Garret's curiosity eventually leads to other questions. For instance, why are babies brought to hospitals if angels deliver them and what does a womb have to do with this whole process? When Garret's father explains that babies grow from an egg inside a woman's body, other questions arise about the role that the father plays in making a baby. When it is further explained that the father gives the mother a seed to add to her egg, new, even more troubling concerns arise about the source of the man's seed. Finally, after more discussion and more questions, Keizer's father patiently explains the whole reproductive process with as much detail, sophistication, and frankness as his own young son can understand. Then, Keizer likes to say, he recently had his own child and he finally found out which version of where babies come from is true: angels or eggs and seeds. He pauses . . . and then adds that both versions are true. He knows that the eggs and seeds story is true because he impregnated his wife just as his father had described and nine months later his wife birthed a child. But, he adds, when his own baby was born and he cut the umbilical cord and first looked into his child's eyes, the moment was so special and sacred and wonderful that *angels* is the only word he had to describe what he felt.

For Keizer, the story is a reminder that, as important as questioning and criticism and inquiry are, they must be balanced by an equally strong commitment to experiencing feelings of wonder, awe, and amazement. Essential components of being human are the capacity to wonder and the capacity to deliberate and to criticize. An educational system that neglects feelings of awe, wonderment, and reverence does so at its peril in the same way that schools that fail to teach their students to think are destined for oblivion.

Like all excellent storytelling about teaching, Keizer's tale meets the criteria Thomas Barone (1992) establishes for what he calls a narrative of "enhanced professionalism." First, Keizer's story is accessible and engaging for most readers, regardless of their background. Second, it is compelling, gripping readers with the posing of a familiar problem and then resolving it with a sense of "wearied elation" in the end. Third, it is morally persuasive, very possibly resulting in the "reconstruction of a portion of the reader's value system" (p. 20). Barone explains the moral power of great stories, an explanation that is quite close to the experience people often have while reading Keizer. Good stories "enable readers to gaze in fresh astonishment upon a part of their world they thought they had already seen. They also allow readers to be better acquainted with people they thought they had already known" (p. 20). Underlying Keizer's story is the contrast between the protagonist who refuses to stop until he both understands and appreciates something and the common practice in schools where superficial rationality and negotiated mediocrity prevail.

CONCLUSION

Kohl, Freire, and Keizer remain hopeful, when learners have the support and encouragement to question and criticize their peers, their teachers, their texts, and their community and when they are also granted occasions to be awestruck by the beauty of their natural surroundings and the power of the human mind. For all three of them, this hope is not just conceptual or ideological. It is hard, practical, and angry. Near the end of his story, Keizer asserts, "we will never improve schools unless we restructure society" (p. 156). He appeals to his colleagues and his fellow citizens to be hopeful for schools and society, but he argues as well that it must be a pointed, even embattled hope. It is a hope, like Freire's, which grows out of love, is intolerant of both injustice and poverty, and fights unyieldingly for education that is fair, inclusive, and audacious. Finally, it is a hope that rejects all limits on learning, affirms everyone's capacity to grow, and demands that no question go unasked and no issue be sidestepped. The more willing we are as educators to take up the most difficult challenges, to explore the most sensitive subjects, and to raise the most daring questions, the greater will be our hope that the future for our students and our students' children will be a bright one.

In summary, we conclude that *hopeful teachers*:

> *Maintain fierce and uncompromising commitments to learners, to more creative and adventurous schools, and to more inclusive and generous communities.*
>
> *Practice a democratic faith that, under the right pedagogical conditions, all learners are highly capable and can respond to virtually any academic challenge.*
>
> *Painstakingly instruct criticism and consistently instill wonder.*
>
> *Believe that hope is a discipline that demands hard work, incisive critique, and committed caring.*
>
> *Cannot conceive of progressive teaching or social change without a foundation in hope.*

STUDY QUESTIONS

Kohl

1. Why does Herb Kohl call himself a "hopemonger"? How should teachers promote hope, in Kohl's view?
2. What do you imagine Kohl believes are the characteristics of a good teacher?
3. What values are expressed in Kohl's concepts of "not-learning" and "creative maladjustment"? Have you ever known someone who exemplified these concepts?

Freire

1. What does "banking education" mean?
2. Why does Paulo Freire value "popular knowledge" in the classroom?
3. What are the purposes of dialogue in education, according to Freire?

Keizer

1. Garret Keizer taught in rural Vermont. What are the educational issues he finds in this setting?
2. Why does Keizer use classical literature in his teaching?
3. Like so many authors in this book, Keizer views teaching as a vocation or calling. What are the implications of this view for what and how he teaches?

REFERENCES

Ashton-Warner, S. (1964). *Teacher.* New York: Bantam Books.

Barone, T. (1992). A narrative of enhanced professionalism: Educational researchers and popular storybooks about school people. *Educational Researcher, 21*(8), 15–24.

Dewey, J. (1955). Creative democracy—The task before us. In I. Edman (Ed.), *John Dewey: His contribution to the American tradition* (pp. 308–315). New York: Bobbs Merrill.

Freire, P. (1970). *Pedagogy of the oppressed.* New York: Seabury Press.

Freire, P. (1994). *Pedagogy of hope.* New York: Continuum.

Keizer, G. (1988). *No place but here.* New York: Penguin.

King, M. L. (1992). The power of non-violence. In *I have a dream: Writings and speeches that changed the world* (pp. 29–33). New York: Harper Collins.

Kohl, H. (1967). *36 Children.* New York: New American Library.

Kohl, H. (1969). *The open classroom.* New York: Vintage Books.

Kohl, H. (1994). *"I won't learn from you."* New York: The New Press.

Kohl, H. (1998). *The discipline of hope.* New York: Simon & Schuster.

Lopate, P. (1976). *Being with children.* New York: Poseidon Press.

O'Connor, S. (1996). *Will my name be shouted out?* New York: Simon and Schuster.

No Place But Here

*From NO PLACE BUT HERE by Garret Keizer.
Garret Keizer pp. 77–80 of No Place But Here © 1988
by Garret Keizer, by permission of the University
Press of New England.*

Sometimes as a way of introducing mythology, and of illustrating why it is not accurate to think of myth as naïve science, I tell my classes how I came to know the facts of life. Young people listen carefully to a talk like that. There's the rare chance they may be missing a fact or two.

One evening just after sunset, I begin, I was sitting in the back seat of a 1955 Chevrolet (full attention from audience—How old was Keizer in '55?— Who else was alive back then?—Did they do it in cars?) parked at the Paterson General Hospital in New Jersey. My father and my grandmother were in the front seat. I was three years old. (Audience relaxes—this'll be a long one.) We were there because my mother was inside having my brother, Henry, though at the time, of course, I didn't know that the baby was going to be a brother or that it would be named Henry if it was. I did know that a baby was on its way, and I asked my father, as I'm sure that all of you have by this time asked your parents: Where do babies come from?

My father, who probably didn't need to be answering such questions at that particular time, told me that the angels bring the babies down from heaven.

Wise guy in back: "You mean they don't?"

"Well, stay tuned and you'll find out."

I'm not sure to what extent I'm remembering that moment accurately, and to what extent it's been colored by the dreams I've had since and by the mind's tendency to revise memories, but when I recall my father's answer I am turning to look out the car window at the black skyline of the city, and there are still just a few red streaks from the sunset, and I imagine the angels my father has just told me about. They're giants. They stand on the city. All I can see are their legs; the tops of their thighs are lost in the clouds. Maybe because it is evening, or maybe because we are in a city where there are many dark-skinned people, the angel legs are all black. And I hear singing—a choir of deep voices singing one note, something like "au," very strong and sonorous. Suddenly, two long black arms come out of the sky, and cradled in their massive hands, swinging gently, lower and lower over Paterson, New Jersey, is a little white baby, our baby.

As time went on, I had some questions for my father: Why did the angels bring babies to hospitals? Wouldn't home be more convenient or church more appropriate? Why did only mothers "have them"? What's a womb? Things of that nature. My father then told me that babies grow from an egg inside a mother's stomach, which seemed a lot less credible than what he had told me before, except that it fitted the facts as I knew them, so I accepted it. But soon there were other problems. For instance, if the baby comes from the mother, why do fathers say that children are their own flesh and blood? Wouldn't they only be a mother's flesh and blood? So my father told me that the man gives the woman a seed from his body to add to her egg and together they form a baby. This answer raised its own set of concerns, namely the precise source of the seed, and my growing fear that it was removed from some place on a man's body by means of an unspeakably dreadful operation, which explained why men were often seen standing around at gas stations and barbershops looking grim. Finally, my questions became too numerous, and my father told me the full story of where babies come from, which given my age and the times in which I grew up, was surprisingly candid and complete.

I was told two versions of the facts of life, one involving angels and one involving seeds and eggs. Two years ago my wife gave birth to our daughter, and I was finally able to figure out which version is true.

I pause to let the class laugh.

Then I say: They both are. I know the second version is true because my wife and I did that thing my father had described, and sure enough, we made a baby. But I also know the original story is no less true, for when I saw the terrific force of my wife's pushing, when the doctor told me I could cut the cord that joined mother and daughter, when a new mouth cried out and a new pair of eyes looked into mine, I was surrounded by something large and dark and soulful and singing, and I can only call it angels because I have no other words.

In class, the point of my story is that there are different ways of making sense out of phenomena, that a technical explanation may not be the same thing as a full account, and that in their seemingly fanciful stories the ancient Africans, Celts, Greeks, Hebrews, Hindus, and Sumerians may not even be *trying* to ask "How does it work?" so much as "What does it mean?"

Here in this essay, the point of my story has to do with two abilities within the human mind, both present from childhood: the ability to be critical and the ability to feel wonder, the ability to doubt and the ability to marvel, the drive to seize the facts of life from out of an awesome obscurity and the tendency to be awed once the facts are known—to ask "why" and to exclaim "ah." With one faculty and not the other we are either machines or savages, droids or druids.

If there are two great commandments for shaping the mind of a student, they are surely akin to these: Thou shalt instruct criticism; thou shalt instill wonder.

Pedagogy of Hope

On the other hand—while I certainly cannot ignore hopelessness as a concrete entity, nor turn a blind eye to the historical, economic, and social reasons that explain that hopelessness—I do not understand human existence, and the struggle needed to improve it, apart from hope and dream. Hope is an ontological need. Hopelessness is but hope that has lost its bearings, and become a distortion of that ontological need.

When it becomes a program, hopelessness paralyzes us, immobilizes us. We succumb to fatalism, and then it becomes impossible to muster the strength we absolutely need for a fierce struggle that will re-create the world.

I am hopeful, not out of mere stubbornness, but out of an existential, concrete imperative.

I do not mean that, because I am hopeful, I attribute to this hope of mine the power to transform reality all by itself, so that I set out for the fray without taking account of concrete, material data, declaring, "My hope is enough!" No, my hope is necessary, but it is not enough. Alone, it does not win. But without it, my struggle will be weak and wobbly. We need critical hope the way a fish needs unpolluted water.

The idea that hope alone will transform the world, and action undertaken in that kind of naïveté, is an excellent route to hopelessness, pessimism, and fatalism. But the attempt to do without hope, in the struggle to improve the world, as if that struggle could be reduced to calculated acts alone, or a purely scientific approach, is a frivolous illusion. To attempt to do without hope, which is based on the need for truth as an ethical quality of the struggle, is tantamount to denying that struggle one of its mainstays. The essential thing, as I maintain later on, is this: hope, as an ontological need, demands an anchoring in practice. As an ontological need, hope needs practice in order to become historical concreteness. That is why there is no hope in sheer hopefulness. The hoped-for is not attained by dint of raw hoping. Just to hope is to hope in vain.

Without a minimum of hope, we cannot so much as start the struggle. But without the struggle, hope, as an ontological need, dissipates, loses its bearings, and turns into hopelessness. And hopelessness can become tragic despair. Hence the need for a kind of education in hope. Hope, as it happens, is so important for our existence, individual and social, that we must take every care not to experience it in a mistaken form, and thereby to allow it to slip toward hopelessness and despair. Hopelessness and despair are both the consequence and the cause of inaction or immobilism.

In limited situations, beyond which lies "untested feasibility" alone—sometimes perceivable, sometimes not—we find the why of both positions: the hopeful one and the hopeless one.

One of the tasks of the progressive educator, through a serious, correct political analysis, is to unveil opportunities for hope, no matter what the obstacles may be. After all, without hope there is little we can do. It will be hard to struggle on, and when we fight as hopeless or despairing persons, our struggle will be suicidal. We shall be beside ourselves, drop our weapons, and throw ourselves into sheer hand-to-hand, purely vindictive, combat. Of course, the element of punishment, penalty, correction—the punitive element in the struggle we wage in our hope, in our conviction of its ethical and historical rightness—belongs to the pedagogical nature of the political process of which struggle is an expression. It would not be equitable that injustices, abuses, extortion, illicit profits, influence peddling, the use of offices and positions for the satisfaction of personal interests—all of these things that make up the reason for which, with justifiable anger, we now struggle in Brazil—should go uncorrected, just as it would not be right for any of those who would be judged guilty not to be severely punished, within the limits of the law.

Dialogue between teachers and students does not place them on the same footing professionally, but it does mark the democratic position between them. Teachers and students are not identical, and this for countless reasons. After all, it is a *difference* between them that makes them precisely students or teachers. Were they simply identical, each could be the other. Dialogue is meaningful precisely because the dialogical subjects, the agents in the dialogue, not only retain their identity, but actively defend it, and thus grow together. Precisely on this account, dialogue does not *level* them, does not "even them out," reduce them to each other. Dialogue is not a favor done by one for the other, a kind of grace accorded. On the contrary, it implies a sincere, fundamental respect on the part of the subjects engaged in it, a respect that is violated, or prevented from materializing, by authoritarianism. Permissiveness does the same thing, in a different, but equally deleterious, way.

There is no dialogue in "spontaneism" any more than in the omnipotence of the teacher. But a dialogical relation does not, as is sometimes thought, rule out the possibility of the act of teaching. On the contrary, it founds this act, which is completed and sealed in its correlative, the act of learning, * and both become authentically possible only when the educator's thinking, critical and concerned though it be, nevertheless refuses to "apply the brakes" to the educand's ability to think. On the contrary, both "thinkings" become authentically possible only when the educator's critical thinking is delivered over to the educand's curiosity. If the educator's thinking cancels, crushes, or hinders the development of educands' thinking, then the educator's thinking, being authoritarian, tends to generate in the educands upon whom it impinges a timid, inauthentic, sometimes even merely rebellious thinking.

Indeed, dialogue cannot be blamed for the warped use sometimes made of it—for its pure imitation, or its caricature. Dialogue must not be trans-

*See, in this regard, Eduardo Nicol, *Los principios de la ciencia* (Mexico City: Fondo de Culture Económica, 1965).

formed into a noncommittal "chewing the fat" to the random rhythm of whatever happens to be transpiring between teacher and educands.

Pedagogical dialogue implies not only content, or cognoscible object around which to revolve, but also a presentation concerning it made by the educator for the educands.

Here I should like to return to reflections I have previously made about the "expository lesson." **

The real evil is not in the expository lesson—in the explanation given by the teacher. This is not what I have criticized as a kind of "banking." I have criticized, and I continue to criticize, that type of educator-educand relationship in which the educator regards himself or herself as the educands' sole educator—in which the educator violates, or refuses to accept, the fundamental condition of the act of knowing, which is its dialogical relation (Nicol, 1965), and therefore establishes a relation in which the educator transfers knowledge about *a* or *b* or *c* objects or elements of content to an educand considered as pure recipient.

This is the criticism I have made and still make. The question now is: will every "expository classroom," as they are called, be this? I think not. I deny it. There are expository classrooms in which this is indeed attempted: pure transferals of the teacher's accumulated knowledge to the students. These are vertical classrooms, in which the teacher, in a spirit of authoritarianism, attempts the *impossible*, from the viewpoint of theory of knowledge: to transfer knowledge.

There is another kind of classroom, in which, while appearing not to effect the transfer of content, also cancels or hinders the educand's ability to do critical thinking. That is, there are classrooms that sound much more like children's songs than like genuine challenges. They house the expositions that "tame" educands, or "lull them to sleep"—where, on the one side, the students are lulled to sleep by the teacher's pretentious, high-sounding words, and on the other, the teacher likewise doing a parcel of self-babying. But there is a third position, which I regard as profoundly valid: that in which the teacher makes a little presentation of the subject and then the group of students joins with the teacher in an analysis precisely of that presentation. In this fashion, in the little introductory exposition, the teacher challenges the students, who thereupon question themselves and question the teacher, and thereby share in plumbing the depths of, developing, the initial exposition. This kind of work may in no wise be regarded as negative, as traditional schooling in the pejorative sense.

Finally, I find yet another kind of teacher whom I do not regard as a banker. It is that very serious teacher who, in conducting a course, adopts a relationship with the subject, with the content, of which she or he is treating, that is one of profound, affectionate, almost loving respect, whether that content be constituted of a text composed by the teacher or a text composed by someone else. Ultimately, he or she is bearing witness to the educands as to

**Paulo Freire and Sérgio Guimaraes, *Sobre Educação—diálogos* (Rio de Janeira: Paz e Terra, 1984).

how he or she studies, "approaches," or draws near a given subject, how she or he thinks critically. Now the educands must have, or create and develop, the critical ability to accompany the teacher's movement in his or her attempt to approach the topic under consideration.

From a certain point of view, this kind of teacher also commits an error. It consists in ignoring the fact that the knowledge relation does not terminate in the object. In other words, the knowledge relationship is not exclusively between a cognizing subject and a cognoscible object. It "bridges over" to another subject, basically becoming a subject-object-subject relation.

As a democratic relationship, dialogue is the opportunity available to me to open up to the thinking of others, and thereby not wither away in isolation.

The Narrative of Freedom

Upon entering the teaching profession, many novice teachers carry with them memories and expectations from their own schooling of distant and rigidly hierarchical relationships between teachers, students, and administrators. They remember that, between student and teacher, the assertions of the teacher are not to be questioned and that the authority of the text is final. They may remember that the term *insubordination* is used to describe and silence those teachers who dare to criticize school policies or to question the bases on which decisions about such policy are made.

Teachers who have recently graduated from their college preparation classes might have studied some critical theories of education and learned how pervasive sexism, racism, and class biases have been in shaping curricula and policy in American education in the past. But they probably lack contemporary models for using critical theory to create more democratic classrooms and for acting as agents for positive change in their own school districts.

Furthermore, new teachers usually aren't given much encouragement to examine their own personal histories to uncover how these biases have shaped, or misshaped, their own views of what education can be. At worst, when teachers avoid self-study, they may unconsciously perpetuate stereotyping and bias in their own classroom practices, just as the Reading Teacher did in Kozol's *Death at an Early Age* (see chapter 3). A different but just as tragic outcome of this lack of self-awareness is that teachers themselves can continue to be victimized by racism and sexism in their own schools, as Jane Tompkins discovered during her fight for tenure at Temple University (see chapter 6). Black teachers are sometimes expected to copy the practices of their white peers, as bell hooks has discovered. Female teachers are urged to mimic the teaching and disciplinary styles of their male colleagues, as if that is even possible.

Teachers who have not been encouraged to honor the authenticity of their experience by, for example, telling the stories of their own education and miseducation are disconnected from the power of that experience for teaching others. Developing a critical consciousness of their own schooling is not a typical requirement in most teacher education programs. But teachers can begin to discover the value of constant self-scrutiny and of confronting injustice in their own past and present lives. They can begin to contribute in a more conscious fashion to the creation of more democratic classrooms and to more honestly respectful relationships between students, teachers, and administrators.

bell hooks is a teacher and a theorist of education for whom recovery of her own story is an important starting place for thinking about classrooms as places in which to "practice freedom." In her view, education at its best frees students to reflect on the social realities of their lives, to hear how the language of their culture shapes their thinking, and to discover or invent new social realities and new identities for themselves. Her theory of education, which she calls *engaged pedagogy*, offers an avenue for both students and teachers to examine the impact of race, gender, and class biases on their education and to develop a critical consciousness in their common pursuit of knowledge. She believes that this kind of education is meant not just for members of oppressed groups but for all students and teachers. An education that liberates is one in which "everyone can claim knowledge as a field in which we all labor" (1994, p. 15).

In her writing, she lays bare the details of her life as a black woman intellectual and teacher who lives and works in a society she describes as "white supremacist capitalist patriarchy." (She has become identified with that phrase, and she even gently mocks herself for using it so often.) Author of more than 15 books, bell hooks is currently Distinguished Professor of English at the City University of New York. Elements of her teaching story are found in many of her books and articles, but this chapter will focus on three of her most recent works: *Bone Black* (1996), her girlhood memoir; *Wounds of Passion* (1997), her story of young womanhood and becoming a writer; and *Teaching to Transgress: Education as the Practice of Freedom* (1994), which is the most extensive statement of her teaching philosophy.

In *Teaching to Transgress*, hooks expresses her gratitude to the "many women and men who dare to create theory from the location of pain and struggle, who courageously expose wounds to give us their experience to teach and guide, as a means to chart new theoretical journeys" (p. 74). She has done no less. In her writing, she breaks down the barriers between the public and private to encourage teachers and students to see connections between their "habits of being" and their intellectual lives. She wants students and teachers to embark on an intellectual quest for wholeness of mind, body, and spirit. In hooks' view, teachers should see themselves as responsible for not just the intellectual but also the emotional and spiritual growth of their students.

While incorporating ideas from feminist and critical pedagogy, hooks sees engaged pedagogy as more demanding in that it requires an active commitment on the part of both teachers and students to becoming self-actualized. Although many students express gratitude when their teachers demonstrate their commitment to this kind of growth, the value of becoming self-actualized is not one that is openly espoused by educators—at least not in these times. hooks has found that the belief that teachers have a responsibility to heal themselves is commonly found in 19th century writing about education. Some of us remember that there was a brief resurgence of interest in training teachers in humanistic approaches to education during the 1970s (see the text titled *Discovering Your Teaching Self*, by Curwin and Fuhrmann, 1975, for a good example of this approach). Today, hooks writes in her characteristically blunt style, the university is seen as a haven for "those who are smart in book knowledge but who might be otherwise unfit for social interaction" (p. 16). Book knowledge is not enough to be an effective teacher. hooks believes that respecting and caring for the "souls" of her students is essential to create classrooms in which learning is most meaningful. Teachers who are not striving to find places of healing within themselves cannot even envision the kinds of personal growth and transformation she believes are at the heart of a "liberatory" education.

FORMATIVE YEARS

Born Gloria Watkins in Hopkinsville, Kentucky, in 1952, she took the name of her great-grandmother Bell Hooks as her pen name with the publication of her first book, *Ain't I a Woman: Black Women and Feminism*, in 1981. Explaining this choice in *Wounds of Passion*, she tells us that since girlhood she was taught that one should serve without calling attention to oneself. Although she was often thought of as difficult and demanding as a young woman, she claims another life in which she wishes to practice humility. hooks wants to remind herself that her ego is not the most important part of her and that she is always more than her writing. She sees this as an expression of her commitment to a spiritual life separate from and sometimes in conflict with her academic life. She hopes that the use of a pen name will help her to practice detachment, a discipline advocated by teachers of engaged Buddhism. Her desire to link theory with practice is inspired by sources ranging from Christian to Buddhist to Marxist.

In her foreword to *Bone Black*, hooks tells us that she intends to tell the story of her struggle to create a self "distinct from and yet inclusive of" the Southern black culture in which she was raised, a world "sometimes paradisiacal and sometimes terrifying" (p. xi). Citing the impact of her first reading of Toni Morrison's *The Bluest Eye*, hooks says that she identified with the main character in the novel, a young black girl who is a critical thinker, who reflects on her experience and wants to theorize her life.

The story she tells is intimate in its details and clear-eyed in its judgments. Gloria Watkins is a girl who wants to be allowed to speak her mind as her great-grandmother did, but to her parents it is just "talking back" (p. 130). She is punished, often severely and so frequently for her outspokenness that she begins to feel persecuted and abandoned. When she challenges her mother to explain why her father should have the right to hit her when he barely speaks to her, the result is more ridicule. Her loneliness is compounded by severe bouts of asthma that keep her sitting up all night in a dining room chair. Home remedies are ineffectual and frequent visits to the doctor too expensive. Her desolation is profound: "Their world is the only world there is. To be exiled from it is to be without life. She cries because she is in mourning. They will not let her wear the color black. . . . Black is a woman's color" (p. 131).

She is told that she is too smart, that men do not like a smart woman, and more importantly, men do not like a woman who talks back. Her mother tells her that she is determined to "break her" (p. 99). They are even afraid, they tell her, that she might be a witch or an old woman born again in a young girl's body. Astonishingly, bell hooks is later able to empathize with her parents' fear of her by theorizing that this young black couple was struggling to realize a norm established by white society even though its costs were greater than could be measured materially:

> Try to imagine what it must have been like for them, each of them working hard all day, struggling to maintain a family of seven children, then having to cope with one bright-eyed child relentlessly questioning, daring to challenge male authority, rebelling against the very patriarchal norm they were trying so hard to institutionalize. . . . No wonder that Mama would say to me, now and then, exasperated, frustrated, "I don't know where I got you from, but I sure wish I could give you back." (1994, p. 60)

Theorizing her experience becomes a "sanctuary" (1994, p. 61) for this young gifted black girl, a place where she can make sense of what is happening to her and where she can imagine how to live differently. Reflecting on and analyzing her circumstances helps her to understand that "theory could be a healing place" (1994, p. 61). Later, she incorporates this insight into her teaching philosophy in which she envisions the classroom as a place of collective liberation where no gap exists between theory and practice.

Her mother's rejection of her is seen from a nascent feminist point of view as a rejection of an invitation to remember loneliness. Gloria sees that this had something to do with marriage: "To be the wife to the husband, [her mother] must be willing to sacrifice even her daughters for his good" (1996, p. 151). And yet, Gloria also sees her mother as giving her a sense that there is more to life than what her uninspiring daily existence has to offer. When she discovers the Romantic poets, she likens her experience of reading them to losing a part of herself and then recovering it in the poems. Gloria memorizes poems and recites them to herself while washing the dishes or ironing. In Emily Dickinson's work she discovers that solitude can feed the spirit. Gloria reinvents herself as a visionary by writing her own poetry "using the poems to keep on living" (1996, p. 132).

Against the background of a home in which she finds harsh judgments and suspicion of her talents, hooks recalls that her education at the segregated Booker T. Washington and Crispus Attucks schools was liberating. In the introduction to *Teaching to Transgress*, she tells us that her teachers at these schools are almost all black women on a mission:

They were committed to nurturing intellect so that we could become scholars, thinkers, and cultural workers—black folks who used our "minds". . . . Though they did not define or articulate these practices in theoretical terms, my teachers were enacting a revolutionary pedagogy of resistance that was profoundly anticolonial. (1994, p. 2)

Her teachers are especially committed to caring for the gifted black students, those in whom they see enormous potential. Part of that caring entails the teachers' knowing a lot about their students' lives—where they live, who their parents and grandparents are, which church they belong to, even how they are treated in their families. Some of those teachers had taught their students' parents, sisters, and brothers. Although segregation means being bussed to a school miles away in the country while white children can walk to their neighborhood schools, for Gloria, school before desegregation is "sheer joy." It is a place where she can forget the self she creates to conform with her family's ideas of whom she should be. At school she can literally reinvent herself "through ideas." This is both thrilling and risky, since some of the ideas she is learning are revolutionary. In hooks' analysis, pleasure and danger share equally in her experience of "ecstasy" in school.

The appeal that this kind of intellectual danger still holds for bell hooks is evident in the influence that engaged Buddhism has had in the formulation of her engaged pedagogy. "Living on the razor's edge" as a way of thinking about the reality of human existence is an idea she quotes from the work of Pema Chodron, a Buddhist teacher, who in turn describes her best teachers as those who "stepped outside the conventional mind and who could actually stop my mind and completely open it up and free it." (cited on p. 207).

In stark contrast with the liberating education Gloria Watkins experiences in those all-black schools, the desegregated high school to which she is later bussed feels like a place of "slaughter, for parts of ourselves must be severed to make this integration of schools work" (1996, p. 154). She knows that when she walks past the principal's office in the desegregated school, she can count on seeing a man who not only doesn't know her name, but also doesn't care about her or her friends. What is expected of the black students there is obedience and not any desire or even ability to learn.

Furthermore, learning in these schools is about "information only." The predominantly white schools offer an education that has little or nothing to do with practicing freedom and certainly nothing to do with resisting racism. It has no connection with the students' identities nor with teaching them how they should live their lives. The white teachers fear the black students whom they herd into the gym in the early morning hours and warn not to "make trouble" while they wait for the white students to arrive. Few of the white teachers she encounters have any vision of education as liberation for their black students, and those who do risk ostracism.

One of the few white teachers she remembers as not being afraid of her is her art teacher, Mr. Harold. He pins the school's problem on racism, not the presence of the black students. He wears black shirts and black pants with funny ties and gets away with it because he is an artist. When Gloria works on a watercolor painting of an important dream she had, he allows her to use nothing but the color black. But he urges her to stay with the painting begun in black and to add color to it. As she becomes enthralled with mixing water with powder to make paint in primary colors, he tells her that he enjoys the sight of a student falling in love with color. Later, when she begins an oil painting of the dream, she tells him that she wants to paint the "wilderness my spirit roams in" (p. 171). He advises her to let the color show what the wilderness is like. By carefully observing and commenting on her learning process and by encouraging her to take risks in her painting, Mr. Harold helps Gloria experience the freedom to express her deepest emotions in art.

Outside of school Gloria Watkins encounters other adults who are important to her growth. At the opening session of an interdenominational religious retreat, she hears a Catholic priest speak and feels that "I have suddenly entered a room where only he and I are present" (1996, p. 176–177) as he speaks of loneliness. Later this priest tells her that he sees her poised on the edge of a cliff, but that she should not be afraid because he believes that, despite the loneliness she feels, she will "leap into life" bringing with her beauty, courage, and wisdom. He tells her to begin to love herself.

On the same retreat, a woman sent to her by this priest gives Gloria a copy of Rilke's *Letters to a Young Poet*, which she reads over and over. In Rilke she finds a writer who gives meaning to the wilderness of spirit she feels. Her response to Rilke's kind and wise words is that "I am drowning and it is the raft that takes me safely to shore" (1996, p. 182). Reading Rilke also enables her to affirm her identity as a poet, since she realizes that words have the power to keep her alive. The only person in her family with whom she can share this discovery is her beloved grandfather, Daddy Gus. He tells her not to be afraid to "look deep into everything" and not to fear the pain she feels. He also advises her that it is her work to find out where she belongs. hooks claims to have found a place of belonging by writing in her journal, where she can make a world for herself.

SCHOLARSHIP STUDENT AND ADVANCED STUDY

Awarded a scholarship for undergraduate study at Stanford University, Gloria Watkins enters her classes there hoping to become an "insurgent black intellectual." Instead she encounters yet another set of lessons in obedience to authority. She is surprised to find that her professors even at this prestigious university are not excited about teaching. Some use the classroom primarily, it seems, to dominate and exert power and control. From them she learns about the kind of person and teacher she doesn't want to be: lacking in the ability to communicate with students, lacking in the ability to facilitate dialogue, and lacking in self-knowledge.

Later, in graduate school, Gloria comes to hate being in the classroom. She sees that while "exceptional" white male students are allowed to determine the course of their own intellectual growth, the rest of the students, and especially those from marginalized groups, are confined to memorizing and repeating back the information deemed most important by their professors. Being a critical thinker is seen as a threat to the authority of those who own the knowledge. Even worse, it is sometimes mistaken as an attempt to mask inferior work. Becoming "clones" of their white peers is the most expected of the black students, a dispiriting realization that undermines her joy in learning. She feels that her classes are boring and lacking in possibilities for transformative experiences.

Gloria finds some exceptions to this in the new Women's Studies courses. She discovers that it is assumed that the knowledge gained in feminist classrooms will not only help the students become better scholars but also improve their lives outside of the classroom. In these classes, professors allow their students to question the political implications of teaching and learning methods. Simultaneously, Gloria discovers the work of Paulo Freire, which she uses to critique the limitations of the feminist classrooms and the scholarship she encounters there. Finding Freire's work, she says, is crucial to her survival as a student. In *Teaching to Transgress*, she devotes a chapter to describing the importance of his influence on her thinking about education. She comes to his work "dying of thirst" for a language with which to describe her struggle to create a politically resistant identity as an intellectual. A sentence of his that states, "we cannot enter the struggle as objects in order later to become subjects" becomes for her a "revolutionary mantra." While wrestling with the meaning of this statement for her own intellectual identity, she writes her first book, *Ain't I a Woman: Black Women and Feminism*. Additionally, her experience of liberatory education in the segregated black schools of her youth enables her to grasp immediately Freire's concept of education as the practice of freedom. She says that, in reading *Pedagogy of the Oppressed*, she feels herself included in ways she never felt reading the feminist books of the 1960s and '70s. In this context, she begins to believe that it is her destiny to become a teacher and a writer, to make the classroom experience a place of liberation for all students.

To her frustration, her classmates in her feminist literature courses are annoyed with her seeming inability to deal "just" with gender. This is their complaint when she presents a paper on Pauline Réage's *The Story of O* as a symbolic narrative of colonialism. In hooks' experience, the only place where it is possible for her to focus exclusively on patriarchy, separate from issues of race and class, is back home where de facto racial apartheid enables her to see gender domination patterns within her own Southern black culture. For example, hooks disagrees with her classmates' assertion that black women have always been liberated because they have always worked outside the home. The white students and teachers in her feminist literature classes seem to want to deny the connection she sees between race and gender, preferring to "think of feminism as this little colony that they own" (1997, p. 206). hooks wants to claim feminism as a field of study for all women and men. Although her arguments are rebuffed by most if not all of the white women in her feminist studies classes, she fortunately finds herself unable to take the advice of her lover, himself a gifted black scholar and writer, to "just sit in these classrooms and be silent" (1997, p. 207).

Her inability to maintain silence has its costs. The first time she takes her oral exams for the Ph.D., she fails despite passing all the written exams and writing the first draft of her book. She makes the mistake of being "totally honest" when asked how she would teach James Joyce. Her response is that she has no intention of teaching his work—that she wants a diverse and unbiased curriculum. Though she has been warned before about not showing the proper deference to her professors, she is stunned by the news of failure and simultaneously awed by her innocence. "How could I have thought I could speak truth to power and not be punished?" she writes (1997, p. 134). The realization that her professors are simply trying to teach her to surrender and submit to their authority shocks hooks. She expects more of a spirit of justice and fair play from them. Fortunately, her ability to survive such onslaughts strengthens her. She begins to appreciate the power of her own idealism and the depth of her determination to speak her mind freely.

bell hooks' memories of her teachers in graduate school contain one bright light. Diane Middlebrook is her favorite professor, a "sexy woman who thinks and writes and takes no prisoners" (1997, p. 143). According to hooks, Middlebrook (as her students called her) is interested not just in her students' minds but also their spirits. Her students come to her class excited. Though hooks is again the only black woman in the class and race is rarely mentioned, "it is as though Middlebrook takes all the issues we have been talking about since girlhood on inside her students and brings them out in the open" (p. 144). Gloria finds the classroom discussions about whether it is possible for women to write creatively and simultaneously have husbands, children, and a full life to be both thrilling and frightening. Confronting these difficult questions about the creative life for women is nurturing, putting an end to silence about them, but also painful in the realization that resistance to thinking about these questions is so powerful. From Diane Middlebrook she learns that there is a place for passion in the classroom. She sees that, in order to let learning flourish, students are best seen as whole persons and not as disembodied minds.

A LIFE IN TEACHING

Becoming a teacher herself, hooks develops her own pedagogy of freedom and wholeness. She finds that creating educational theory is itself a way in which to practice freedom. For example, a first principle in her theory is that the classroom should be an exciting place. She finds that the role of excitement in higher education is suspect because many teachers believe that emotion interferes with, rather than enhances, serious learning. Although the public may applaud Hollywood's depictions of passionate teachers as seen, for example, in *Dead Poets Society*, she finds that caring passionately for one's teaching and one's students and showing that passion doesn't feel safe to most teachers. Even behavior as innocent as unrestrained laughter is seen as vulgar and antithetical to the proper degree of decorum in many classrooms, especially those in prestigious colleges and universities. hooks finds that displays of emotion are sometimes perceived as a sign of lower-class origins and are thought to reveal a lack of identification with the middle-class norms of the academy. But when teachers allow emotional expression in their classrooms, students respond by saying they especially enjoy such courses. Suspicion is then aroused that, when enjoyment prevails, no real learning can be taking place. Real learning is hard and disagreeable and should induce a slight drowsiness in students. In hooks' view, this repression of emotional expression and students' self-censorship of deeply held convictions actually undermines the democratic exchange of ideas in the classroom.

bell hooks wants teaching to be a joyful activity and sees this view as an act of resistance in itself, given the degree of boredom and apathy often found in American classrooms. In colleges and universities, teaching is usually the least valued of professional activities, and students don't find pedagogical theories as hip or cool to study as they find feminist or Marxist theory. To claim the classroom as a place of radical possibility is itself a radical act.

Excitement in the classroom requires spontaneity and the absence of a rigid agenda that determines what will and will not be discussed in the classroom. Students must be allowed to interject their own concerns and needs and to be seen as individuals. In hooks' view, this doesn't preclude the possibility of their full engagement with serious ideas. Many professors are unwilling to take the risks necessary to allow their classrooms to become places where real pleasure in learning is encouraged for fear of losing control of their agenda. In Freire's words, "the teacher confuses the authority of knowledge with his or her own professional authority, which she or he sets in opposition to the freedom of the students" (p. 54, 1970/1993). Encouraging students to participate in agenda setting in the classroom is to transgress, to move beyond the boundaries of what is considered acceptable. What hooks proposes is very similar to what Ira Shor carries out in his narrative *When Students Have Power* (see chapter 3), which is not surprising since both hooks and Shor are close students of Freire.

Valuing the presence of everyone in the room is another necessary ingredient for an exciting classroom, in hooks' view. It begins with the professor's recognition that every student has resources to contribute to the creation of a learning community in the classroom. This entails the professor's teaching the students how to hear each other's voices by showing sincere interest in and appreciation of the contributions of each student. One of the differences between the banking model of education and hooks' engaged pedagogy is the professor's belief that students can teach each other and the professor. In Freire's words again, "the teacher is no longer merely the-one-who-teaches, but one who is himself taught in dialogue with the students, who in turn while being taught also teach" (1970/1993, p. 61). hooks contends that professors should be empowered by their interactions with students, and she tries to show in her books how much influence her students have had in her intellectual work. In addition, throughout the course of the semester, she encourages them to evaluate her class, to critique it and make suggestions all along rather than to wait for the evaluation forms at the end of the semester, a practice that is again strikingly similar to Shor's. Even beyond the classroom, she says, "I journey with students as they progress in their lives. In many ways, I continue to teach them, even as they become more capable of teaching me" (1994, p. 205).

In addition, there can be no spectators in the classroom. Although professors often encounter students for whom a passive role is the only one in which they feel comfortable, hooks insists that it is the teacher's obligation to challenge these students to participate. She insists that the notion that only the professor is in charge of classroom dynamics must be deconstructed. As her reputation for being an exciting teacher grows, she encounters more students who wish to attend class to watch the "star" in action. But the silent spectator has no place in her vision of the exciting classroom. Teaching is much more than a spectacle for an audience to appreciate; it is establishing the conditions for students to find their voices and to articulate new possibilities.

This insight leads her to write *Teaching to Transgress: Education as the Practice of Freedom* for both teachers and students. hooks wants this book to serve as an "intervention" to educate both students and teachers about the possibilities and the risks of engaging classroom experiences. As she tells it in the introduction to the book, one semester she had a class that "completely failed on the communal level" (p. 8). It was a dull class that she grew to dread facing at 8:00 in the morning. In her view, one of the reasons it fails is the early morning hour, when at least a third of the class is still sleepy. But additionally, and for reasons she still doesn't understand, she finds this class full of "resisting" students who do not want to participate in a class that requires them to consider new ways of learning. This experience teaches her that it takes more than the will and desire of the teacher to make the classroom a communal, exciting experience. In *Teaching to Transgress*, she includes excerpts from an article published in the *Village Voice* by one of her students named Gary Dauphin, who writes of the joys and the problems he encounters in working with her. In this book she allows her voice to be only one of many offering an account of her teaching.

Sometimes students misunderstand the implications of her engaged pedagogy and expect that an inversion of hierarchy will take place in her classroom, such that students from marginalized groups will be granted a privileged status. hooks writes of a group of black female students in a course on African American writers who expected her to "decenter" the voices of privileged white students in the class so that they could experience what it felt like to be an outsider. She sees this as replacing one dictatorship with another. To the disappointment of students who expect to feel more comfortable and perhaps not to have to work as hard for her as for their other professors, she insists on creating space for everyone to speak.

Engaged pedagogy requires that students connect theory with their own lived experience. Thus confessional narratives and testimonials are encouraged as ways for students to recreate theory in the classroom. In hooks' classes, these are not meant to be merely a way for students to vent their anger or to serve as therapy sessions, although she hopes that her classes will offer knowledge that heals rather than wounds. She writes that she is "most thrilled when the telling of experience links discussion of facts or more abstract concepts to reality" (p. 86). She finds it productive for professors to be the first to bring their own experiences to bear upon discussions. It is only fair for teachers to be vulnerable if they expect their students to take similar risks. This practice also displaces the view of the professor as the all-knowing interrogator. Finally, when listening to everyone's experience is validated as a way of expanding knowledge, the students seem less inclined to compete for voice, as sometimes happens when the classroom seems to belong to one group more than it does to another.

Assigning an autobiographical paragraph about an early racial memory in classes in which students are reading Toni Morrison's novel *The Bluest Eye* is an example of how hooks implements her desire to bring the passion of experience into her classroom. Each student reads the paragraph aloud to the class, enabling the students to recognize the diversity of their experiences and the limits of considering the experience of only a few. hooks is eloquent in describing her intent:

> In the classroom I share as much as possible the need for critical thinkers to engage multiple locations, to address diverse standpoints, to allow us to gather knowledge fully and inclusively. Sometimes, I tell students, it is like a recipe. I tell them to imagine we are baking bread that needs flour. And we have all the other ingredients but no flour. Suddenly, the flour becomes most important even though it alone will not do. This is a way to think about experience in the classroom. (p. 91)

One of the risks of engaged pedagogy lies in the inherent unpredictability of the dynamic in an open classroom. Many teachers fear unpredictable interactions in their classrooms because of the challenges they pose to both their skills for interacting with people from backgrounds unfamiliar to them and to their own capacity for learning and personal growth. Not only must every student be permitted to speak, but the teacher must be capable of speaking differently to different classes as a function of the particular concerns of those students. The "engaged voice" of the teacher is always "evolving in dialogue with a world beyond itself" (p. 11). This is one of the ways in which to promote educational renewal. If some teachers "seek asylum" (p. 165) in academe because of their fears of the world outside the sacred groves or because of an inability to heal their own wounds, they will be incapable of creating classrooms in which personal growth and transformation are possible.

An existential fear that they will lose their right to be teachers once they discover their humanity is one factor, hooks believes, that blocks many teachers from critiquing their own practices. She claims that her own ability to remain flexible is due in part to the fact that she never became attached to an image of herself as a professor, that her identity as a teacher was never tied to validation from others in academe. She expresses bitterness toward colleagues who "willingly betrayed the promise of intellectual fellowship and radical openness that I believe are the heart and soul of learning" (p. 205). Refocusing her attention on her own commitment to the art of teaching has helped hooks to overcome her disappointment in her colleagues' seeming unwillingness to pursue self-understanding and personal growth.

Not knowing (see Eleanor Duckworth on the power of not knowing in her 1997 book *The Having of Wonderful Ideas*) is also part of the experience of engaged classrooms. There are times, hooks admits, when:

> the mountaintop is difficult to reach with all our resources, factual and confessional, so we are just there collectively grasping, feeling the limitations of knowledge, longing together, yearning for a way to reach that highest point. Even this yearning is a way to know. (p. 92)

A concomitant risk for those who aspire to create excitement in their classrooms is "burn-out." hooks wants schools and universities to recognize that teachers need time away from teaching to rejuvenate themselves. She has felt this lack of time off to be damaging to her own teaching. hooks fears that the lack of institutional support for engaged pedagogy prevents many from attempting it and eventually exhausts many of those who practice it year after year, sometimes to increasingly large classes and class loads. She suggests that teachers insist on limits on the number of students enrolled in their classes. She also recommends the practices of job sharing and job switching to create fresh opportunities to learn from colleagues in new environments.

Teachers must also deal with the awesome responsibility of actually changing lives when they educate their students for critical consciousness. This is another avenue by which hooks allows her students to teach her. She recalls an incident from her years teaching a course on black women writers in the African American Studies department at Yale University. The students were exploring the topic of internalized racism among black women. One of her female black students returned from a break declaring that, after years of straightening her hair, she had decided to let it go natural. hooks writes "I still remember the fear I felt when she testified that the class had changed her" (p. 196). bell hooks experienced this young woman's transformation in her appearance as a "direct challenge that I had to face and affirm" to continue her advocacy of uniting theory and practice.

The need for compassion for the dilemmas of the engaged classroom extends also to the students. While classes can and should be enjoyable, teachers and students need to recognize that experiencing difficulty is a stage in intellectual development. hooks accepts that a "cozy, good feeling" might occasionally be an obstacle to grappling with difficult dilemmas. She acknowledges that there is pain involved when students find themselves giving up familiar ways of thinking. Students sometimes experience feelings of estrangement from family members and friends, where before only comfort was found. She writes, "I have not forgotten the day a student came to class and told me: 'We take your class. We learn to look at the world from a critical standpoint, one that considers race, sex, and class. And we can't enjoy life anymore.' " (p. 42)

hooks has learned to deal with this discomfort directly by inviting class members to share their experiences of how they have changed their views of life outside the classroom and how these changes have been received. This discussion builds a sense of community in the classroom as students realize they are undergoing transformations together. She encourages them to "creatively invent ways to cross borders" (p. 183). She also encourages her students to believe in their ability to become agents of change in the creation of a more just society. She wants them to see themselves as not just passive observers or as victims. A passage from one of her students' journals illustrates the beginning of a critical consciousness:

> . . . I cannot go back and change years of believing that the most wonderful thing in the world would be to be Martin Luther King's wife—but I can go on and find the strength I need to be the revolutionary for myself rather than the companion and help for someone else. So no, I don't believe we can change what has already been done but we can change the future and so I am reclaiming and learning more of who I am so that I can be whole. (p. 196)

hooks admits that not all of her students enjoy studying with her. At the beginning of her career, she found this unsettling because, like most novice teachers, she wanted to be liked and admired by all of her students. With experience she learned that the rewards of engaged pedagogy are sometimes delayed, as Jane Tompkins learned as well. Some of her students need more time to appreciate the challenges she poses to their ways of thinking and being in the world. Some of them contact her years later to express their appreciation for what they learned in her classes.

CONCLUSION

bell hooks concludes her story with the confession that, after 20 years of teaching, she finds that she is "often most joyous in the classroom, brought closer here to the ecstatic than by most of life's experiences" (p. 206). The final paragraph in *Teaching to Transgress* is an inspiring summation of her view of the potential of engaged pedagogy:

> The academy is not paradise. But learning is a place where paradise can be created. The classroom, with all its limitations, remains a place

of possibility. In that field of possibility we have the opportunity to labor for freedom, to demand of ourselves and our comrades, an openness of mind and heart that allows us to face reality even as we collectively imagine ways to move beyond boundaries, to transgress. This is education as the practice of freedom. (p. 207)

In summary, we conclude that *emancipatory teachers:*

> *Embrace diversity because learners come from many different places and espouse many different points of view.*
> *Encourage creative conflict because honest differences must be shared before unity can be created within diversity.*
> *Practice honesty because learning in depth is impossible without it.*
> *Maintain humility because each of us has such a limited point of view and because there is always so much more to learn.*
> *Seek to liberate all learners from conditions and circumstances that impede human flourishing.*
> *Believe that education is, above all, the practice of freedom.*

STUDY QUESTIONS

1. Why does bell hooks recount the story of her own schooling in her books on education?
2. What influence did feminist theory have on hooks' views of education?
3. What influence did Freire's work have on hooks' views of education?
4. Why does hooks see her education in segregated schools as liberating?
5. What does hooks mean when she says that theory building can be liberating?
6. What are the elements of hooks' "pedagogy of freedom"?

REFERENCES

Curwin, R. L., & Fuhrmann, B. S. (1975). *Discovering your teaching self: Humanistic approaches to effective teaching.* Englewood Cliffs, NJ: Prentice Hall.

Duckworth, E. (1997). *The having of wonderful ideas.* New York: Teachers College Press.

Freire, P. (1970/1993). *Pedagogy of the oppressed.* (M. Bergman Ramon, trans.) New York: Continuum.

hooks, b. (1981). *Ain't I a woman: Black women and feminism.* Boston: South End Press.

hooks, b. (1994). *Teaching to transgress: Education as the practice of freedom.* New York: Routledge.

hooks, b. (1996). *Bone black: Memories of childhood.* New York: Henry Holt & Co.

hooks, b. (1997). *Wounds of passion: A writing life.* New York: Henry Holt & Co.

Teaching to Transgress

Excerpt

While I wanted teaching to be my career, I believed that personal success was intimately linked with self-actualization. My passion for this quest led me to interrogate constantly the mind/body split that was so often taken to be a given. Most professors were often deeply antagonistic toward, even scornful of, any approach to learning emerging from a philosophical standpoint emphasizing the union of mind, body, and spirit, rather than the separation of these elements. Like many of the students I now teach, I was often told by powerful academics that I was misguided to seek such a perspective in the academy. Throughout my student years I felt deep inner anguish. Memory of that pain returns as I listen to students express the concern that they will not succeed in academic professions if they want to be well, if they eschew dysfunctional behavior or participation in coercive hierarchies. These students are often fearful, as I was, that there are no spaces in the academy where the will to be self-actualized can be affirmed.

This fear is present because many professors have intensely hostile responses to the vision of liberatory education that connects the will to know with the will to become. Within professional circles, individuals often complain bitterly that students want classes to be "encounter groups." While it is utterly unreasonable for students to expect classrooms to be therapy sessions, it is appropriate for them to hope that the knowledge received in these settings will enrich and enhance them.

Currently, the students I encounter seem far more uncertain about the project of self-actualization than my peers and I were twenty years ago. They feel that there are no clear ethical guidelines shaping actions. Yet, while they despair, they are also adamant that education should be liberatory. They want and demand more from professors than my generation did. There are times when I walk into classrooms overflowing with students who feel terribly wounded in their psyches (many of them see therapists), yet I do not think that they want therapy from me. They do want an education that is healing to the uninformed, unknowing spirit. They do want knowledge that is meaningful. They rightfully expect that my colleagues and I will not offer them information without addressing the connection between what they are learning and their overall life experiences.

This demand on the students' part does not mean that they will always accept our guidance. This is one of the joys of education as the practice of freedom, for it allows students to assume responsibility for their choices. Writing about our teacher/student relationship in a piece for the *Village Voice*, "How to Run the Yard: Off-Line and into the Margins at Yale," one of my students, Gary Dauphin, shares the joys of working with me as well as the tensions that surfaced between us as he began to devote his time to pledging a fraternity rather than cultivating his writing:

> People think academics like Gloria [my given name] are all about difference: but what I learned from her was mostly about sameness, about what I had in common as a black man to people of color; to women and gays and lesbians and the poor and anyone else who wanted in. I did some of this learning by reading but most of it came from hanging out on the fringes of her life. I lived like that for a while, shuttling between high points in my classes and low points outside. Gloria was a safe haven. Pledging a fraternity is about as far away as you can get from her classroom, from the yellow kitchen where she used to share her lunch with students in need of various forms of sustenance.

This is Gary writing about the joy. The tension arose as we discussed his reason for wanting to join a fraternity and my disdain for that decision. Gary comments, "They represented a vision of black manhood that she abhorred, one where violence and abuse were primary ciphers of bonding and identity." Describing his assertion of autonomy from my influence he writes, "But she must have also known the limits of even her influence on my life, the limits of books and teachers."

Ultimately, Gary felt that the decision he had made to join a fraternity was not constructive, that I "had taught him openness" where the fraternity had encouraged one-dimensional allegiance. Our interchange both during and after this experience was an example of engaged pedagogy.

Through critical thinking—a process he learned by reading theory and actively analyzing texts—Gary experienced education as the practice of freedom. His final comments about me: "Gloria had only mentioned the entire episode once after it was over, and this to tell me simply that there are many kinds of choices, many kinds of logic. I could make those events mean whatever I wanted as long as I was honest." I have quoted his writing at length because it is testimony affirming engaged pedagogy. It means that my voice is not the only account of what happens in the classroom.

Engaged pedagogy necessarily values student expression. In her essay, "Interrupting the Calls for Student Voice in Liberatory Education: A Feminist Poststructuralist Perspective," Mimi Orner employs a Foucauldian framework to suggest that

> Regulatory and punitive means and uses of the confession bring to mind curricular and pedagogical practices which call for students to publicly reveal, even confess, information about their lives and cultures in the presence of authority figures such as teachers.

When education is the practice of freedom, students are not the only ones who are asked to share, to confess. Engaged pedagogy does not seek simply to empower students. Any classroom that employs a holistic model of learning will also be a place where teachers grow, and are empowered by the process. That empowerment cannot happen if we refuse to be vulnerable while encouraging students to take risks. Professors who expect students to share confessional narratives but who are themselves unwilling to share are exercising power in a manner that could be coercive. In my classrooms I do not expect students to take any risks that I would not take, to share in any way that I would not share. When professors bring narratives of their experiences into classroom discussions it eliminates the possibility that we can function as all-knowing, silent interrogators. It is often productive if professors take the first risk, linking confessional narratives to academic discussions so as to show how experience can illuminate and enhance our understanding of academic material. But most professors must practice being vulnerable in the classroom, being wholly present in mind, body, and spirit.

Progressive professors working to transform the curriculum so that it does not reflect biases or reinforce systems of domination are most often the individuals willing to take the risks that engaged pedagogy requires and to make their teaching practices a site of resistance. In her essay, "On Race and Voice: Challenges for Liberation Education in the 1990s," Chandra Mohanty writes that

> resistance lies in self-conscious engagement with dominant, normative discourses and representations and in the active creation of oppositional analytic and cultural spaces. Resistance that is random and isolated is clearly not as effective as that which is mobilized through systemic politicized practices of teaching and learning. Uncovering and reclaiming subjugated knowledge is one way to lay claims to alternative histories. But these knowledges need to be understood and defined pedagogically, as questions of strategy and practice as well as of scholarship, in order to transform educational institutions radically.

Professors who embrace the challenge of self-actualization will be better able to create pedagogical practices that engage students, providing them with ways of knowing that enhance their capacity to live fully and deeply.

9

Writing Your Teaching Story

Becoming a teacher is, in part, a process of constructing a new identity for yourself. This process happens in a particular context that can support or undermine your burgeoning identity. Easy beginnings for new teachers (Huberman, 1995) are characterized by good relationships with students who are open to learning, a supportive principal, a helpful supervising teacher, and a clear sense of purpose. When these conditions hold, your sense of vocation is quickly strengthened. For others, the beginning is painful. Students who reject your efforts, supervisors who constantly monitor and criticize your activities, and other teachers who reject or exclude newcomers or who try to instill self-doubt about your methods, all contribute to a less than easy start. Under these conditions, even the most dedicated new teachers begin to wonder why they ever decided to go into the profession. Thus, the story you tell of your induction experience, your own narrative of apprenticeship, will be shaped in large part by the support you receive in the process of finding yourself as a teacher.

For most of us, it takes a long time before we feel firmly established in our identity as a teacher. In fact, studies reviewed by Carter and Doyle (1996) indicate that it takes teachers an average of 4 to 7 years before they feel confident and settled into their teaching roles. It might take longer for teachers who are transferred frequently between grade levels and courses within their first 5 years of teaching. Unfortunately, this is not an uncommon practice in some school districts. New teachers have the least seniority and the fewest choices about where to teach and what subjects to teach. Solidifying an identity under these conditions can be difficult.

Even among some experienced teachers who have found their footing in the classroom, identity issues arise again if teachers discover that, as Anita Plath Helle put it, they have let the entire educational apparatus shape the selves they have become (Helle, 1991, p. 53). One teacher wrote that, during her second year, "I felt my personality and my identity eroding as I yelled at the students, kowtowed to the administration, and argued with my colleagues" (Isenberg, 1994, p. 26). When this happens, teachers talk of feeling disconnected from themselves and of trying to reconcile the demands of teaching with the ideals that led them into the profession in the first place (Helle, 1991).

Writing your own teaching narratives, and writing responses to others' narratives, provides an opportunity to assert your identity as a teacher, to refine your teaching philosophy, to find ways to communicate it more clearly to diverse readers, and to engage in self-assessment and self-improvement. Narratives of teaching can help you cope with the difficult circumstances surrounding the quest for one's identity as a teacher. The stories told by teachers in Mary Renck Jalongo and Joan Isenberg's book titled *Teachers' Stories: From Personal Narrative to Professional Insight* (1995) attest to the fact that there are many obstacles to overcome and conflicts to resolve even years after one's career has begun. The authors of that book use narratives based on the actual experiences of classroom teachers confronting challenges to their teaching philosophy, or to their competence, to prepare novice teachers who will inevitably face similar challenges. In addition, they encourage novice teachers to generate their own narratives as a way to articulate and to shore up that fragile identity.

In the process of writing your narratives, you will find that the ability to call upon a set of "strong and stable images" (Carter & Doyle, 1996, p. 134) to describe and to guide your practice in the complex world of the classroom is one key to the achievement of a sense of mastery as a teacher. The acquisition of these images takes time, experience, and reflection. Here again other teachers' stories can be sources of abiding inspiration for the formation and nurturance of such images. An example is the image of "classroom as home," as explicated by a teacher named Stephanie whose practices, and the narratives she generated about them, are documented by Connelly and Clandinin (1985).

In the last analysis, the learning and growth of students is central to a teacher's identity and satisfaction. That is one aspect of most teachers' sense of self that is firmly established at the start (Nias, 1989). Most beginning teachers already see themselves as people who are strongly committed to the welfare of their students (Pagano, 1991). They believe that the work they do with their students will be the ultimate and the most important test of their success as a teacher. They evaluate conditions outside the classroom with reference to whether they facilitate or impede the important work they do with students (Nias, 1989).

In caring for them, teachers realize that students bring their personal narratives to the classroom and, to a large extent, the ability of teachers and students to connect depends on the ability of the teacher to hear and appreciate the students' stories. This notion of the teacher's sense of self as dependent on her ability to connect with her students is reflected in the theory of Nel Noddings, which addresses the primacy of the caring relation in education (Witherell & Noddings, 1991). Noddings believes that "to educate is to take seriously both the quest for life's meaning and the meaning of individual lives" (p. 3). In the teaching relationship, we are called upon to apprehend the narratives of our students to be able to envision the possibilities they embody. Understanding our own narrative truth helps. As Maxine Greene put it, "There must be links, after all, between what we are trying to make of ourselves and what we are striving to make possible in the lives of our students" (Greene, 1995, p. 65).

Ultimately, the teacher's sense of self as a teacher is formed and given meaning in the context of her relationships with her students. No matter how ironic the quest for identity is in a society characterized by prejudices of race, gender, and social class (Graham, 1995), good teachers commit themselves to creating classrooms and relationships within them in which all students can engage in that quest. As Peter Abbs (1974) put it, in advocating for the use of autobiography in teacher preparation:

> The centre of education resides in the individual. If we are to achieve a genuinely human education we must return again and again to the person before us . . . the individual who is ready, however dimly and in need of however much support, to adventure both further out into his experience and further into it, who is ready, in some part of himself, to risk himself in order to become more than he now is." (p. 5)

There is a complication in this scenario. Noddings points out that the student, the one-cared-for, must recognize and respond to the efforts of the teacher in order for there to be a caring relationship between the two. If teachers' identities as such are largely dependent on how successful they feel in reaching their students, then we are facing a dilemma. Many of the stories of teachers told herein are stories of rejection, at least initially, by some students. The title "I Won't Learn From You" could be the label for a whole genre of such stories.

To become a teacher who can stay the course, one must develop a sense of self that is not entirely dependent on the responses of others. Because good teachers care deeply about both the students they teach and the importance of what they're teaching them, this is difficult. But the very sturdiness and resilience that teachers demonstrate in the face of rejection can itself be an important lesson to students. Bill Ayers writes, "teachers, whatever else we teach, teach themselves" (1993, p. 129). That may be especially true with our students who believe they have no intention of learning from us.

NARRATIVE IMAGINATION IN TEACHERS

> Narrative art has the power to make us see the lives of the different with more than a casual tourist's interest—with involvement and sympathetic understanding, with anger at our society's refusals of visibility . . . We see that circumstances shape not only people's possibilities for action, but also their aspirations and desires, hopes and fears. (Nussbaum, 1997, p. 88)

One of the most important qualities a teacher can bring to his classroom is the capacity to hear, understand, and appreciate the stories of his students. A teacher must be able to see his students both as people who are very much like himself and as individuals with experiences so different from his own that he must listen carefully to their stories to discern their meanings.

In her book *Cultivating Humanity: A Classical Defense of Reform in Liberal Education,* Martha Nussbaum advocates the development of such a "narrative imagination" as a core value for education. She reminds us that the history of such an education is an ancient one. Athenians in ancient Greece attended performances of tragic dramas written to cultivate the moral development of Athens' young citizens. The spectators at these drama festivals identified with the tragic hero, a decent person caught up in oppressive circumstances.

The Greek tragedies transported their spectators between worlds. In viewing the tragedies, Nussbaum tells us, the young male citizen of Athens was invited to experience lives he might, depending on his luck and his character, actually inhabit: those of slaves, beggars, exiles, and those of generals and rulers. He was also invited to identify with those whom he would never become: wives, daughters, mothers, and people from other countries, including Persians and Africans. Thus the dramas explored both similarity and difference. The young man was confronted with the fact that people with thoughts and feelings very much like his own had to face shame and grief brought on by circumstances for which they were not entirely responsible. He was invited to think about what that might mean for living a moral life.

Nussbaum points out that one of the things that characters in dramas teach us is that, in many important ways, we are not all "brothers under the skin." Our circumstances shape our emotions, thoughts, and ambitions. By both identifying with and failing to identify with characters in stories, we learn what life does to other people and to us.

The character of Akmir in Herb Kohl's story "I Won't Learn From You" is a good example of this point. When we used this story in one of our classes for prospective teachers, some of our students confessed a failure to identify with Akmir and an inability to see him as a sympathetic character. Some other students in the class were more readily able to understand that the experience of being shaped by anger was something that could have happened to them. In fact, it had happened to some of them. Dialogues between "identifying" and "failing to identify" students about modern tragedies such as his can help prospective teachers become aware that some of their future students might have stories like Akmir's to tell. They have the opportunity to hear other students speak from his perspective and to think about how they would respond to a student like him before the real-life test in their own classrooms. If we want to educate all our students, we should be interested in using powerful stories such as Kohl's as a way to foster critical thinking about the habits of mind and heart our society sustains. Including stories about students like Akmir in teacher education programs is itself a way to expand our ability to recognize and include the outcasts of our society in the story of American education.

An anonymous reviewer of this book in its early manuscript form worried that individual reflection on such stories would not "change things." Martha Nussbaum asks us to appreciate a compassionate imagination inspired by literature; even though it doesn't lead immediately to political change, that shouldn't make us underestimate its worth. She claims that the interpretive abilities we gain by engaging ourselves with the lives of characters we've encountered in literature are essential for our participation in a democracy. This is particularly true if we have allowed ourselves to be disturbed by challenging characters. It's easy to identify with people like ourselves who find themselves in tough circumstances. The real test of our capacity for empathy comes when we try to understand the motivations of those whose actions and beliefs seem very threatening to our values. But by expanding our imaginations to encompass other points of view, we are granted glimpses of lives beyond the blinders of our conventional perceptions and beliefs.

Finally, we would be missing an important practical use for the narrative imagination if we ignored Shirley Pendlebury's (1995) incisive analysis of its value in both understanding and evaluating good teaching. She argues that sound practical reasoning in the classroom requires "situational appreciation," a way of seeing that is best nurtured by stories. She asks, how do we understand the child who is one day responsive and eager to learn and the next day sullen, angry, and resentful? Her claim is that it is by understanding the child's personal narrative. She states, "to act rightly is to be narratively engaged, for it is in the context of human stories that we are best able to see the salient features of different human situations. . ." (p. 61). She argues further that the language of stories should be used to evaluate a teacher's practice, for that is the language that is best suited for describing the "goods and ends" of teaching: "the obstacles overcome or still looming large; conflicts resolved, displaced, or deepened; turning points for better or worse; climaxes and culminations" (p. 64). A challenge for teacher education is to find ways to develop the capacity for a narrative imagination in our students, so that we may use the language of narrative to understand and describe what we are doing and why.

NARRATIVE IN THE SERVICE
OF EDUCATIONAL RENEWAL

> We project to our students not who we are but the kind of person we would like to be or what we would like others to think of us as being. . . After years of such trying, we often wind up better than we were at the start, which is surely one of the great rewards of teaching. (Jackson, 1992, pp. 242–243)

As teachers most of us recognize that we are "role models" for our students. We know that our students scrutinize our behavior and our language for clues to who we are and who we hope to be. And so we try to be at our best when we're on display in the classroom. But eventually all of us have at least one moment in the classroom when the utterly unexpected happens, and all eyes turn to us to see how we handle it. Nothing can be more revealing of character than those moments when we can't fall back on our familiar scripts and we must improvise a response on the spot. In that moment, we, and simultaneously our students, discover what we're really made of. Sometimes we surprise ourselves by finding more compassion than we thought we had or a more agile intellect than we thought we could muster. Some of the best teaching stories describe moments like these, moments when teachers start to renew themselves.

Charles Taylor (1976) claims that a defining characteristic of selfhood is the capacity to ask ourselves the question, "Is this the kind of being I ought to be, or really want to be?" (p. 281). Asking the question, he says, entails our concern with evaluating the worth of potentially conflicting desires and goals. Furthermore, the worth of various desires or goals is evaluated with respect to the particular kind of life we hope to lead.

The choices between conflicting goals and desires might be easier to make if it weren't for a couple of complications the world offers us: first, the moral choices we are sometimes called upon to make are choices between two "goods," and second, it is sometimes difficult to sort out just what our choices are and what's at stake in the midst of the complexity of everyday life. To be aware of these complications and to take responsibility for the radical choices we do make is part of what we mean by self-renewal.

In the world of schools, as Joseph Featherstone (1995) put it, "New teachers often don't realize that there are sides to take, and that they are called upon to choose" (p. 12). What's more, the sides can be difficult to discern in that noisy world. Shirley Pendlebury (1995) claims that the process she calls "narrative redescription," in which teachers tell the stories of tough choices they've made, is the most helpful one for discerning both the issues at stake and the particulars of the situations in which the choices arise. Teachers who are responsible in the sense that Taylor describes, and who have written their own stories of the choices they've made, can be our best guides in our quest for educational renewal.

Romantic as this notion is, the quest for renewal might be one of the most practical endeavors a teacher can undertake. A sense of moral purpose provides a guiding vision that can help in making choices in everything from curriculum decisions, to discipline decisions (such as those the teacher Barbara Morgan faced in Pendlebury's article), to deciding whether to go back to the job for one more year. If Joseph Featherstone is right that "you will never survive your years as a teacher by listening to what passes for vision now in the United States" (p. 16), you need to feed your desire to become a better teacher with something better—such as the visions, hopes, and dreams of the teachers whose narratives are honored herein. Thus, a partial answer to Parker Palmer's question "How can educational institutions sustain and deepen the selfhood from which good teaching comes?" (1998, p. 4) is that they can encourage the reading of stories that appeal to our better desires and help us develop our own sense of moral direction.

NARRATIVE IN SERVICE OF
'THE UNDIVIDED SELF'

> The courage to live divided no more . . . comes from this simple in-
> sight: no punishment anyone lays on you could possibly be worse than
> the punishment you lay on yourself by conspiring in your own dimin-
> ishment. (Palmer, 1998, p. 171)

In his recent book, *The Courage to Teach: Exploring the Inner Landscape
of a Teacher's Life* (1998), Parker Palmer advocates living an undivided life, one
in which we have found ways to reconcile the conflicting claims of the institutions we inhabit, including schools, with the claims of our own hearts and
minds. This can be difficult, he says, for teachers who love education so much
that they refuse to allow their schools to sink to their lowest forms. Once again,
narratives of teaching can provide both inspiration and guidance in reconciling
the hopes and dreams we bring to our teaching careers with the sometimes-
harsh realities we encounter in schools.

The conflicting emotions felt by teachers living divided lives are depicted
in "The Scary Part Is That It Happens Without Us Knowing" (Featherstone,
Gregorich, Niesz, & Young, 1995). In this chapter, two teacher-educators, He-
len Featherstone and Lauren Jones Young, and two student teachers, Patty
Gregorich and Tricia Niesz, describe the lessons they learned about how the
reality of schools can cause painful conflicts for student teachers who value
the transformations they have recently undergone in a progressive teacher education program. The beliefs that Gregorich and Niesz had developed as students and that seemed fundamental to their new identities as teachers were
challenged by the practices in the urban elementary schools in which they
chose to begin their apprenticeships. Excerpts from Niesz's student teaching
journal are particularly illuminating and disturbing. She wrote that "two years
of intense learning [in her teacher education program] has to contend with a
life of living and doing school. New teachers are pressured to give up ideals either to fit in to a school or because they don't know how to reconcile idealism,
theory, and learning with the real world. The scary part is that it happens without us knowing" (p. 202).

Featherstone and Young's responses to Niesz's journal entries include
their observation that beginners are rarely satisfied with the inadequate ap-
proximations of good teaching that are the best one can hope to strive for in
the first year. But more trenchant is their observation that "one powerful en-
emy is yourself." As Niesz observed, the pull toward authoritarian images of
teaching is almost irresistible when the culture of the school doesn't support
the models learned and prized in the college of education. It was only by seek-
ing out the voices of teachers who had originally inspired them to go into
teaching that Niesz and Gregorich were able to continue to honor the selves
that had embraced those visions.

In the fourth week of her student teaching experience, Niesz wrote in her
journal that she had figured out a way to keep her motivation up—by rereading

articles and books from her education classes. Among them was Herb Kohl's *36 Children* (1967). She writes that, on rereading it, she is struck by "how teaching . . . seemed like a fight against society's idea of what teaching is supposed to be" (p. 198). And in her postmortem analysis of her student teaching experience, Niesz writes that the best she felt was the day when, instead of working on a lesson plan, she reread the most inspiring pieces from her teacher education classes. In both reading and writing about other teachers' attempts to live an undivided life in school, Niesz, Gregorich, Featherstone, and Young learned about the value of narrative in that quest for wholeness.

A decade before, the authors of *Women's Ways of Knowing* described their interviews as containing some "poignant accounts in which teachers seemed trapped against their will into the banker role" (p. 214). These teachers hadn't yet found ways to reconcile their desire to bring themselves into the classroom with their images of how a class "should" be conducted. On the other hand, the idea that teachers can be entirely self-made is one of the cultural myths that Deborah Britzman (1986) wishes to dispel. The culture of schools reinforces this misconception by discouraging examination of the historical and sociological roots of the school culture. Seeing one's personal teaching narrative as reflective of the pressures imposed by such myths is liberating and conducive to the development of the "undivided self."

AUTHORSHIP OF YOUR TEACHING STORY

Expressing "authorship" of your teaching life through the stories you tell can help you discover and claim your authority and responsibility for the direction your teaching takes. Mark Tappan and Lyn Mikel Brown (1991) claim that teachers can develop morally by authoring their own stories and by learning the lessons these stories tell about the moral experiences in their lives. In telling your teaching stories, you learn from the events you recount all over again, by reconsidering what happened, what your choices were, what you thought and did, and how it all turned out. To tell a story you must authorize a perspective. If that perspective reflects your values, then your identity, your authenticity, and your moral agency are reinforced. You articulate who you are now as a teacher and that, in turn, influences who you become.

To whom you address your story is an important concern. A story written for or told to your teacher may naturally take a different shape than the "same" story told to your parents, to your friends, or to yourself in your journal. All of these audiences might and should be sympathetic ones, but part of authoring is taking into account your varying purposes in telling your story to different audiences. Most of us are more willing to show our vulnerability to, and to seek a response from, people who have already proven their sensitivity and concern for us.

Assuming that the story you write will be read by an instructor in a teacher education program, your teacher's response will ideally be one that indicates that she has heard, understood, and appreciated your point of view.

That response, while encouraging, should also support, as Tappan and Brown put it, "continued authorization of that perspective—that is, it must support the gradual emergence of authorship" (p. 185).

One source of difficulty in advocating the writing of personal narratives by students as part of a teacher education curriculum is that our varying locations in society, our differences in gender, race, and class backgrounds, can lead us to misread another's perspective. This difficulty is compounded if questions of authorization are entangled with questions of power, as in the case where the autobiography is to be graded. Passing judgments of that sort on the satisfactoriness of a student's story can undermine our intention to foster more authorship, in the sense described previously.

We have to help each other out by listening carefully to each other's stories, clarifying our intentions when they're unclear, and explaining our narrated actions to the best of our ability. This process of clarification can be as helpful to the writer as it is to the readers. Readers, in turn, must be prepared to be open-minded, slow to judge, and willing to read about painful and difficult events, which often yield the richest lessons for both reader and writer. Students need to respect the right of teachers and other students in the classroom to engage themselves with difficult and sometimes controversial narratives.

It seems that almost everyone approaches the task of writing teaching stories with similar concerns. Most of us have hesitated in writing an autobiographical essay either because our lives seem too uninteresting or, if eventful, for fear that we'll never be able to convey the full meaning in words. However, the process of writing about our lives seems to result in an expansion of the meaning in them, sometimes by stumbling on cause and effect, as Eudora Welty put it, and generally by seeing connections between events that we hadn't before apprehended. The best place to start is by keeping a journal.

JOURNAL WRITING FOR GROWTH

In the development of your identity as a teacher, your journal can be a place to remember who you are and figure out who you want to be. In your journal you can be honest with yourself about what's going on in your life and in your classroom. It is also a place where you can attend to yourself in a caring fashion. In a private journal, the only risk you take is that the chance that you will undergo a real transformation in your thinking.

In Mary Louise Holly's useful book on journal keeping for teachers titled *Writing to Grow* (1989), a teacher named Craig reflects on the experience of coming to the brink of new insights in his journal:

> For years I had so much to say about education and now I had a safe and supportive forum to speak. I wrote voluminously while I had all this to say. Old thoughts and narrative accounts of daily events provided an abundance of materials. But then the trouble started. When the time came when the only way to go was deeper analysis and show-

downs with the big questions I choked. First I didn't want to deal with them. I ask kids "why" questions but am reluctant to deal with them myself. (Holly, 1989, p. 12)

Craig learned that writing for oneself is a powerful tool for gaining self-knowledge. He began with a journey back in time, catching up with whom he had become and how he got there by recounting all the teaching stories he had never written before. He ended up face-to-face with the big questions that he wasn't sure he was ready to tackle. Something in writing our stories just naturally leads us to what Vivian Paley calls the "growing edge" and the possibility of becoming our own best teachers.

There are many ways to keep a journal and many books to consult on journal keeping. Perhaps the most helpful book for teachers is Holly's *Writing to Grow*, in which she demonstrates how to write vignettes, portraits, life maps, autobiographical essays, logs, time lines, pocket journals, sketchbooks, double entry journals, and many more types of writing. All of these techniques are illustrated with examples from the logs, diaries, and journals kept by beginning and experienced teachers.

In addition to the tips on techniques, *Writing to Grow* contains three chapters devoted to extensive excerpts from the journals of three teachers written over more than a year. The reader sees how the journal can evolve from a place where teachers simply document their days to a place where they begin to have a dialogue with themselves, posing questions and then attempting to answer them. It is interesting to read how these teachers' attempts to answer their own questions begin with self-talk in the journal but sometimes lead to taking action. For example, a teacher named Judy asks herself early in her journal keeping why she feels so threatened by the administrators in her school. Somewhat later she notes that she is beginning to "speak out more" (p. 34) to her principal about her observations. She writes that she sees him as more of a person and that, while she wishes he were more approachable, she no longer feels threatened by him. She notices that she is also becoming more sensitive to other people as a result of her journal keeping. In her last entry recorded in the book, Judy writes that working on her journal is "a chance to sit down and actually confront myself . . . levels of writing became a way of thinking . . . an author for no one but myself" (p. 36). These examples encourage us to begin keeping teaching journals, or if we already do, to experiment with different formats.

Meetings between teachers to discuss their journals are an important component of the journal-keeping project that Holly documents in her book. The success of those meetings, and how important they became to the journal keepers, is consonant with Carter and Doyle's (1996) finding that nearly all reports of the use of biography in teacher education programs recommend that personal narratives be discussed in a collaborative context. In general, a high degree of mutual support in a context that encourages evocation of memories and experiences is helpful for making the most of the journal-keeping and narrative-writing experience.

Finally, Joanne Cooper (1991) makes the interesting point that journal writing is a way that teachers can nurture themselves. Journal writing puts us in relation to ourselves so that, in the words of Nel Noddings' (1984) ethic of care, we become both the one who is caring and the cared-for. Noddings reminds us that "the one-caring must be maintained, for she is the immediate source of caring. The one-caring then properly pays heed to her own condition" (1984, p. 105). Journal writing gives us an opportunity to listen to and appreciate all the parts of our selves and to encourage and support our attempts to expand our awareness and to become better teachers.

Journal writing can lead very naturally to writing stories about your teaching. Sometimes the stories won't be written until years after the journal entries are made. But if we don't have time to write all the stories we want to, we can always go back to the journal to revisit those events that stimulated our growth.

HOW TO WRITE A TEACHING STORY

The first thing you need to accept is that you probably won't know what your story will look like until you've written it. Don't worry about feeling lost at the beginning and even in the middle of your writing. If you follow the writing process approach advocated by many good writing teachers (see the reading list at the end of this chapter), you'll end up with a better story than you think you're capable of writing.

So let's say that your education professor has asked you to write a story about your memories of being a student or, if you've already been teaching, the experience of learning to teach. The first thing to do is to generate as many images, words, and phrases you can think of when you reflect back on your years of schooling or teaching. A very useful technique for both generating and organizing these memories is called *clustering*. Many books on writing describe this process of drawing a circle around a key word or phrase and then drawing "branches" off this circle. At the end of the branches you write words or phrases that elaborate on or describe aspects of the central word. It's best if you can generate some memories that involve your senses (sights, sounds, tastes, smells, textures) and your emotions (joy, sorrow, frustration, anger, resentment, embarrassment, pride). The richer your sensory memories and the deeper your feelings, the more insightful your story can be.

After you've generated two or three clusters, it's time to do some free writing. This is a time-honored technique in the process approach to writing, and there are many descriptions of free writing in the books listed at the end of this chapter. Quite simply, you put your pen to paper and write for at least ten minutes without stopping to edit, correct punctuation, reread, or worry about how well you're writing. Do this for at least one cluster. Free writing is nothing like a first draft. But it's a first step if you want to access the deepest meanings of your topic. Ultimately, there's something mysterious about how free writing works. Peter Elbow, author of *Writing Without Teachers* (1973), who is often credited with inventing the technique, believes it works at an unconscious level to help you find connections between seemingly disparate memories.

If one of your free writing exercises leads you directly into generating a first draft, then start your story. If you've done several free writes on different topics and can't decide which one to choose for your paper, follow the advice of Sheila Bender, author of *Writing Personal Essays* (1995), and choose the topic that generates the most intense emotions for you. This might seem like paradoxical advice, especially if you believe that strong feelings will interfere with getting the job done or done well, but it works as mysteriously as free writing does to enrich your final essay. If you have documents you've saved from your student teaching or from your own schooling (lesson plans, report cards, class pictures), it can be helpful to look at them to trigger more memories and to access the sensory and emotional aspects of the experience you want to write about. (For an extended discussion of this process, see the chapter titled "Picture This: Using School Photographs to Study Ourselves" in Mitchell & Weber, 1999.) This is not necessarily easy or fun. You'll come face to face with who you used to be, and that's usually a less mature person than who you are now. It can be reassuring to keep in mind what the existential psychologist Rollo May wrote in his book *Love and Will* about memory—that you will not remember something until you are ready to take some stand toward it.

Then you start writing. If you're already a fluent and skillful writer, you are on your way. If you're not fluent, it's especially important to get an early start on the writing. Consult the books on writing again if you need tips on how to organize an essay. If you've done the free writing and generated some more memories from looking at documents and photos, you'll have a lot more material than you expected. It will take time to find the words to describe the experience and to decide on a sequence for your thoughts. If you have the time to work on it for at least 15 minutes every day for a week or so, that's better than trying to write the whole essay in one sitting. Sleeping on it seems to help you generate better ways to organize your thoughts.

Polish the draft, read it to sympathetic friends, and get their responses (see Bender, 1995, for excellent advice on how to seek helpful responses and provide them for other writers). It's important to remember that this process of writing a teaching narrative isn't complete until you have shared it with other teachers who have written their own.

Twenty Topics for Narrative Essays

1. The best teacher I knew
2. The worst teacher I knew
3. Another teacher from whom I've learned a lot
4. The best part of me as a teacher
5. What I want my students to learn from me
6. The students who have helped me become a better teacher
7. The books that have helped me become a better teacher
8. When learning was easy for me

9. When learning was difficult for me
10. My most memorable class
11. The best principal I've known
12. The most helpful evaluation I've received
13. When I changed my teaching methods
14. How my subject "chose me"
15. Ways I've managed to work in or around "the system"
16. Ways I've tried to teach justice and fairness in my classroom
17. Ways I've helped a new teacher
18. Ways I've mentored my students
19. Ways I've tried to grow as a teacher
20. Ways I've written about my teaching

Questions for Writing Different Types of Narratives

Narrative of social criticism

1. How can you help your own school, and your own classroom, reflect the democratic ideals espoused by Kozol?
2. What would student empowerment look like in your classroom?
3. How can you find ways to challenge and engage your own students, as Marva Collins does, to allow their love of learning to flourish?
4. What are the moral and social commitments at the foundation of your philosophy of teaching?

Narrative of induction and apprenticeship

1. How has a mentor influenced your teaching? What was the most helpful advice you received as a teacher?
2. Describe a turning point or critical incident in your first years of teaching that changed you as a teacher.
3. How do you find a sense of meaning and purpose in your work?
4. Has there been a theory or method of teaching your subject that changed your approach?

Narrative of reflective practice

1. How have you worked to combat sexism, racism, and class biases in your own classroom and school?
2. How has the growth of your knowledge about yourself affected your teaching?
3. Have you ever been "creatively insubordinate" even in some small way in your teaching?
4. How do you talk about your teaching with other teachers?

Narrative of journey

1. How did you come to choose teaching as a career?
2. Can you trace the developmental stages of your teaching career?
3. How did you make your teaching style your own?

Narrative of hope
1. Have you ever "not-learned" something or recognized a student who decided to "not-learn" something?
2. Have you ever found yourself objecting to the labeling or categorizing of yourself or a student?
3. How have you tried to honor the "lived experience" of your students?

Narrative of freedom
1. How do you think your drive toward self-actualization affects your teaching?
2. How do you deal with spontaneity and unpredictability in your classroom?
3. How do you try to bring the "passion of experience" into your classes?
4. How do you deal with students' pain at giving up old ways of thinking?

Books of Advice on Writing Personal Essays and Memoirs

Barrington, J. (1997). *Writing the Memoir.* Portland, OR: Eighth Mountain Press.

Bender, S. (1995). *Writing Personal Essays: How to Shape Your Life Experiences for the Page.* Cincinnati, OH: Writer's Digest Books.

Elbow, P. (1973). *Writing Without Teachers.* New York: Oxford University Press.

McDonnell, J. T. (1998). *Living to Tell the Tale: A Guide to Writing Memoir.* New York: Penguin Books.

Rainer, T. (1997). *Your Life as Story: Discovering the "New Autobiography" and Writing Memoir as Literature.* New York: Tarcher/Putnam.

REFERENCES

Abbs, P. (1974). *Autobiography in education.* London: Heinemann Educational Books.

Ayers, W. (1993). *To teach: The journey of a teacher.* New York: Teachers College Press.

Belenky, M. F., Clinchy, B. M., Goldberger, N. R., & Tarule, J. M. (1986). *Women's ways of knowing: The development of self, voice, and mind.* New York: Basic Books.

Bender, S. (1995). *Writing personal essays: How to shape your life experiences for the page.* Cincinnati, OH: Writer's Digest Books.

Britzman, D. P. (1986). Cultural myths in the making of a teacher: Biography and social structure in teacher education. *Harvard Educational Review,* 56: 442–456.

Carter, K. & Doyle, W. (1996). Personal narrative and life history in learning to teach. In J. Sikula (Ed.), *Handbook of research on teacher education* (2nd ed., pp. 120-142). New York: Macmillan.

Connelly, F. M., & Clandinin, D. J. (1985). Personal practical knowledge and the modes of knowing: Relevance for teaching and learning. In E. Eisner (Ed.), *Learning and teaching the ways of knowing* (pp. 174–198). Chicago: National Society for the Study of Education.

Cooper, J. (1991). Telling our own stories: The reading and writing of journals or diaries. In C. Witherell & N. Noddings (Eds.), *Stories lives tell: Narrative and dialogue in education* (pp. 96–112). New York: Teachers College Press.

Elbow, P. (1973). *Writing without teachers*. New York: Oxford University Press.

Featherstone, H., Gregorich, P., Niesz, T., & Young, L. J. (1995). The scary part is that it happens without us knowing. In W. Ayers (Ed.), *To become a teacher: Making a difference in children's lives* (pp. 193–214). New York: Teachers College Press.

Featherstone, J. (1995). Letter to a young teacher. In W. Ayers (Ed.), *To become a teacher: Making a difference in children's lives* (pp. 11–22). New York: Teachers College Press.

Graham, R. J. (1995). Stories of teaching as tragedy and romance. In H. McEwan & K. Egan (Eds.), *Narrative in teaching, learning, and research* (pp. 195–210). New York: Teachers College Press.

Greene, M. (1995). Choosing a past and inventing a future: The becoming of a teacher. In W. Ayers (Ed.), *To become a teacher: Making a difference in children's lives* (pp. 65–77). New York: Teachers College Press.

Grumet, M. (1988). *Bitter milk: Women and teaching*. Amherst, MA: University of Massachusetts Press.

Helle, A. P. (1991). Reading women's autobiographies: A map of reconstructed knowing. In C. Witherell & N. Noddings (Eds.), *Stories lives tell: Narrative and dialogue in education* (pp. 48–66). New York: Teachers College Press.

Holly, M. L. (1989). *Writing to grow: Keeping a personal-professional journal*. Portsmouth, NH: Heinemann.

Huberman, M. (1995). Working with life-history narratives. In H. McEwan & K. Egan (Eds.), *Narrative in teaching, learning, and research*. New York: Teachers College Press.

Isenberg, J. (1994). *Going by the book: The role of popular classroom chronicles in the professional development of teachers*. Westport, CT: Bergin and Garvey.

Jackson, P. (1992). Reflections on teaching ourselves. In D. Burleson (Ed.), *Reflections: Personal essays by 33 distinguished educators* (pp. 232–244). Bloomington, IN: Phi Delta Kappa.

Jalongo, M. R., & Isenberg, J. P. (1995). *Teachers' stories: From personal narrative to professional insight*. San Francisco: Jossey-Bass.

May, R. (1969, 1995). *Love and will*. New York: Delacorte Press.

Mitchell, C., & Weber, S. (1999). *Reinventing ourselves as teachers: Beyond nostalgia*. Philadelphia: Falmer Press, Taylor & Francis, Inc.

Noddings, N. (1984). *Caring: A feminine approach to ethics and moral education*. Berkeley, CA: University of California Press.

Nias, J. (1989). *Primary teachers talking: A study of teachers at work*. New York: Routledge.

Nussbaum, M. C. (1997). *Cultivating humanity: A classical defense of reform in liberal education*. Cambridge, MA: Harvard University Press.

Pagano, J. (1991). Moral fictions: The dilemma of theory and practice. In C. Witherell & N. Noddings (Eds.), *Stories lives tell: Narrative and dialogue in education* (pp. 193–206). New York: Teachers College Press.

Palmer, P. (1998). *The courage to teach: Exploring the inner landscape of a teacher's life*. San Francisco: Jossey-Bass.

Pendlebury, S. (1995). Reason and story in wise practice. In H. McEwan & K. Egan (Eds.), *Narrative in teaching, learning, and research* (pp. 50–65). New York: Teachers College Press.

Tappan, M. B., & Brown, L. M. (1991). Stories told and lessons learned: Toward a narrative approach to moral development and moral education. In C. Witherell & N. Noddings (Eds.), *Stories lives tell: Narrative and dialogue in education* (pp. 171–192). New York: Teachers College Press.

Taylor, C. (1976). Responsibility for self. In A. O. Rorty (Ed.), *The identities of persons*. Berkeley, CA: University of California Press.

Witherell, C., & Noddings, N. (Eds.). (1991). *Stories lives tell: Narrative and dialogue in education*. New York: Teachers College Press.

10

Conclusion

N arratives of teaching are a marvelous, even indispensable source of good pedagogy. They model effective and creative instructional practices, they spur teachers to reflect deeply on their efforts to engage students, and they compellingly depict the educational conditions that foster human growth. Stories of teaching deliver realistic and haunting descriptions of classroom life, reminding us that good teaching remains a complex, challenging, and exciting enterprise. These stories also offer some valuable perspectives on making a meaningful life, and they provide teachers at all levels of experience with guidance in reconstructing their personal and professional identities.

To sum up, we refer back to William Schubert's (1991) preliminary findings about the dispositions and skills that the best teachers appear to share, and we review incidents from the narratives that reinforce Schubert's claims. As you may recall from chapter 1, the six qualities or characteristics that we found to be most relevant were that these teachers:

1. Maintain a sense of mission about the importance of teaching;
2. Exhibit a love and compassion for students;
3. Determine ways to build on student strengths;
4. Exhibit a clear sense of meaning and direction or are in the process of revising the same;
5. Guide their work with a quest for that which is worthwhile and just;
6. Are actively involved in self-education (Schubert, p. 220).

MAINTAIN A SENSE OF MISSION ABOUT THE IMPORTANCE OF TEACHING

It is remarkable what a clear sense of mission and purpose all of these teachers maintain. For bell hooks and Ira Shor, school is a place to embrace democracy and participation, to challenge the current social order and the perspectives of those in power. It is a place to heighten the critical consciousness of students, to invent new social realities, and to bring unimagined possibilities to fruition. For them, education is about freedom and emancipation, and everything they strive to do as teachers ultimately relates to loosening the shackles of convention and stasis.

For Garret Keizer and Herb Kohl, school must teach criticism and analytic thought, but it also must instill wonder and spread joy. For both of them, there are basic skills that must be carefully taught, such as reading and writing in sightfully, but teachers must also establish a climate, they maintain, that invites pleasure in learning and encourages students to express awe when encountering the remarkable and unknowable. Carving out a large place for wonder, imagination, hoping, and dreaming should be one of the imperatives of all teaching, right along with helping students to live fuller, richer lives. The narrative of hope is a particularly poignant reminder that teaching and living, learning and being are inextricably linked, and that schools can make a difference in creating a more humane future. Perhaps there must also be recognition, as Inchausti found as he struggled with his students over the devastation of the Holocaust, that even when hope dims, meaning can still be salvaged. It may be useful to note what Victor Frankl (1984) learned during his own travails as a concentration camp prisoner. What really matters, he asserted, "is to bear witness to uniquely human potential at its best, which is to transform a personal tragedy into a triumph, to turn one's predicament into a human achievement" (p. 135).

Vivian Paley's mission is to make school as friendly and as hospitable a place as possible, to provide the conditions for children to flourish and to be themselves. Finding many ways for them to express themselves is one way to do this; giving them many opportunities to talk with each about how they see themselves and the world is another. Providing occasions for children to reflect on their learning, to be actively involved in problem solving, and to use their minds as productively as possible is a dimension of this mission. But an equally important dimension is giving the children constant practice in showing respect, appreciation, and even love for one another. Paley seeks, in other words, to do nothing less than to help her children become fully rounded human beings.

EXHIBIT A LOVE AND COMPASSION FOR STUDENTS

It seems fitting to pick up where we left off and to invoke Paley again. Her unconditional love and concern for her students, regardless of their behavior or their apparent disabilities, is inspiring. The case of Jason—the boy who would be a helicopter—stands out. Refusing to label him or to constrain him more than necessary, Paley is able to reach Jason and understand him a little bit better. Her patient, deliberate approach is not a cure-all; it does not transform Jason's relationships with his peers. But her genuine interest in Jason and her transparent concern for him wins his trust and builds his confidence.

Marva Collins is justly renowned, like Vivian Paley, for the love and affection she showers on her students. Every story she tells, every idea she imparts furthers in some way compassion, decency, or mutual respect. Her interactions with students are physically close and emotionally affirming. As she has said, her curriculum is purposely over the head of the students, but she instills in them the confidence and self-esteem they need to negotiate even the most difficult academic material.

Jane Tompkins, too, develops strong attachments to her students and concludes that perhaps it is the caring relationships she creates with them, more than the content she imparts, that matter. Of course, it takes her a long time to come to this conclusion, but by the end of her story it is clear that the enduring connections she makes with students are, for her, one of teaching's chief satisfactions.

In *Small Victories* (1990), Samuel Freedman's remarkable account of an outstanding teacher's struggle to outlast the New York City school bureaucracy, Jessica Siegel, the story's protagonist, spends most of one evening weeping in admiration and awe over her students' autobiographies. Their life stories are such powerful testimonies to the courage and perseverance they have shown in the face of adversity that she can only conclude that her students are heroes. This theme is repeated many times in the literature of teacher narratives. Garret Keizer reveals a similar admiration for those students in rural Vermont who proudly affiliate with the Future Farmers of America. Herb Kohl develops an enduring respect for the many students who respond so enthusiastically to his experimental teaching at Other Ways, his alternative storefront school in downtown Berkeley. Mike Rose, too, comes to view as heroes the returning veterans he is assigned to teach, primarily for the resilience they exhibit in persevering as learners despite years of negative experiences in school. By showing these students the respect and admiration they deserve, the teachers in their lives make education, often for the first time, a meaningful and purposeful activity.

DETERMINE WAYS TO BUILD ON STUDENT STRENGTHS

These stories do not exhaust all of the skills and dispositions that teachers need, but they address many of the most important. Teachers in these stories invariably have a firm grasp of the subject matter they are attempting to teach but also eagerly seek out creative and imaginative pedagogical approaches that build on student strengths and interests. Whether it is Jane Tompkins using actual whaling settings to launch discussion of *Moby Dick*, or Herb Kohl teaching poetry through maps of the city of Berkeley, or Vivian Paley and Marva Collins inviting students to act out the stories they read, these teachers search relentlessly for ways to build excitement and make meaning.

These teachers also encourage their students to engage in useful, horizon-broadening dialogue. For Vivian Paley, the very test of a good classroom atmosphere or of solid educational processes is the extent to which they promote useful dialogue. When a strategy like the time-out chair doesn't meet this test, Paley rejects it. For Inchausti, classroom discussion is an occasion for students and teacher to explore their deepest feelings and reveal their greatest doubts. The exchange over the book *Night* becomes a transformative experience, one which forces the entire class to confront the limits of their knowledge and the practical lessons for conducting their own lives. Ira Shor places classroom discussion at the heart of the entire educational process and sees it not only as the most important mode for learning and interpreting content, but also as an opening for negotiating every aspect of the class's collective deliberations. Indeed, how the group will conduct itself in dialogue becomes a major topic of dialogue itself.

bell hooks' desire to make teaching and learning joyful activities is another way that teachers can build on their student strengths. Her injunction to make education an occasion for celebration, for honest expression of our emotional experience and frank disclosure of the ways in which the dominant culture often squelches our creativity and spirit, is her version of "engaged pedagogy." The sort of spontaneous and flexible environment she creates not only does not interfere with the consideration of serious and profound ideas; it actually facilitates such consideration. When students feel that their problems and their experiences are honored and given authentic space in the classroom, their willingness to explore the connections between these experiences and the larger society's public problems is greatly enhanced. hooks' approach is reminiscent of C. Wright Mills' (1959) notion that one of the ways to shed light on public problems is to begin with individual biographies and to examine the links between personal troubles and more generalized public issues.

In their book titled *Teaching in America* (1999), Gerald Grant and Christine Murray offer an intriguing chapter on the essential acts of teaching. The first act they explore is that of knowing the students, and the skill they treat at greatest length in this regard is listening. Surely, listening to their students is one of those habits that the authors of these narratives most widely share. Whether it is Vivian Paley painstakingly documenting her kindergartners' exact words or Ira Shor "backloading" his own commentary to create space for neglected voices or Jane Tompkins trading her professorial authority for student dominated discussion, careful listening on the part of the teacher is the key to success. As we have shown, it is also one of the keys to building on student strengths.

EXHIBIT A CLEAR SENSE OF MEANING AND DIRECTION

Most of the stories we have examined remind educators that clarity of vision for the future depends in part upon an understanding of what has gone wrong in the past. By studying these narratives, teachers can be more effective in mounting their own critique of schools and in generating more satisfactory alternatives.

Aspiring teachers and veterans alike must take time to observe and study policies and practices that inhibit growth and to consider some of the reasons why such policies and practices have been so resistant to change. All of these narratives should also inspire teachers to reject schooling practices that stigmatize, debilitate, or impair and to recognize that these structures are products of human-made institutions and therefore alterable.

These stories should also provide teachers with a renewed sense of purpose about the place and value of teaching. They return teachers to their roots, encouraging them to reflect on their original reasons for pursuing a career in teaching and stimulating them to construct or to reconstruct a personal philosophy of teaching and learning. Readers of these stories are forced to confront philosophies of education that focus on student limitations and to engender new directions for schooling that hold out the promise of fostering every child's growth.

Narratives can be used to encourage aspiring teachers to visit local schools, encouraging them to observe everyday practices closely for evidence that these schools convey an inclusive, affirming, and challenging ethos. Similarly, the experiences of Kozol, Collins, and Shor should remind us how insidious bigoted practices can be and how wide-awake we must remain to resist such practices. Both beginning and veteran teachers should form the habit of intensively observing schools and of taking careful note of ordinary, everyday actions that either affirm or diminish students.

For Howard Gardner, unleashing human capacities to think and create provides the chief direction for good teaching. This means recognizing the multiple areas in which students can demonstrate excellence, the many ways to measure progress apart from the standardized tests that so often distort learning capacity, and the many people in addition to professional teachers who can help enhance student understanding. Regardless of how scholars weigh the strengths and weaknesses of Gardner's theory of multiple intelligences, many teachers believe that his writings have changed the educational landscape by emphasizing that students often enjoy ability in disciplines and fields that are undervalued by traditional academic institutions. His findings have helped many schools to design activities and introduce classes that allow these undervalued abilities to flourish. He has simultaneously been a severe critic of standardized tests (in part resulting from his own boyhood experiences with these tests) and has proposed a variety of other forms of assessment that capture students' abilities to adapt to actual problems and difficulties that emerge from everyday living. Finally, he has urged educators to exploit the many natural teachers who reside in the local community and to involve them in designing projects and supervising apprenticeships that give students opportunities to learn new skills under the guidance of experts from a variety of fields. All of these suggestions have a single purpose—to acknowledge the vast range of students' learning capacities and to develop these capacities as fully as possible.

Although James Herndon has a very different notion about the meaning and direction of schooling, his focus emerges as clearly as does Gardner's. His goal is to help students make their own choices wisely and thoughtfully and thereby to experience the satisfactions of individual independence and freedom that he believes should accompany their transition to adulthood. He does this by refusing to impose premature control on students' activities and by letting their natural interests and energy shape the direction of their own education. His decisions to welcome "slambook season" and to encourage charting the Top 40 popular songs are two examples of granting students the freedom to construct their own education. His "habit" of making a wide range of stimulating materials available to students—from record players to multiple copies of dramatic stories—is another way in which Herndon directs his students and yet allows them wide latitude in making choices. The guidance he provides is nonauthoritarian but significant. It is never, however, guidance for its own sake. It is always in the patient service of educating students for self-control and self-expression.

GUIDE THEIR WORK WITH A QUEST FOR THE WORTHWHILE AND JUST

No theme emerges from the teacher narratives we have chosen as strongly as the notion that these teachers constantly measure their accomplishments against a standard of what is worthwhile and just for students and for the larger society. Paulo Freire's standard of what is worthwhile and just has to do with mutual respect, social equity, and love. He challenges all groups to move toward unity in diversity. He exhorts them to take up the hard issues and to explore them in powerful and challenging ways, while maintaining an atmosphere of solidarity and love. Such an atmosphere, however, has nothing in common with sentimental niceness or superficial consensus. It is an atmosphere that accepts how contentious the discussion of difficult issues can be, but it is also at bottom guided by the sense that every voice is invited and every view needed to reach deeper understanding.

Mike Rose seeks schools that support a new, more pluralistic vision of democratic community. It is a vision in which teachers employ diverse strategies to discern undetected abilities and multiple methods to unleash those abilities. Rose's conception does not compromise on educational excellence, nor does it shrink from promotion of the basics of reading, writing, computing, and thinking well. But it does call on educators to move toward standards that "celebrate the plural, messy human reality of it" and that embrace "the rich mix of speech and ritual and story that is America" (p. 238). For Rose, this means that teachers assume there is academic potential in even the lowest performing students, but that, so far, this potential has gone unrecognized and untapped. It is up to teachers to devise approaches and means to bring those abilities to the surface and to allow these students to take their full place as participants in a democracy. As Rose has also indicated, however, this is a most challenging expectation. It requires teachers to cross boundaries of class and culture, to be creative in motivating performance, and to be watchful and alert so that when signs of ability do emerge, they can be affirmed and made the basis of still higher student achievement.

Patricia Schmidt's quest for the worthwhile and just may appear more modest but is, in reality, no less ambitious. For her, self-understanding and self-awareness should be the goal of education, not in isolation from those around us, but, as she says, "in connection and feeling connected to the world" (p. 176). Through self-understanding compassion for others develops, relationships blossom and grow, and educational meaning emerges. When education is too authoritarian and restrictive, when it does not give free rein to the development of one's individuality, one's moral artistry, then the quest for educational renewal is blocked and the pursuit of education's larger purpose is suppressed. Schmidt finds herself turning again and again to Arnold Jersild's classic study of teacher development to support her view. In his book *When Teachers Face Themselves* (1955), Jersild argues that education is emptied of both meaning and purpose unless opportunities are available for both teachers and students to engage in regular self-examination. He goes so far as to say that most of what we do educationally cannot be sustained unless self-understanding and self-reflection are important aspects of what is taught. For Schmidt, it was only after her discovery of reader response theory and the freedom she enjoyed as a graduate student to pursue the implications of this theory for her teaching and herself that education finally acquired the meaning that it was meant to have all along.

For Garret Keizer, schools have a role to play in preparing students to become more effective advocates of a restructured and reinvigorated society. He argues that society's high expectations for schools can never be realized until the surrounding community confronts the entrenched injustices that handicap many of its most talented people. For instance, he laments the fact that raising the self-awareness and social consciousness of young people won't do much good until society's dim awareness of the youth in its midst is greatly heightened. This seeming paradox fades, however, when Keizer's conception of schooling is framed as preparing students to be social critics who thoughtfully diagnose society's weaknesses and inequities and who learn how to work confidently and actively for social justice. This is not Keizer's only purpose for schooling; it is probably not even the one he would advance most vigorously. But it is a goal that emerges almost inescapably as he witnesses schools struggling to make up for the societal burdens that hamper so many students.

Drawing again on the work of Grant and Murray (1999), good teachers are modelers and one of the things they model best is a love of ideas. Repeatedly, we witness the teachers in these stories unabashedly exhibiting their passion for books recently read, theories conscientiously mastered, notions enthusiastically absorbed. One of Herb Kohl's entire stories is premised on a book that opened up whole new worlds to him. bell hooks' first love is literature, and most of what she explores with her students emerges from the stories they read together. Marva Collins' greatest satisfaction is sharing the lessons of great, enduring classics with her children. Patricia Schmidt's professional and personal breakthrough occurs as a result of discovering Louise Rosenblatt's reader response theory. There are many other such examples, but suffice it to say that invariably a very large dimension of these teacher narratives is the power of books, ideas, and ways of reenvisioning the world. For nearly all of these teacher-writers, the intellectual side of life is an important part of what is worthwhile and just.

TEACHERS ACTIVELY INVOLVED IN SELF-EDUCATION

Good teachers are constantly learning, and one important source of their on-going enlightenment is their colleagues. Brother Blake is a master teacher who imparts to Robert Inchausti everything he comes to know about the craft of teaching. Others, like Herndon or Schmidt, find their mentors within themselves or in writers who are physically distant from them. These stories underscore the need for teachers to cultivate supportive and constructively critical colleagues who can collaborate with them in forging a culture of affirmation and continuous improvement in schools. Whether it is students just getting into teaching or teachers who have been working at it for 20 years, processes must be established to allow people to confide in one another, to observe classes, and to come to see one another as valuable resources for increasing effectiveness.

Any kind of professional development program for novices or veterans should provide opportunities for teachers to work in pairs or small groups as a way to promote a kind of professional affinity, build trust, and fully exploit the wise counsel that only colleagues can provide. There should be activities encouraging mutual critique of teachers' thinking, writing, and teaching, and there should be opportunities for teachers to articulate what they are hoping to gain from interaction with their colleagues. Certain dispositions such as appreciation, humility, and mindfulness must characterize such discussions if they are to be mutually helpful (Brookfield and Preskill, 1999).

The narratives of reflective practice and of journey are especially valuable when viewed as an integrated whole. Teachers should get in the habit of reflecting regularly on their teaching, perhaps by maintaining a journal. Vivian Paley's many works of reflective practice are made possible by her careful, consistent, and voluminous journaling and by the painstaking way in which she tape records many of her class sessions. Usually with the help of a theme such as race, gender, or rules of play, she carefully documents what transpires in her classes and then, at a later time, reflects on the meaning of these experiences. She builds up a formidable record of how her classroom changes over time and how her thinking about particular issues changes as well.

Journal writing is also an excellent way to gain a perspective on the course of one's professional life. A different kind of journaling, it relies less on a record of daily experience and more on a recording of fairly distant memories of events, thoughts, and feelings. Here the teacher is more memoirist than journalist, but the entries set down still have an impact on one's daily practices. Indeed, there is something especially exciting about the interplay between regular accounting of one's teaching practices and occasional stabs at considering and recording those experiences over the long haul. Teaching is importantly shaped by one's sense of self, and the experiences one accumulates as a professional have an important impact on the capacity for self-renewal. Growing consciousness of the spiraling transactional relationship between everyday self and the self of one's life course is not only stimulating in itself, it can give teachers a sense of themselves over time that helps to counteract burnout and other common maladies that potentially afflict the disengaged veteran teacher.

Finally, of course, the writing of one's teaching autobiography is an important form of professional development, a crucial vehicle for self-education and personal growth. All of the stories we have featured in this book were written, in part, to provide their authors with an opportunity for extensive reflection and self-examination. The process of coming to know ourselves better and of composing richer, more authentic selves is incalculably enhanced through the writing of our professional histories. Like the authors of these books, teachers should spend time reflecting on their work and find ways to write down what they have learned and share it with others. It can be one of the central ways in which teachers find renewal and generate new energy and enthusiasm for the challenges ahead.

TEACHERS AS ENABLERS

Another closely related way to think about the teachers featured in this book is as enablers. For Ken Macrorie (1984), enablers are teachers "who help others to do good works and extend their already considerable powers" (p. xi). Although enablers are distinctive in many ways, they also tend to hold certain qualities in common. They challenge learners to do their best, while simultaneously creating a classroom atmosphere in which learners are affirmed and celebrated for what they already are accomplishing. Risk taking is encouraged and mistakes are expected, but errors never lead to punishment, only more learning. Additionally, trust and honesty are important to enablers. Being forthright about what one knows and doesn't know is part of the process of creating a trusting environment, as is finding the human and material resources to enable learners to flourish. Encouraging the excitement and exhilaration that accompanies significant accomplishment is also part of enabling. For enablers, strong emotions are as welcome as powerful thinking. Finally, enablers want learners to do good work that matters to them as learners and human beings. It is not work imposed by an authoritarian figure, but work that results from the genuine merging of the aspirations of both teacher and learner.

There is perhaps no more appropriate synonym for the teachers in this book than enabler. Vivian Paley and Marva Collins stand out as enablers. They do all they can to establish the respect, to engender the relationships, and to encourage the exploration that will allow children to discover unknown parts of themselves and exceed their potential. Herb Kohl and Garret Keizer are classic enablers. The stories they tell, the activities they dream up, and the dialogues they facilitate are all designed to enable, to give learners the tools they need to remake a more caring and just world. James Herndon and Jane Tompkins are committed enablers as well. They don't impart knowledge so much as free up students to make choices and identify interests that will allow them to pursue their most intense passions and, in the end, do their best and most meaningful work.

Teachers who enable aren't particularly interested in getting credit for helping their students to learn. They willingly accept their often unacknowledged, behind-the-scenes role. What matters to enabling teachers is that learners keep learning and that they develop a lifelong affection for the pleasures of acquiring knowledge. This quiet, unassuming, self-effacing attitude that many of the finest teachers project leads to our discussion of the final topic in this book—the fourth stage of teaching.

THE FOURTH STAGE

In the first chapter of this book, we refer to Daniel Lindley's (1993) argument from his book *This Rough Magic* that the best teachers proceed through three stages as professionals. They begin as novices who struggle to meet the demands of children and to turn their knowledge of subject matter into teachable form. By the second stage, they have a solid understanding of the students for whom they are responsible and are capable of teaching them the subject or subjects they have always loved. Most teachers stop at the second stage. Those fortunate individuals who reach the third stage are able to invest their teaching with their own unique identities, to bring themselves to bear on the things they teach and the interactions they enjoy with their students. As Lindley says, "teaching becomes an idiosyncratically creative act, an extension and expression of her whole being. With this come moments of pure joy, or clarity, or fun that were previously only imagined" (p. 14).

It is our contention that the teachers featured in the narratives discussed in this book all reach Lindley's third stage of teaching. They all display a moral and pedagogical artistry that is uniquely their own, and their teaching is inseparable from who they are as professionals and human beings. Although they have suffered through moments of despair and loss and have committed many errors and mistakes, they all feel they are responding to a call and have experienced moments of great joy and insight as teachers.

What we have not yet revealed is that Lindley believes there is a fourth stage of teaching. And as Lindley says, this stage happens "in the student" (p. 127). The fourth stage is the art of letting go, of celebrating the student's final separation from the teacher. For the teacher, there is the quiet, unheralded satisfaction that comes from knowing that you had something to do with helping a student become an independent learner. But the process is so subtle and imperceptible that the student does not acknowledge the role of the teacher. The student understands only that she is now prepared to take her place in a democratic society and perhaps assume the role of teacher herself. At this stage, teaching is not primarily an expression of the teacher's identity but, as Lindley says, "becomes an expression of the inner adult now alive within the student, empowering the student in magical but insensible ways" (p. 130).

In this final fourth stage, then, the teacher gives of herself generously and selflessly, without expectation of anything in return. The intrinsic pleasure of enabling a student's development is one reward to be savored. But there is another. As Lindley suggests, the teacher enjoys the privilege of being a part of the student's "imaginal world," of getting inside the student's thoughts and drawing them forth with new vigor, strength, and precision. The image of the teacher in this example can be likened to Plato's midwife who helps to birth a new identity, almost literally guides the making of a new consciousness. And there is a sense that with each act of birthing, a part of the teacher—at the very least a part of her psychic energy—is imparted to the student and lost forever to the teacher. It is at this rare final stage that great teachers willingly relinquish parts of themselves to make possible the building of future generations. In the end, rewards and honors lose their luster; even words of gratitude, as pleasant as they are, carry little enduring value. There is only the inner satisfaction of giving one's life for something larger than oneself and knowing that the next encounter with a student might yield something powerful, wonderful, or even sublime.

The teacher-writers in the narratives we have explored know these things; they have, after all, lived these things. And fortunately for us, they know as well that the only way to capture the wonders and mysteries of these fourth stage encounters is to put them into some kind of story. When the finest teachers are also excellent writers, the chances are that the stories they tell will reveal something profound about the vocation of teaching and, for that matter, about life itself. This is why we have labored over these stories, why we have gone to such lengths to tell you about them. As we have said many times, these stories are not only guides to great teaching and learning, they are guides as well to living full, rich lives. The time we spend reading these stories is time well spent not only learning more about teaching, but also learning more about each other and ourselves.

REFERENCES

Brookfield, S., & Preskill, S. (1999). *Discussion as a way of teaching: Tools and techniques for democratic classrooms.* San Francisco, CA: Jossey-Bass.

Frankl, V. (1984). *Man's search for meaning.* New York: Washington Square Press.

Freedman, S. (1990). *Small victories.* New York: Harper and Row.

Grant, G. & Murray, C. (1999). *Teaching in America: The slow revolution.* Cambridge, MA: Harvard University Press.

Jersild, A. (1955). *When teachers face themselves.* New York: Bureau of Publications, Teachers College Press.

Lindley, D. A. (1993). *This rough magic: The life of teaching.* Westport, CT: Bergin and Garvey.

Macrorie, K. (1984). *20 teachers.* New York: Oxford University Press.

Mills, C. W. (1959). *The sociological imagination.* New York: Oxford University Press.

Schubert, W. (1991). Teacher lore: A basis for understanding praxis. In C. Witherell and N. Noddings (Eds.). *Stories lives tell: Narrative and dialogue in education* (pp. 207–233). New York: Teachers College Press.

INDEX